ARABIA IMPERILLED:
THE SECURITY IMPERATIVES OF
THE ARAB GULF STATES

ARABIA IMPERILLED:
THE SECURITY IMPERATIVES OF
THE ARAB GULF STATES

MAZHER A. HAMEED

MIDDLE EAST ASSESSMENTS GROUP

The Middle East Assessments Group (MEAG) is an independent public policy research organization dedicated to the analysis of political, economic and social issues with bearing on stability and security in the Middle East. MEAG sponsors a program of research and analysis which draws on the experience and insight of individuals directly involved in Middle East affairs as well as on more traditional sources of information. These resources are used to identify and weigh options for U.S. policy. Through publications, seminars and consultation, MEAG provides public and private sector decision-makers with assessments of regional developments and trends and their impact on U.S. interests.

Library of Congress Cataloging-in-Publication Data

Hameed, Mazher A., 1950-
 Arabia imperilled: the security imperatives of the
Arab Gulf States.

 Bibliography: p.
 Includes index.
 1. Persian Gulf States—Politics and government.
2. Persian Gulf States—Strategic aspects. 3. Persian
Gulf Region—Politics and government. 4. Persian Gulf
Region—Strategic aspects. 5. Persian Gulf Region—
Relations—United States. 6. United States—Relations—
Persian Gulf States. I. Middle East Assessments Group.
II. Title.
DS247.A138H36   1986   355'.033053   86-5364
ISBN 0-937783-00-5

In memory of Rodney F. Basil,
whose insight, concern and
involvement with Middle East affairs
remains a major source of inspiration.

TABLE OF CONTENTS

LIST OF ILLUSTRATIONS

FOREWORD

If we are to believe either Biblical accounts or the judgments of historians, mankind's origins lie to a large extent in the region of the Persian Gulf. No doubt, it is an exaggeration—though one that underscores an important truth—to observe that mankind's destiny in the 21st century may also lie in precisely the same region of the world. Reflecting its dominant position in world oil reserves, its own political volatility, and its proximity to the Soviet Union, the Persian Gulf remains today the strategic vortex of international politics.

Nevertheless, concern in this country over the military security and political stability of the Gulf has plummeted since the days of the second oil shock, the fall of the shah, the rise of Khomeini, and the hostage crisis. Such complacence is short-sighted, however. It reflects the current oil glut and the belief that the energy problem has gone away. But the oil glut reflects internal cartel dynamics and temporary market conditions more than longer-term geological—and *geopolitical*—reality. Even today, a war rages between Iran and Iraq—as it has for much of the past six years. If the forces of Khomeini were to crush the regime of Saddam Hussein (and possibly establish another Shi'ite republic in Iraq), the geopolitical and oil market consequences would be severe and swift. Within the Persian Gulf, Khomeini would then have achieved a position of preponderant power. The Gulf states would be obliged to defer to Tehran—among other things in oil production policies. The OPEC cartel would be revivified and reshaped under Iran's domination— and would reflect Iran's high-price policies and hostility toward the industrial world. Since Iraq's forces are far better equipped and are likely to hold, such an outcome may appear to be a low-probability event. Nonetheless, it is of sufficient seriousness that the continuing war between Iraq and Iran merits far more than the widespread indifference displayed in the West.

There is another matter of equal potential importance. The collapse of oil prices (as of 1986) means a revival of oil consumption in the industrial world and simultaneously a decline in oil production in high-cost producing areas. The United States is herself the *preeminent* high-cost oil producer. If prices remain low and if no compensatory policies are adopted, by 1990 the United States will be importing roughly nine million barrels a day—assuming the oil is then available on the world market. Moreover, because of the decline in domestic production, the United States would then have passed the 50-percent mark in terms of oil dependency. Thus, by the early 1990s at the latest, the United States and the entire industrial world will have been driven back to dependency upon the oil resources of the Persian Gulf. Once again we shall be obliged to face on a daily basis the questions of the political stability and the military security of the Persian Gulf region. Since this is a few years away at best, it would seem appropriate for us to shed the complacence and the indifference regarding developments in the Persian Gulf, and to focus now on the forces at work in that region.

In this regard Mr. Hameed has provided us with a most timely book, providing a wealth of information regarding this most critical region of the world about which so little is known in this country. It provides both an introduction to and analysis of the complex politics of the Gulf. It is a primer, that in addition is both well-balanced and thoughtful. Mr. Hameed describes the political and economic forces at play in the region. He examines both the balance of military forces and the tensions that lie behind them. He underscores the weaknesses of the structure that the United States put in place (during our preoccupation with Vietnam) to compensate for British withdrawal from the Gulf. He examines the evolution of Iraq and its significance for the region, especially in the light of the Iranian-Syrian axis. With the passage of the years the importance of these forces will steadily grow. In just a few years, perhaps regrettably, we shall once again be thoroughly immersed in Persian Gulf developments. For all these reasons, Mr. Hameed's book deserves careful study.

James Schlesinger

Washington, D.C.
April 1986

xii

PREFACE

Background

This book discusses the nature of the geopolitical environment in the Gulf, the evolution of U.S. concern with that issue, the nature and range of threats to U.S. interests there and the political, economic, and other Gulf resources that can be marshaled to protect those interests. Our focus is not the Gulf itself, however; the assessment is based upon those U.S. interests that are affected by Gulf security. It is apparent that a number of important developments have reduced the immediate vulnerability of key U.S. Gulf interests; it is no less evident that the Gulf remains a key to Western security. What, then, can and should be done to further reduce American vulnerabilities and to guard against new and emerging threats to U.S. interests? What are those interests and, in view of recent developments, how secure are they?

In his State of the Union Message of 1980, the president of the United States, indicating that the security of the Persian (or Arabian) Gulf was directly related to America's own security, pledged that "an attempt by any outside force to gain control of the . . . Gulf region will be regarded as an assault on the vital interests of the United States of America and [that] such an assault will be repelled by any means necessary, including military force."

The years since this warning was issued have produced a number of signal events and developments—in the Gulf, in areas proximate to it, in the United States, and in the West—that have had a major impact on Gulf security and on the U.S. relationship with the Gulf states. Among these developments, several stand out:

• Rapid increases in the price of crude oil led to a number of important oil discoveries. Development has already begun on some of them, dramatically increasing competition for market shares.

• The combined effect of increased energy prices, consumer slow-downs, new conservation efforts, and fuel switching placed sudden and unexpectedly effective brakes on demand.

• The Iran-Iraq War did not end rapidly. It continues, and its by-products have been slowly increasing the breadth and levels of violence throughout the Gulf.

• The emergence of Iran as a center of both Islamic resurgence and revolutionism also increased the rhetorical tension through vitriolic propaganda; added to the diversity of political violence through the use of indirect and low-level attacks; and spread that violence throughout the Gulf.

• The planning and construction of alternative pipelines through which to ship Gulf-produced petroleum have provided some security against a "closure" of the Gulf.

• The sharp reduction in oil producers' expenditures has begun to establish a ceiling on business and investment opportunities.

• Substantial changes in the military equation in the Gulf have left oil producers stronger, but, paradoxically, more vulnerable.

• The United States, following the administrative identification of forces for rapid deployment to the Gulf, has (under the U.S. Central Command [CENTCOM]) begun to pre-position equipment, exercise troops, and establish the necessary support links and contingency facilities to play a deterrent, or if necessary, a combat role in certain types of potential Gulf threat situations.

• The Arab Gulf countries (except Iraq, still involved in the war with Iran) have also begun to make some headway in planning their own collective self-defense. While its effectiveness can only extend to limited threat situations due to restricted manpower and equipment bases, the Gulf Cooperation Council (GCC) does offer some evidence of enhanced deterrence and defense in the future.

• The Afghan resistance has engaged occupying Soviet forces in a long-term insurgency, reducing the probability of any immediate threat from that quarter while increasing the likelihood of an extended presence of Soviet forces there.

U.S. Interests in the Gulf

The principal U.S. interest in the Gulf has long been its oil resources. Changes in the petroleum situation—general growth in crude production and producers, on the one hand, and more stable and in some cases declining demand, on the other—clearly attenuate over the short term what was not too many years ago a fragile balance. At the same time, consumer agreements for sharing in periods of shortage, while they may produce more rational allocation and distribution of petroleum should major shortfalls occur, also ensure that such shortages will not be confined to one or more target countries; they will be shared by all, including the United States.

More important, the Gulf as an aggregate remains the "swing producer" in the oil trade. Although no single country in the Gulf any longer produces a great enough proportion of Free World oil to induce crisis through unilateral production cutbacks, any contingency that interrupted the flow of all or most Gulf oil would certainly generate a major Western economic crisis and severely affect NATO's viability as a military deterrent if it endures for any substantial period of time (despite high, and in some cases record-level, stocks among Western governments).

Saudi Arabia's importance is particularly noteworthy in the context of potential oil interruptions. A cut-off of Gulf oil that did not include Saudi production would be ineffective, because, due to the enormous Saudi production capacity, that country alone could match most current Gulf petroleum exports, More important, Saudi Arabia is the one Arab Gulf producer that has alternative routes (i.e., non-Gulf routes) for the export of its petroleum. (Saudi Arabia has opened one pipeline on the Red Sea, and will soon have a second ready for operation.) Indeed, one of the Saudi pipelines also carries Iraqi crude.

The Gulf Arab states have consistently favored a stable pricing system, and preferably one coordinated with consuming countries. Saudi Arabia and the smaller Gulf states have fought bitter battles with the "price hawks" of Organization of Petroleum Exporting Countries (OPEC), the oil producers' organization, to maintain stable prices, and have urged other OPEC members to recognize the interdependence of the producer and consumer countries in the world economy. When the "price hawks" refused to listen to reason, Saudi Arabia held out for lower prices and produced sufficient oil to create a surplus, thereby exerting downward pressure on prices. While even these actions have not stilled the demands for higher prices from a few producers, Saudi and GCC country policies have helped prevent irrational pricing procedures and higher prices. Indeed, their actions helped create the current, so-called glut, and have exerted strong downward pressures on prices.

A decade of enormous capital flows into the Gulf producer countries in exchange for the oil flowing out of them has created a new kind of Gulf and Western cooperation, however. The international monetary system, and the stability of Western key currencies, particularly the U.S. dollar, which is the principal means of exchange in petroleum commerce, are now directly and heavily affected by decisions and actions taken by the Gulf countries acting as a group, or by Saudi Arabia as the major financial power of the Gulf (and one of the premier financial powers of the world). This is not to suggest that the U.S. economy is as directly or immediately dependent upon Saudi Arabia's financial decisions as it once was on the kingdom's petroleum decisions; it *is* to say that new, important, and perhaps more far-reaching areas of interdependence have come to supplement the former ones.

The new interdependencies are hardly reason for alarm. U.S. policy has always favored use of the dollar in international finance, and it is clearly an American interest of no minor consequence that this practice continues. The result—that foreign powers will come to hold large quantities of dollars—is clear, but it is equally clear that the greater the role of the dollar in foreign economies (such as the oil producers'), the more directly any damage to the U.S. economy is transferred to their own economies. The producers have been among the staunchest defenders of the dollar and the American economy, and little wonder, since they too are captive to the dollar's destiny. Saudi leaders, in particular, have been quite outspoken for many years about the importance of Western economic stability and the shared interests that this objective creates. Under these circumstances, "interdependence" is certainly neither too strong nor too euphemistic a term to describe the mutual interest in maintaining a strong U.S. economy, the backbone to the Western economies as a group.

The economic importance of the Gulf states is not limited to production of oil and support of the international monetary system and Western economic stability. The Gulf oil producers have undertaken their own major economic assistance programs that materially aided Islamic countries friendly to the West. Their support of Pakistan and Somalia are cases in point. These assistance programs reduce the burden of aid on the United States and its allies and at the same time provide what is frequently vital help to countries important to U.S. security interests.

The countries of the GCC—Bahrain, Kuwait, Oman, Qatar, Saudi Arabia, and the United Arab Emirates (UAE)[1]—continue to supply the oil that makes the sustained combat power of the North Atlantic Treaty Organization (NATO) viable. This is more than an economic factor; it is clearly strategic and political, as well. Denial of the Gulf to the Soviet Union—not merely to Soviet expansionist designs, but to political control or hegemony—remains vital to the West. Soviet control over the Gulf, whether effected directly or indirectly, would mean not less than Soviet control over Western industrial strength and therefore defensive capacity. In this very immediate and vital sense, the Gulf remains a critical area for American security.

However, there are other—less existential but more immediate—political ways in which the Gulf is relevant and important to U.S. interests. All the members of the GCC are "moderates"—they are opposed in principle to the use of violence to effect change, and favor evolutionary development rather than radical or extremist approaches. Politically, all have cooperated with the West, and maintain friendly relations with the United States. Only Kuwait has long-established diplomatic relations with the Soviet Union (Oman and the UAE opened formal relations in late 1985), and neither the people nor the governments of the Gulf states are oriented in that direction politically or socially. The United States has contingency basing arrangements, is allowed virtual home-porting rights for some of its naval units, and has informal arrangements for cooperation with various of the GCC governments.

In addition to a legacy of political and some defense cooperation with the West, the Gulf states have taken more active postures in their international relations. In both Somalia and Egypt, for example, Saudi Arabia used its own approach to diplomacy to secure the ouster of Soviet advisors; both countries became key American allies. Saudi Arabia has also taken the lead in condemning the Soviet invasion of Afghanistan and in ensuring that the continuing Soviet occupation retains the highest priority in Middle East and Islamic councils.

It is not only with respect to Soviet ambitions in the area that the GCC states and the West hold common views. Both are deeply concerned about the growth of religious extremism, across all faiths, in the Middle East and in nearby areas. Both the Gulf countries and the West have also consulted about the increase in political violence in the Middle East, and particularly about the use of ter-

---

[1] The UAE consists of the following seven sheikhdoms: Abu Dhabi, 'Ajman, Dubai, Fujaira, Ras al-Khaima, Sharjah, and Umm al-Qaiwain.

rorism. Both have suffered terrorist violence. The rise of Iranian extremism and the spread of Iranian revolutionary fervor in the Gulf is of direct concern to the West and the Gulf as well, and it is in the Gulf that the Iranian revolution will either be contained or will receive the fuel it needs to spread.

As a result of their oil wealth, of the influence their production is believed to have in the West, and of their own financial assistance to a variety of countries, the Gulf states, particularly Saudi Arabia, have assumed a prominent role in the politics of the Third World. Over the last decade, the GCC countries have become participants in a variety of peacekeeping or mediating activities, some directly related to or supportive of U.S. actions in troubled areas such as Lebanon. Saudi Arabia's position as guardian of the Muslim holy places provides additional stature for that country in the Islamic family of nations, and its leadership of the Islamic world has often led to that group's support of specific U.S. policies or opposition to Soviet initiatives.

Threats to U.S. Gulf Interests

Arrayed against, and spread around, the Gulf countries are a variety of threats taking an even greater variety of forms. The Gulf War between Iran and Iraq demonstrates that even conventional military operations cannot be excluded. More likely—and more manageable—threats arise from adversary use of low-level violence, violence such as sabotage, terrorism, political agitation, or coups (for example, the one Iran attempted to effect in Bahrain).

Complicating the process of defending the GCC states is the dispersion of potential hostile activity. Iran's Gulf coast runs for about 1,000 kilometers (km) more or less parallel to the GCC countries' coastlines, and at a distance of only between 50 and 350 km. In concrete terms this provides virtually no warning time against air attacks, and abundant opportunities for harassment by air or sea. Should the Iraqi government (currently on excellent terms with the GCC states) change as a result of internal developments, an Iranian military victory, or some combination of the two, Iraq's land borders with the GCC totaling more than 1,150 km and the proximity of large Iraqi air and ground forces to Kuwait renders virtually impossible any attempt to blunt an invasion prior to its achieving some objectives. Israeli aircraft already frequently violate Saudi airspace, and are well within range of the kingdom's new Red Sea oil port and industrial showcase at Yanbu. Saudi Arabia also has extensive (over 1,300 km) land borders with the Yemens, borders that have always been tense and remain so. Across the Red Sea—the West's new oil safety valve if something happens to interrupt oil transport in the Gulf—lies Marxist Ethiopia, allied with the People's Democratic Republic of Yemen (PDRY or South Yemen), with a coastline of 900 km only 600 km from Saudi Arabia, and host to Soviet forces on the Dahlak Islands.

The GCC occupies over 2.5 million square km, an area about one third that of the continental United States. While the principal targets for capture or harassment are clustered in the Gulf, major political centers could also be attacked from any direction with a variety of goals in mind.

The GCC and Gulf Security

In addition to those problems posed by potential threat countries, the GCC must overcome the significant impediments posed by its own youth and composition—members have not purchased interoperable arms and have little experience in joint operations or planning. Moreover, the GCC states are developing countries and suffer shortcomings, such as in skilled manpower, that are typical of such countries.

The GCC does not lack equipment, and in fact adequate quantities of high-performance systems are available in the aggregated inventories of the members. However, the procurement of these weapons was not well planned from the standpoint of either collective or individual requirements, except in Saudi Arabia and to some degree in Oman. There is little prospect that even a tenth of the firepower and defense potential available in the smaller states' inventories can be realized, which in turn places a burden out of all proportion on Oman and, especially, Saudi Arabia.

Ultimately, with their limited population base, the GCC states cannot become a potent offensive force; nor can they reach the level of military strength of the threat forces. However, since there is no practical possibility of their seeking to attack and defeat their neighbors, such a level of power is unnecessary. What is required is the ability to make hostile attack sufficiently costly (and clearly unsuccessful in capturing GCC resources) that it is manifestly unwise—in other words, providing deterrence. Yet, given the value of the Gulf targets, deterrence necessarily involves a limited but clear strike capability, and it is the absence of this capability that may be the most significant deficiency in the GCC.

Realistically, only two GCC states—Oman and Saudi Arabia—have any capability to defend themselves against attack without external support. Saudi Arabia is and will continue to be the backbone of the GCC. It alone has the strategic depth, the human resources, and the organization for defense planning to carry out GCC-wide defensive operations. Perhaps even more important, most of the social and political problems impeding military modernization in the smaller GCC states obtain to a much less significant degree, or not at all, in Saudi Arabia. Already, in the tanker crisis of 1984, it was to Saudi Arabia that the smaller states looked in order to protect petroleum cargoes. The kingdom does have the ability to defend itself, and to some extent the rest of the GCC, against some range of threats, but lacks necessary deterrent strike capabilities.

In order to defend the Gulf front, Saudi Arabia should acquire improved radar and weapons systems that would optimize a limited but effective deterrent strike capability. For other fronts, important to the GCC only because Saudi Arabia is the core of its defense, Saudi Arabia should obtain an improved command, control, communications and intelligence (C^3I) system. The kingdom must continue to take the lead in coordinating the defense of the GCC, even if this requires ad hoc bilateral agreements to supplement GCC-wide cooperative accords.

The current decline in the West's oil vulnerability is a healthy development that has reduced the immediate level of concern with the Gulf. It is both politically reasonable and analytically correct to weigh the level of petroleum vulnerability heavily in the measure of the Gulf's importance to the United States. At the same time, it would be an error—and an error Washington has avoided—to assume the short-term amelioration of the once-critical oil vulnerability erodes the significance of the Gulf to the point where its security is of marginal interest to the United States.

Substantial Soviet efforts to make further inroads in the Gulf and the continuing attention devoted to Gulf developments by European and Japanese, as well as American, strategic thinkers, political leaders, businessmen, and bankers reflect the salience of the area and its enduring relevance to American security. If the West's short-term vulnerability to Gulf developments has declined—and, fortunately, it has—this change has served to place the Gulf in its proper perspective, a perspective that reveals the region to be one of several critical nodes in the global system.

It is in the clear and incontrovertible interest of both the United

States and the moderate Gulf countries to cooperate in the construction of a viable GCC defensive system and the improvement of the American capacity to bolster that system should it be challenged by the Soviet Union. For the local defenders, the Gulf states, and those whose critical interests are at stake, the best defense is *deterrence*, a defense that obviates its own employment.

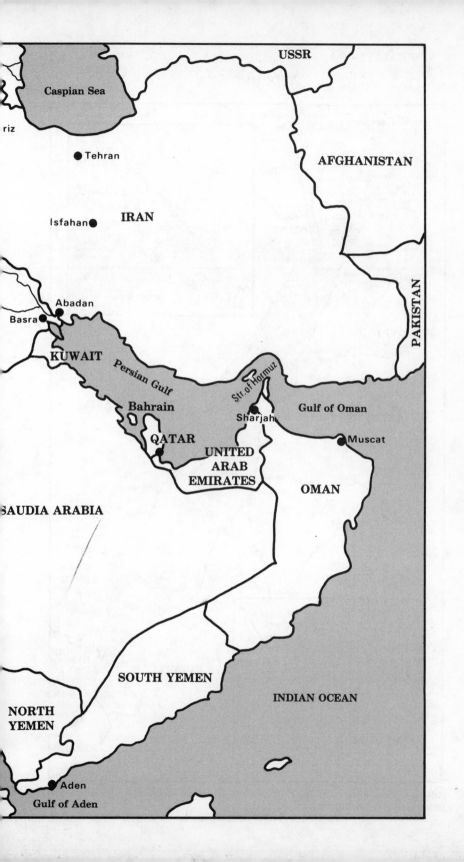

THE RED SEA

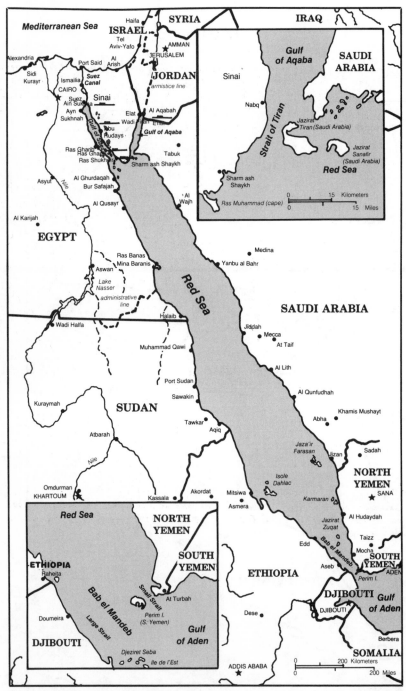

Adapted from Cordesman, *The Gulf and the Search for Strategic Stability* (Boulder, Colo.: Westview) p. 791.

THE ARABIAN PENINSULA

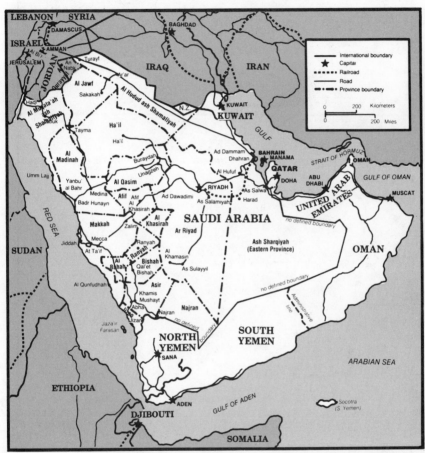

Adapted from Cordesman, *The Gulf and the Search for Strategic Stability* (Boulder, Colo.: Westview) p. 86.

I

GEOPOLITICS OF GULF SECURITY

The Gulf's importance to the United States derives from its hydrocarbon resources. Yet, the political system in which those resources are extracted and supplied is a complex one that, even apart from its own internal dynamics, operates in the interstices of regional (i.e., Middle East) and global political, economic, and military relations that establish many of the parameters for Gulf defense.

Introduction

This chapter discusses the politics of the Gulf and the relationship to its states both of other Gulf countries and of external powers. The chapter introduces regional alignments and organizations related to security, and places Gulf power relationships in their geographical, as well as political, context.

Political Geography of the Gulf States

Background

Like most regions of the world, the Persian/Arabian Gulf is characterized by striking asymmetries of size and power among its component states. (See Table 1.1) Iran's 42.5 millions of population live

1

in 1,644,000 square km. By contrast, Kuwait's 17,000 square km host 1.75 million inhabitants, of whom over 1 million (almost 60 percent) are foreign, and on Bahrain's 678 square km reside 400,000 Bahrainis. Similarly, the size of local armed forces varies from about 2,800 in Bahrain to about 650,000 in Iraq, and much larger forces in Iran and Iraq if irregulars and paramilitary forces are included. Iraq has over 4,500 tanks and about 580 combat aircraft, many of them highly advanced, while Bahrain has no combat aircraft or tanks.

Clearly, the interactions of Gulf states are not relations among equals. Historically, the strongest countries *on* the Gulf lay in the north—Iran and Iraq—but the principal power *in* the Gulf was Britain. For over a century, the United Kingdom maintained a *pax britannica* in the Gulf, but that state continued at least as much because the Gulf languished in obscurity as because of any muscle exerted by the British. (Indeed in the postwar crisis over continued Soviet occupation of Iran, it was the United States, not the United Kingdom, that was required to face down Moscow.) Whatever its potential strategic value for geographic, economic, or other reasons, it would not be off the mark to characterize the Gulf as a backwater of world politics prior to the 1960s.

Iran, after the return of the shah in 1953, and Iraq, after turning

TABLE 1.1

VITAL STATISTICS OF GULF STATES
(January 1985)

State	Area (km²)	Population (000)	Size of Military	Mil. Budget ($US mill.)	Combat a/c	Tanks
Bahrain	678	400	2,800	253	0	0
Iran	1,644,000	42,500	600,000	17,370	50	1,000
Iraq	437,400	14,900	642,500	10,300	580	4,900
Kuwait	16,900	1,750	12,500	1,360	49	240
Oman	300,000	1,000	21,500	1,960	52	20
Qatar	11,400	275	6,000	170	11	24
Saudi Arabia	2,240,000	7,000	51,500	22,700	203	450
UAE	77,700	1,300	43,000	1,900	43	178

to the Soviets for arms, were the primary military powers on the Gulf littoral. In the 1960s they engaged in an arms race that left Iran with an especially impressive arsenal. But before the late 1960s neither had any real capability to project and support sustained military power significantly beyond its borders. Even in the early to mid-1970s, despite Iranian expeditionary forces' experience in Oman and Tehran's acquisition of mobility-enhancing technology, it is not clear whether the imperial Iranian armed forces could conduct sustained combat operations against a major foe well outside Iran. It is clear that Iraq could not.

American concern about Gulf security is of recent date, although the involvement of the United States in Gulf military affairs stretches back almost to World War II. A U.S. air base was constructed at Dhahran in the immediate aftermath of the war, and the U.S. Middle East Force (MIDEASTFOR) of the U.S. Navy emerged at approximately the same time. However, the American air base was of little importance, and MIDEASTFOR was, and to a great extent remains, a political force. In fact, the United States deferred to and benefited from the *pax britannica* of the Gulf.

The Cold War focused U.S. attention on Iran and Turkey, countries sharing long borders with the Soviet Union, and with other states of the "Northern Tier." While regional experts pointed to the value of the Gulf, the limited American imports of oil, the relatively minor commercial investment there (by contrast with that in Europe), and, again, the presence of the British tended to limit real concern to the northern Gulf.

As the Gulf's importance grew in the mid to late 1960s, the British were reaching a decision to withdraw. American policymakers were concerned about the resulting "power vacuum," and debated how security and stability could best be maintained in the post-U.K. Gulf. Faced with a decision on whether (or to what extent) to project real U.S. power into the Gulf to replace the British, the American government instead opted for a "twin-pillar" policy that envisaged U.S. encouragement and support of Iran and Saudi Arabia in order that they might assume the mantle of policemen of the Gulf.

The twin-pillar policy had several faults. First, it naively assumed that Iran and Saudi Arabia would cooperate on the basis of common interests rather than coming into conflict as a result of divergent interests. Second, the policy overlooked the disparity between Iran and Saudi Arabia. Third, Washington underestimated and misread Iraq. Fourth, the nature of and limits on the power of the "pillars" were never understood.

Iranian-Saudi cooperation was troubled by growing differences on oil production and pricing. Since petroleum revenues were the lifeblood of security planning, and therefore of security itself, these differences were certainly not solely economic.

Iran was far and away the superpower of the Gulf. Its armed forces exceeded those of Iraq by 20-300 percent in most categories of key weapons systems and by 75 percent in manpower. More important, given the criticality of quality as against quantity in modern armed combat, Iran's armed forces were characterized by higher morale and better-quality personnel; its weaponry was more advanced and better maintained; its training, better and more rigorous; its officer corps, superior and less politicized; and its superpower relationship, stronger and more reliable. Saudi Arabia was not in the same military class as either Iran or Iraq, as Table 1.2 demonstrates.

While the United States and Saudi Arabia did enter into programmatic efforts to upgrade Saudi defensive capabilities, the process was long term and not without major impediments. Only in the latter half of the 1970s did it begin to show results in the kingdom's ability to absorb greater quantities of more sophisticated weapons systems, quantities still limited by the small Saudi population relative to its northern neighbors. For the immediate period after the twin-pillar policy entered into force, however, the emphasis was directed toward the construction of a military infrastructure ade-

TABLE 1.2

EVOLUTION OF THE
THREE PRINCIPAL GULF POWERS, 1970–1980

	1970			1980		
	Iran	Iraq	S. Arabia	Iran	Iraq	S. Arabia
mil. mnpwr. (000)	161	94.5	60	240	242	67
tanks	>750	685	90	1,735	2,750	380
APCs	>750	>200	—	>825	2,500	>350
Strk a/c	32	124	24	265	217	—
Intrcp a/c	138	105	51	166	115	136
maj. naval comb. vessels	11	—	—	11	—	—

4

quate to support the anticipated growth in men, arms, and responsibilities. Thus, the enormous systems and manpower gap between Iran and Saudi Arabia widened dramatically in the decade of the 1970s.

Military order of battle (OB) was not the only distinction between Iran and Saudi Arabia, however. The shah of Iran, in part *because* of his country's military superiority, viewed himself as the appropriate successor to the United Kingdom, the new Gulf policeman, and saw the special relationship evolving with the United States as reinforcement of that role. Yet, Iran's oil resources were already on the decline at the levels of production reached in the mid-1970s, and it was anticipated that Iran would "run out of oil" by the end of the century or sooner if those rates were sustained. The proximity (across the Gulf) of vast quantities of reserves in the population-poor and weak Arabian Peninsula was assumed not to have escaped the shah's notice. His acquisition (real and planned) of a number of air-cushion vehicles raised alarms in the kingdom, where many began to wonder about the shah's intentions.

Such concerns were not reduced by Iran's record. In 1971, Iran seized control of Abu Musa and the Tumbs, Gulf islets theretofore controlled nominally by components of the then-newly-formed UAE. (The Islamic Republic has maintained its claim to and control of these islets.) Moreover, Iran's unilateral armed provocations in the disputed Shatt al-Arab and support of Kurdish rebels in Iraq inflamed already sensitive Iranian-Iraqi relations.

Nor was the myopia concerning the Saudi-Iranian relationship the only problem in implementing the twin-pillar policy. The development of U.S.-Iran relations was so rapid and intensive in the late 1960s that Iraq, which never claimed the role of Gulf policeman but never acquiesced in Iran's assertion of such a role either, was pushed to a more aggressive articulation of what its leaders felt were their country's rights. The Iran-Iraq arms race—which early ceased to be an arms race so unbalanced was it—was asymmetrical because while Iran armed principally against Iraq, Iraq was dealing with an active and dangerous insurgency (supported by Iran) and felt compelled to respond to armed challenges arising in the Fertile Crescent (e.g., from Syria) as well as to the Iranian procurements. (Once Iran had far outdistanced Iraq in the arms race, the shah began to argue that his government needed arms to defend itself against the Soviets, to protect the Gulf, and so forth.) The only country prepared to provide the arms Iraq sought on acceptable terms was the Soviet Union, and in many respects the U.S. government policy of providing the shah with anything he wanted (short of nuclear weapons) had the effect of pushing the Soviet-Iraqi relationship well beyond the levels Baghdad would have preferred as well as of further fueling Iraqi arms procurement (which, in turn, ignited several competitive procurement spirals outside the Gulf).

Finally, even the military limits of power constraining the twin pillars were ill understood in Washington in the 1969-71 period, when it seemed to suffice to increase the weapons inventory of regional powers, making those inventories relatively superior to those of all who might challenge the status quo, to create a viable security system. In fact, however, weapons inventories may grow, personnel levels may increase, training may improve—all without materially enhancing the ability of a country to *project* that power beyond its borders (which, after all, is the essence of a regional policeman's duties). Force projection requires concepts of force structure, advances in C^3, capabilities in long-range supply and support (including maintenance), and experience in maneuver that all eluded Saudi or even Iranian forces in the 1960s and 1970s. Thus, leaving aside the political problems facing Iranian-Saudi cooperation in asserting a new security system, the physical ability to implement such a regime was still at least a decade away.

Position and Status of Individual States

The North

Despite the very significant improvements that have been made in Saudi defensive capabilities (see below), the overwhelming preponderance of military power remains in the north. Manpower differentials between Iran or Iraq, on the one hand, and the other Gulf states, on the other, are so great as to outweigh the technology advantages Saudi Arabia enjoys in some areas. The size of the Saudi force structure, both actual and projected, does not provide the kingdom the opportunity to envisage an offensive role for its forces, in terms of conquest, with respect to either of the larger powers to the north. This is the case even more clearly with the other lower Gulf states.

Since September 1980, Iran and Iraq, the two major powers of the Gulf, have been at war with each other. The war has been portrayed as merely a contemporary version of a conflict that has endured for over a millennium between Persian and Arab, Shi'a and Sunni. There are elements of this age-old ethnic conflict in the present war, certainly. Moreover, there are a number of other elements—disputes over the role of each country in the Gulf; rivalry between sectarian and secular ideologies; and a clash between the

GEOPOLITICS OF GULF SECURITY

personalities of the ruling elites. All this contributes to the venom of the war. However, it is quite clear that Iran and its revolution constitute a fundamental challenge to the existing system of international relations in the Middle East and beyond. This is a major factor in the war, and the principal reason it has not been possible to end it after so many casualties on both sides and an apparent stalemate on the ground.

The virulent revolutionary ideology and uncompromising political tactics of Iran have placed Iraq in the unaccustomed position of defending the status quo in the Gulf. Iraq has become a bastion of regional stability, altering its previous posture toward Israel and aligning itself with the moderate Arab states. In the face of the Iranian threat this new posture is eminently comprehensible, but how durable is it? Has Iraqi pan-Arab Ba'thism changed permanently?

There is strong evidence to suggest that the linkages and interdependencies occasioned by the war may well endure beyond its conclusion. Certainly, Iraq will have a significant need for maximum revenue for reconstruction and for continued development, and the pipelines through Saudi Arabia cannot easily be dismissed as unimportant linkages in these circumstances. The Jordanian-Iraqi relationship may well endure, and the Iraqi-Syrian rivalry will certainly remain. King Hussein has moderated his position vis-a-vis Syria, but is under no illusions about his future in a Syrian-dominated system. Thus, there is good reason to believe that the new Iraqi posture is not an ephemeral one.

At the same time, it is prudent to raise alternative possibilities—in both countries. It is conceivable that, following the departure of Ayatollah Khomeini from the scene, Iran will reduce its revolutionary zeal, or at least its commitment to pursue fundamental change through subversion, terrorism, and war. It may be that with or without Khomeini the internal schisms that his autocratic and arbitrary rule has spawned will lead to another upsurge of either violent domestic upheavals or separatist movements along the periphery of this very heterogeneous country. While Iran is overwhelmingly Shi'a, the Sunni regions along Iran's northwest and southeast borders have chafed self-consciously under the Shi'a intemperance that is new to them. To date, however, there has been an unsteady but still marked progress in rationalizing the process of future leadership selection, a process that is expected to be tumultuous but is unlikely to introduce change of the magnitude suggested here. Moreover, the separatism that exists along Iran's periphery appears to have *diminished*, not increased, in effectiveness, if not potency over the last few years.

While the possibilities of fundamental change in Iran that we have adduced cannot be excluded, major shifts in Iraq appear to be more likely. There can be no question of Saddam Hussein's overall authority and control at the present time, yet evidence is abundant that his control is in no way as complete as Khomeini's. He has been forced to make policy shifts deemed necessary only very gradually due to opposition from within the armed forces, resistance on the part of the public, or alternative power centers inside the Ba'th itself. Moreover, Iraq's posture has changed, which reflects its pragmatism and therefore potential to shift once again, while Iran's has remained fundamentally unidirectional since the advent of the Islamic Republic. And in fact none can be certain of the future of Saddam Hussein's tenure in Iraq, especially if the war should continue to cost heavily in lives, treasure, development, and expectations.

Should Iran score a complete and victorious military breakthrough—a highly unlikely eventuality—the Saddam Hussein regime would be removed and an Islamic republican government installed. Alternatively, the breakthrough could be incomplete but decisive enough to ensure the ouster of the current leadership and its replacement, perhaps within the Ba'th, by a government nominally independent of but in fact completely responsive to Iran. In either case, Iraq would become a land-bridge between Iran and Syria, and the revolutionary entente between these two would have become the most powerful coalition in the Middle East.[1]

There are other situations that could alter the position of Iraq. The government in Baghdad has been extremely dissatisfied with the quantity and quality of support it has received from the Gulf Arab states in its war with Iran, a war seen in Baghdad as one in defense of the interests of all the Arab states against the threat from Iran. The opening toward the United States, a renewal of relations Saddam Hussein has sought for some time and certainly seems to value, may prove itself to be without value. The Iraqi leadership, recognizing the realistic political constraints on the United States, has kept its options open by maintaining good relations with the Soviet Union as well. There is considerable pressure still in Iraq within the party to rely on the Soviet Union rather than the United States; what effect will this have if the United

---

[1] It cannot be denied that the minority 'Alawi regime in Damascus would be discomfited at the prospect of the fundamentalist colossus to the east, but perhaps not more than by the present hostile Iraqi government to the east, since Assad's Syria has cooperated fully with Iran in trying to unseat Saddam and extensively with Iran in Lebanon as well.

8

States proves unforthcoming? Even during the war there have been occasional cases of provocation toward the Gulf states. Should a peace finally arrive on the front with Iran through whatever means, how certain can anyone be that Iraq, with essentially the same political leadership in place as during more aggressive, interventionist years, will not again turn its attention toward the smaller Gulf states. The border conflict with Kuwait, for example, remains unresolved; will Baghdad not use its extraordinarily large, well-equipped, and now experienced army to extort or even force a settlement on its terms?

Saudi Arabia

Saudi Arabia remains a critical country in the Gulf. While the kingdom's military resources do not compare in size with those of Iran or Iraq—and never will—they have steadily developed and today have a considerable defensive capability in the Gulf context. Saudi Arabia remains the only one of the three major Gulf countries that is irrevocably committed to stability and security in the Gulf and to its Western orientation.

Saudi Arabia is an attractive target, even more so in a period of oil glut. The kingdom remains the key producer in the Gulf and in OPEC. Without Saudi production, the balance is unstable; with it, there is a surfeit. This is especially true if Iran should be in a position to control the other Gulf producers, which would be likely if it triumphed over Iraq. Moreover, Saudi Arabia's proven reserves remain by far the largest in the world, a magnet to countries like Iran whose reserves will be exhausted much sooner. And Saudi Arabia's financial resources have made it one of the world's premier financial powers with the resources to influence not only regional governments, but, ironically, even more the Western industrialized economies.

The importance of Saudi Arabia lies not in its military strength but in its political orientation and economic resources. In recent years, Riyadh has been the region's most active capital in the search for means to dampen the self-destructive fires of conflict, and to reinforce the stability of the moderates and their ability to resist the pressure and attacks of extremist, revolutionary groups. In this context, the government of Saudi Arabia, with little exportable military power, has provided extraordinary quantities of financial aid to those under the greatest pressure; and has cooperated closely with other governments, notably the United States, in trying to bring about a settlement to such flashpoints as Lebanon.

9

The government in Iran has made no secret that its ultimate target is not Iraq, but Saudi Arabia. And in fact the Iranians have already perpetrated a large number of subversive acts in the kingdom. Meanwhile, Saudi Arabia, for its part, concluding that the weakness of the Gulf is its own weakness, has moved quickly and decisively in recent years to broaden and strengthen the security resources in the Gulf, stressing regional cooperation rather than simply arms acquisition. (See below, Chapter IV.) Saudi Arabia enjoys close and cooperative relations with all the smaller Gulf countries, as well as with Iraq, and has worked assiduously to develop better and more effective exchange of information with the Gulf sheikhdoms on all security threats, internal and external. Saudi Arabia has also taken the lead in rationalizing oil prices, and to this end has taken the lion's share of the production cuts in the current glut.[2]

The Saudis have a number of advantages their smaller neighbors do not, and they realize it. They have size, which provides a certain strategic depth unavailable to the smaller Gulf states. (However, from a security point of view, the most valuable Saudi resources likely to serve as a target, the oil fields, lie close to the borders and to international waters.) The Saudi government has also had a degree of stability foreign to some of the smaller Gulf states, and benefits from a level of legitimacy within the country that probably exceeds that of all of the other Gulf nations and of most countries in the region.

Saudi Arabia also benefits from a position of regional leadership conferred on the kingdom by virtue of its oil resources, which are thought to provide influence in the West, its financial strength, its subventions to a number of other countries, and from its religious stature amongst Muslim nations as the guardian of the Muslim holy places at Mecca and Medina. Ever since the reign of the late King Faisal, Saudi Arabia has also had a reputation of moral leadership in policy, a position Iran's new leadership has tried, so far in vain, to attack.

The Smaller Gulf States

In the years following the British withdrawal from east of Suez, the smaller Gulf countries—Bahrain, Kuwait, Oman, Qatar, and

---

[2] In late 1985, Saudi Arabia was forced to abandon its long-held role of swing producer as a result of repeated violations of quota agreements by other OPEC members. The present Saudi policy is expected to be temporary, and is intended to restore discipline within OPEC.

the UAE—appeared to many the artifacts of a previous era, short-lived anachronisms in a turbulent area. Despite some internal problems, and not inconsiderable external challenges, all five have survived and developed. They are far from secure nation-states; all face major difficulties in the years ahead. But they have already outlived the doomsday forecasts of the pessimists.

The five smaller Gulf countries are often lumped together by outsiders for matters of convenience, leaving the impression that they are all similar. In fact, of course, their differences are as great as those of other countries in the Middle East. Apart from the obvious geographical propinquity, and the fact that they are all Muslim states, the smaller Gulf countries have in common only the shared external threat from the larger Gulf states to the North and East, a tradition of social conservatism, and a history of isolation from the processes of world politics.

Bahrain is a small island state with a population slightly over half Shi'a (the only one of the smaller Gulf states whose citizens are predominantly Shi'a). While Bahrain once depended on oil production for its revenue, the small reserves and relatively high production-to-reserves ratio alerted the Bahraini leadership to the dangers ahead, and it wisely moved toward more downstream operations, especially refining. Bahrain has been trying to establish itself as the Gulf entrepot—its banking, commerce, and communications center. While it does not appear that the island will ever capture this niche, these kinds of operations have led to a healthier diversification of the economy. Bahrain was the headquarters of MIDEASTFOR for many years, and the force continues to benefit from regular use of the island's facilities. The completion of a causeway between Saudi Arabia and Bahrain means the latter is no longer an island politically, whatever its geographical designation. It virtually guarantees a swift and intensive Saudi reaction to threats against Bahrain.

Kuwait has had a long history of oil production, which continues to be the small country's primary source of income. Kuwait's parliament takes a more active role in politics and government than is common in the Gulf, and its press is perhaps the freest and most vigorous in the Arab world since the tragedy in Lebanon. The large number of Palestinians, well organized and highly politicized, have been an especially important political factor in Kuwait. After Saudi Arabia, Kuwait has been the most active GCC participant in regional politics, and Kuwait has also learned to "buy off" threats where possible.

The bulk of *Oman*'s territory lies outside the Gulf, but the tip of the Musandam Peninsula, which is subject to Oman's sovereignty,

11

makes Oman a Gulf state and an important one given the strategic value of the peninsula in terms of control of Gulf waters. Long isolated from the world by the father of the current sultan of Oman, the country has emerged rapidly and actively over the past 15 years. Oman succeeded in overcoming a dangerous insurgency sponsored by external leftist forces, and is therefore deeply sensitive to issues of stability in the area. Oman, often marching to a drummer different from that of the other GCC states, has an agreement with the United States permitting use of certain Omani facilities on a contingency basis, has jointly exercised its own with U.S. forces, and has supported most U.S. efforts to bring peace and security to the area. Oman is exploiting its very limited oil reserves.

Qatar is another oil producer, but in small quantities (Qatar's gas reserves are much more promising). Its population is by far the smallest of the Gulf states, even though in area Qatar is two thirds the size of Kuwait. Qatar, like the other Gulf states, is trying to use its oil income to move into the 20th century, but without destroying the underlying fabric of society. This has proved especially difficult in a country with a population so small that expatriate labor is required in relatively greater proportions than in the other Gulf countries.

Finally, the *UAE* consists of seven sheikhdoms that used to form the Trucial Oman states. Their population, area, and oil resources are very unevenly distributed, with the lion's share of the wealth located in Abu Dhabi and, to a lesser extent, Dubai. Of all the Gulf states, the UAE, the establishment of which was accomplished in the 11th hour of the British withdrawal, was itself troublesome and rancorous. None of the UAE sheikhs was eager to give up any of his own authority or his state's autonomy. However, there has been a steady accretion of power by the central UAE government and a diminuation of power of the individual states. In practice this has also meant a growth in the individual power of Abu Dhabi within the federation. The small, scattered sheikhdoms, with chaotic borders and petty rivalries, cover a large spectrum in levels of development, administrative efficiency, security preparedness, and even awareness of the outside (or proximate) world.

These small countries vary greatly, but, taken together, share a number of common interests, principal among which is high vulnerability and therefore a shared and profound concern about the stability and security of the Gulf they all share. They all depend upon petroleum commerce, even if in different ways and to different degrees. They all look to Saudi Arabia to take the leadership role in the Gulf, despite past conflicts with the kingdom in some cases, because of its size, resources, and links to the West. Due to their

12

small populations and the rapid development and economic expansion all have experienced, they share a major problem, too—the heavy presence of expatriate labor. This is a problem of several dimensions—economic (the great need for foreign labor, the fluctuating supply and demand), social (the explosive presence of large numbers of non-nationals whose customs are foreign to and often disruptive of the social order), political (local disdain of foreign labor, and foreign resentment of personal treatment and administrative discrimination), and security (foreign loyalties often hostile to the local public order).

Relationships of the Gulf States

Alignments and Coalitions

The most important institution in the Gulf is unquestionably the GCC. Members of the GCC are Saudi Arabia and all of the smaller Gulf states. Neither Iran nor Iraq is a member, and the Iraqi government, which long proposed some form of Gulf security regime, seemed to resent (and may still resent) exclusion, which was justified by GCC members on the basis that Iraq was engaged in a war with Iran to which the other GCC members were not, and did not wish to become, parties.

The GCC is an organization with ambitious and wide-ranging objectives in a variety of domains. Nevertheless, its *raison d'etre* is unquestionably security. It was established, largely at Saudi initiative, to improve security coordination and cooperation among the conservative Arab Gulf states (i.e., the Arab Gulf states exclusive of Iraq). It has succeeded in upgrading cooperation, but has so far fallen short of the hopes the Saudi government had originally invested in it. (See Chapter IV below.)

Iraq's exclusion from the GCC should not be taken to imply that Baghdad is isolated in the Gulf from fellow Arab states. On the contrary, Iraq's relations with other Gulf countries are on the whole very positive, active, and diverse. The Gulf countries have provided enormous economic support to Iraq in order to enable Baghdad to continue to hold the line against Iran. Some of the Gulf states see Iraq as the first line of defense against Iranian expansion, Shi'a consciousness, and revolution and subversion in the Gulf. Moreover, Iraq and the Gulf Arab states consult frequently on matters of common concern.

Another institution bringing together the Arab Gulf states, but including others as well, is the Organization of Arab Petroleum

13

Exporting Countries (OAPEC). All the Arab states in the Gulf except Oman are members of OAPEC, along with Algeria, Libya, and Syria. This organization is a forum for discussing oil policies and problems and for addressing and consulting multilaterally on issues of interest to OPEC in order to maintain the greatest degree of Arab agreement possible within the larger organization. Since OPEC includes only two other Arab oil producers (i.e., non-Gulf Arab oil producers, Algeria and Libya—Syria is not a member of OPEC), OAPEC is a powerful bloc within OPEC. Its wealth, and the importance of its members' subsidies to other Arab governments, give OAPEC substantial influence in the Arab world when they are in agreement on policy.

In addition to formal organizations, informal alignments are important in the Middle East. However, they are much less complex and conflictual in the Gulf due to the cooperation all smaller Arab Gulf countries share with each other and with Saudi Arabia. The growth of problems such as the large-scale presence of expatriates and the movement of Arabs among the Gulf states was a primary reason for the formation of the GCC, which is important as a means to improve cooperation in monitoring these flows.

Saudi Arabia led the way toward greater cooperation among the Arab Gulf states, apart from Iraq, in the 1970s by initiating efforts to resolve the plethoric boundary disputes in the Gulf. Most of these disputes have now been resolved, and although a few remain, none threatens the extensive cooperation that has blossomed among these countries.

The Regional Powers

Iraq and Iran are not as closely linked to the other Gulf states as the latter are to each other, although both do interact with at least some of their Gulf neighbors and in Iraq's case cooperation is in fact extensive. Both, however, are more closely aligned with other regional powers.

The Islamic Republic of Iran is relatively isolated in regional politics, but has had cooperative ties with Syria since the time of the revolution. The principal foundation for the cooperation is the mutual antipathy of the two governments toward Saddam Hussein's Iraq, but they have also worked together on a number of other fronts, have developed extensive linkages, and have been associated in enterprises such as the terrorist bombing of U.S., French, and American contractor facilities in Kuwait in December 1983. Libya,

14

too, has worked ever more closely with the Tehran regime since the revolution. Despite differences in outlook, and Libya's much warmer relations with the Soviet Union, the two countries share regional enemies and friends.

Jordan, Iraq's principal regional ally since 1979, has served as strategic depth (sheltering Iraqi aircraft early in the war), political advocate in the region and beyond, and line of communications (LOC). Enormous quantities of goods are offloaded at Aqaba, then trucked to Iraq from Jordan. Consequently, these two countries have developed even more far-reaching economic cooperation. The support of most of the Arab world is behind Iraq in varying degrees, so that only a handful of Arab states are not involved in some kind of interaction with Iraq. The most notable case of cooperation beyond the Gulf and Jordan is Egypt, which has supplied the Iraqi armed forces with vast amounts of equipment and some manpower for the Gulf war. Indeed, the Iraqi-Jordanian entente appears to be evolving toward a tripartite alliance of Iraq, Jordan, and Egypt. Jordan has already renewed diplomatic relations with Egypt, and Iraq is expected to follow suit at some time in the near future.

The North

Pakistan and Iran cooperated extensively while the shah was in power, and Pakistan, facing major security threats in the north and east, has been loath to encourage additional problems on its border with Iran. Thus, Pakistan and Iran have maintained correct relations, and have even cooperated to a degree in some security-related areas, such as support of Afghan insurgents. They both have problems with the Baluchi people. Pakistan's primary interest in the Gulf is located on the Arab side, however, and especially in Saudi Arabia. The two countries share a conservative, profound Sunni Muslim faith that infuses both daily life and political outlook. In addition, Pakistan has assisted the kingdom in certain areas of security planning, while the money thereby generated and other Saudi subsidies have been of enormous help to poor Pakistan.

Afghanistan has had its own problems, and was never deeply involved with the Gulf. Rather, it is the Gulf that has been involved in Afghan issues, at least since the Soviet invasion of the country at the end of 1979. Saudi Arabia has taken an extremely active role in support of the Afghan guerrillas, and has tried to persuade other countries to increase their own tangible support to the insurgents. Some observers have suggested that the Soviet move into Afghanistan was designed to put the Soviet Union in a better position to interdict oil supplies from the Gulf to the West, and others even raised the specter of a Soviet military move into the Gulf from the new positions in Afghanistan. It is clear that the Gulf governments as a group have felt more vulnerable and less secure since the invasion. The resistance's strong Muslim component[3] has tended to increase Muslim awareness of and sensitivity to the Afghan issue.

The South

The Indian Ocean to the south of the Gulf has seen an increasing level of competition for superpower presence in recent years, spurred on by the unremitting crises of the Indian subcontinent and the Gulf itself. The United States and the Soviet Union have now all but abandoned their talks on naval limitations in the Indian Ocean, and the U.S. naval base at Diego Garcia has increased far beyond the original planning concept. So frequent and intense have been Gulf crises that the United States has at times had more than one carrier task force near the Gulf. (Carriers generally eschew the waters of the Gulf itself, since its narrow confines would tend to negate the advantages of carriers and to heighten their vulnerability.) The deposition of the shah of Iran was a setback to U.S. military and naval flexibility in this area, but Iran was never a major Indian Ocean power, even though the shah apparently had this item on his agenda prior to his departure.

The West

Because the Arabian Peninsula is principally occupied by Saudi Arabia, it is dealt with in the context of the security situation in Saudi Arabia itself. A factor of increasing salience in Gulf security is the Red Sea. The Red Sea remained a strategic backwater longer than the Gulf, and indeed to some extent remains outside the attention of most major powers. However, the importance of the Red Sea has grown as its relationship to the Gulf and its resources has grown. Specifically, because Saudi Arabia early recognized the potential dangers of instability in the Gulf, the kingdom has constructed pipelines that will carry its oil across the country from the Gulf littoral, where the oil fields are, to the Red sea coast. This initiative makes the Red Sea an alternative to the Gulf as a key

---

[3] There are also secular elements in the resistance, but the dominant tone has clearly been a Muslim one.

LOC connected with the petroleum trade. At the time the construction was undertaken, the Red Sea was stable and dominated by countries either friendly to Saudi Arabia or friendly to the oil-consuming countries and therefore unlikely to endanger the new adjunct to the "oil lifeline." However, over the past decade the political tenor of the Red Sea has also changed. Along the littoral are now found Marxist Ethiopia and South Yemen; an unstable Sudan; and a vacillating North Yemen.[4] The strongest naval powers in the Red Sea remain Israel and Egypt. Saudi Arabia and Egypt have left their old rivalries to history, but the extension of Egyptian military power outside the Arab-Israeli context has never given Saudi Arabia a cause for rejoicing. (The two were at odds for many years, and fought a war of surrogates in Yemen from 1962 to 1967.) While Saudi Arabia can look to neither as an ally, they do not constitute any threat to the shipment of oil through the Red Sea.

Role and Power of External States

The external states relevant to a study of Gulf security are limited. They consist of (1) the United States; (2) the Soviet Union; and (3) the major Western European naval powers (France and Britain). Clearly, these countries, like the Gulf states themselves, are characterized by disparate levels of capabilities, diverse types of interests, and different kinds of intentions.

The United States

The United States has had interests in the Gulf for a long period, although it would be accurate to say that those interests for many years did not weigh equally as much, relative to American interests in other regions, as they do now. American interests in the Gulf were essentially commercial and financial, and neither set was viewed as critical before the late 1960s or the early 1970s when a greater appreciation of the shortfall in the availability of petroleum and the implications of that shortfall began to grip the policy community, and after upward pressure on prices had already been in evidence for some time.

Geographical definitions are often means of expressing bureau-

---

[4] Jordan and Djibouti are also Red Sea states, but are not dealt with in that context. Jordan has no real naval power in the Red Sea. Djibouti is potentially important because of the French power based there.

17

cratic interests. U.S. strategic interests in the northern Gulf do in fact antedate the oil issue; they reflect the postwar American policy of containment. However, in that era, it was not the Gulf, but rather the "Northern Tier," that American policymakers addressed—the Northern Tier of Turkey and Iran and Iraq that bordered on the Soviet Union. Thus, the United States had a strategic interest in the Gulf, but generally failed to acknowledge it as such.

Despite an extended period of defense cooperation with Saudi Arabia, no serious concern about the security of the Gulf per se arose prior to British withdrawal. Even then, the Gulf was viewed more in the context of another potential trouble-spot than as an area where important and immediate U.S. interests were at stake. The oil crisis of 1973-1974 dramatically altered the lens through which U.S. leaders saw the Gulf. When the shortage was real, rather than potential, the American economy paid a heavy toll, even if it was less costly than to Europe's. As a result, U.S. policymakers began to look at the Gulf in terms of *the security of the flow of oil.* While the Soviet threat was mentioned in this regard, a variety of statements from senior American policymakers suggests strongly that the primary concern was ensuring the flow of oil to the West— even if over the resistance of the producer states.

Concomitant with the growing interest in coercive means of keeping the oil flow open, there arose a new awareness of the vulnerability of the West to hostile interdiction of the flow of petroleum, interdiction from extra-regional forces. Moreover, American imports from the Gulf, which had been negligible earlier, grew rapidly in the early 1970s. Until the criticality of Gulf oil to Western economies and defenses was dramatized by the 1973-1974 oil crisis, little credence was placed in the likelihood of hostile disruption of the oil flow, and therefore little priority was given to countering such disruption. Suddenly, oil disruption loomed much larger as a threat to U.S. vital interests, and the range of disruption scenarios was considered seriously. The Soviet invasion of Afghanistan, while patently a result of other problems, again brought home the vulnerability of the region and the limitations on the U.S. ability to project its power into the area to protect the vital oil LOCs and sea lanes of communications (SLOCs).

This is the historical context in which the U.S. Rapid Deployment Joint Task Force, now CENTCOM, was established. Ironically, as CENTCOM is truly coming on line with real capability, the *immediate* criticality of Gulf oil supplies and the perception of the threat to them are receding. Still, none can question the reality that the United States and the West remain heavily dependent upon the oil of the Gulf for both economic and defense reasons. Any threat to the continued supply of oil from the Gulf is a direct and serious threat to the vitality of the Western economy and viability of NATO.

For political reasons that are complex and multi-faceted, most Gulf countries have determined that under current conditions it would be counterproductive to grant the United States military facilities or treaty rights as in days of old. The American position on several issues, most notably the Palestinian question, has generated such *popular* disquiet that an overly intimate relationship with the United States could prove politically costly. As the same time, all of the smaller Gulf countries and Saudi Arabia have a long record of cooperation with the Western countries and all see in the Soviet Union a potential or actual threat. Thus, despite real differences on emotionally charged issues, to be unable to cooperate with Western countries' efforts to build improved regional security in the Gulf is clearly neither the interest nor the objective of these countries; it is merely a sad—and dangerous—fact of life. (Only Oman, whose internal crises in the mid-1970s placed the Arab-Israeli issue in a different perspective, has granted the United States facility rights.)

While it has not been possible or prudent to proffer bases, some of the Gulf countries have cooperated in a variety of other security-related ways with the United States. And to some extent, especially in the case of Saudi Arabia, their arms acquisitions from the United States and close cooperation in defense infrastructure construction can be seen as opening opportunities for cooperative interaction in the event of absolutely critical need. Meanwhile, several of the Gulf countries have felt more secure with the steady improvement of the American over-the-horizon presence near the Gulf. The pre-positioning of U.S. supplies, the greater ship-days of U.S. naval deployments, and the significantly enhanced mobility of forces dedicated to CENTCOM responsibilities have relaxed some Gulf concerns about the reliability of the United States in case of major contingencies. By contrast, the conditions the United States insisted were prerequisite to a stronger American hand in cooperation with others in bringing the so-called tanker war to a definitive end raise new concerns about the ability of the United States to address low-intensity warfare, in this case in international waters.[5]

---

[5] At one period during the height of the "tanker war," fear that Iran might launch some sort of naval attack on one of the Arab Gulf states ran high. At this stage, the United States sought to reach agreements with one or more of the states concerning contingency cooperation in the Gulf. Despite having received some preliminary indications of interest, U.S. officials emerged from the experience empty-

The Soviet Union

The Soviet Union has always tended to look at the importance of the Middle East in terms of denial rather than control, notwithstanding the famous discussions with the Nazis on Soviet interest to the South. From this standpoint, good relations with the regional states are desirable, but the absence of good relations is not necessarily a problem *as long as the West does not improve its own security position as a result.* Since 1955, Moscow has always had at least one regional partner in the Middle East, and since 1958 the Soviet Union has generally enjoyed good relations with at least one Gulf state. For many years this was Iraq, but Iraq, though still on good terms with the Soviet Union, is no longer dependent upon or oriented toward Moscow.

The most important Gulf state from the Soviet viewpoint is undoubtedly Iran, primarily because Iran shares a long border with the Soviet Union. For years, the Soviets tried to improve their relations with the shah—and in fact the two countries did pursue trade relations rather vigorously—but to no avail; the shah remained committed to the United States. While Soviet-Iranian relations have been anything but good since the advent of the Islamic Republic, Moscow has scored a major gain as a result of the sharp deterioration of the once-intimate U.S.-Iranian defense tie, which has become a relationship of bitter antipathy.

Denial of Iran to the West as a minimum, influence over Iran as preferable, and control as yet more desirable are not Moscow's only attitudes toward the Gulf. Soviet leaders, recognizing the importance of Gulf resources to the West, aspire to a greater position of influence in the Gulf and, ultimately, to raise doubts about the security of the flow of petroleum from the Gulf to the West. Interruption of that flow of vital resources is not a policy, but a contingency. Rather, it is the ability to exercise significant influence over the region that the Soviets see as the desirable objective. Whether this influence is better secured through diplomacy and support, as is normally the case, or through the threat or use of force, as may occur at infrequent but critical junctures, is a tactical issue dictated by circumstances.

Diplomatically, militarily, and in all other ways, the Gulf has proven slow-going for the Soviets. They have an embassy in Kuwait, as well as in Baghdad and Tehran, but are without diplomatic representation in Saudi Arabia or the smaller Gulf countries, a

---

handed and even less optimistic about the long-term possibility of rationalizing Gulf security with the United States.

measure of the distrust and fear in which they are held there. Diplomatic relations between Oman and the UAE, on the one hand, and the Soviet Union, on the other, have yet to be translated into a formal Soviet diplomatic presence in the two countries.

Western Europe

Western Europe is vitally concerned with Gulf security, since it is heavily dependent upon the Gulf for oil. However, only two European states maintain any military or naval power for projection to this theater—Britain and France.[6] While the United Kingdom was long the dominant force of the Gulf, its ability to use force to influence events there is now marginal, and it maintains no proximate facilities of any size, but deploys a small naval force to the area intermittently and maintains a few hundred advisors in Oman, including some SAS (Special Air Services) units. France does keep some naval power in the area: its Indian Ocean naval command, based in Djibouti, includes five frigates and about ten other ships; other French forces deployed in Djibouti include one mixed regiment and an air squadron; the South Indian Ocean unified command, based in Reunion, has a manning of about 3,500 personnel.

---

[6] Interestingly, both Britain and France have moved toward alternative sources of power. The United Kingdom has turned to the North Sea for oil, while France has spent heavily on the development of nuclear power.

II

THE SECURITY ENVIRONMENT

Although the Western presence and interests in the Gulf are usually considered in their most tangible form—notably, the need for petroleum—there are in fact a wide variety of Western interests in the Gulf, some deriving from its location, others from its resources, and yet others from the prominence of the Middle East in international politics. These interests are often far less tangible, but they are only somewhat less important. Particularly for the United States, as a superpower, it is certain that events which take place in any region deemed important to world politics inevitably affect American standing, power, and efficacy as a principal member of the global community; and American standing, power, and efficacy in turn directly affect the direction and course of international peace and security everywhere in the world.

Introduction

This chapter reviews the nature and origin of threats to Western interests in the Gulf, considering economic and social threats as well as political and security threats. It also addresses the alignment of forces in the Gulf and the stability of that alignment in terms of the threats to Western interests.

Western Interests in the Gulf

A brief consideration of the nature of Western interests in the Persian/Arabian Gulf is necessary prior to a discussion of the threats to those interests. Not very many years ago, the Gulf was truly a backwater of global intercourse; this is no longer the case. Today, Gulf states are critical pillars of the international monetary system, as well as suppliers of the basic building blocks on which the foundation of Western economy rests. International commerce as well as international finance depends heavily upon some of the Gulf countries. Consequently, Western interests in the region are broader than many realize.

The most well-known Western interest, and certainly one of the most immediate importance, is the continued availability of petroleum in adequate quantities and at acceptable prices. Despite the diversification of energy supplies in terms of origin and type, European and Japanese economic welfare, and indirectly therefore the American economy, which is increasingly international, remain dependent upon petroleum supplies from the Gulf. Natural gas from the Gulf (Iran) has also taken on an added importance in recent years, as more and more of it is exploited effectively rather than being flared.

The security impact of the petroleum trade remains important. It is not merely the economies, but also the defenses of Europe that require Gulf oil in order to function, so that NATO is a primary beneficiary of, and indeed is dependent on, the supply of oil from the Gulf. Preventing Soviet control over the resources of the Gulf is not a question of aggressive Western policy or intentions, then; it reflects absolutely vital issues of self-defense.

With the current "oil glut" that emerged in the 1980s, the importance of the Gulf is often seen to have declined. In fact, the surfeit of oil has not diminished the importance of Middle East oil to the West or, derivatively, the United States; it has merely reduced the importance of individual producers. The current surplus amounts to between 0.5 and 2 million barrels per day (MBD). Gulf oil production today equals about 10 MBD. Saudi Arabia's production has averaged around or perhaps slightly less than 2.5 MBD during 1985, and well below the kingdom's production capacity of almost 10 MBD or even its OPEC quota of about 4.5 MBD. Complete interruption of oil from the Gulf would introduce disaster today as

24

MAP 2.1
OIL INSTALLATIONS IN THE GULF

Adapted and Updated from Cordesman, *The Gulf and the Search for Strategic Stability*, (Boulder, Colo.: Westview) p. 294.

it did a decade ago to the global economy. Saudi Arabia's production alone no longer makes the difference between adequate and inadequate supplies of petroleum for the West, but its production *capacity* continues to be a critical offset to a complete cut-off from the Gulf.

No less important than the natural resource requirements in the Gulf are its financial resources. The countries of the Gulf today provide vital support for the international monetary system. Their capital investment in Europe and the United States has been and remains an enormous contribution to the dynamism of the Western economies, and their financial support has made possible an entirely new system for assistance to developing countries, a system that dramatically reduces the proportionate responsibility of the Western economies. The role of the Gulf states, particularly Saudi Arabia, in maintaining the value of the dollar and the maximum degree of international financial stability cannot be overlooked. This is not an altruistic situation on either part: rather, financial cooperation is vital to both the West and the Gulf.

Finally, the political role of the West in the Middle East and Gulf cannot be overlooked. U.S. and Western interests there extend well beyond merely the protection of vital economic resources. American credibility—which is basic to the viability of the entire fabric of Western defense, based as it is on deterrence—is also a primary consideration. The United States has extended guarantees of security in the Middle East that are well known. In the Gulf, every president since Franklin D. Roosevelt has assured Saudi Arabia of American support for its external security, and as recently as 1980 the president indicated that the United States would defend "with force, if necessary," the Gulf area.

Nor is the security of the Gulf merely a question of Western credibility. The significance of Saudi Arabia as the seat of the Islamic holy places of Mecca and Medina is also great. The Islamic world extends from the Atlantic to the Pacific, and embraces much of Asia and even parts of Europe. Among Islamic countries number some of America's long-time allies, like Pakistan and Turkey. Other Islamic countries or countries with large Islamic populations are key friends of the West or provide critical basing rights, countries like Egypt, Oman, Indonesia, and the Philippines. While the West is driven by stronger secular impulses in many domains such as business and defense, this characteristic does not obtain with respect to the Islamic world, where religion remains a central motivating force in every element of people's lives. The moral leadership that inheres in the status of protector of the Islamic holy sites is a valuable resource too often overlooked in the West.

Threats to Western Interests in the Gulf

Political Interests

The principal threats to Western interests in the Gulf derive from non-political vulnerabilities, but are political in nature. Foremost among these are threats to Gulf stability emanating from within or outside the Gulf. Internal threats to the stability of the Gulf governments are more pronounced, immediate, and likely than external threats. However, the internal problems in the Gulf at this time are all manageable except for the influence of outside pressures and activities in support of subversive or other dissidents inside the Gulf states. There is not a single government in the the Gulf, from the northern tier of Iran and Iraq, to the southern tip of (Iran and) Oman and the UAE, that is without internal opposition. How the opposition manifests itself and the degree of outside support may vary, but opposition is ubiquitous.

Political opposition is considered a healthy sign in developed countries, but that is after the development of a strong and stable political culture. The Gulf countries have yet very fragile political orders, and opposition is not to a set of policies or directions but to the political order itself. The reason this opposition, whether from the Right or Left, is a threat to Western interests in all cases relates to the interdependence of the Gulf states, particularly the states of the GCC and, in a different sense (a threat-defined sense), those countries and Iraq. A drastic change in the political order in one Gulf state could, and in some cases most likely would, engender powerful pressures that might consume the entire Gulf Arab community of nations, and with it the states on whose stability Western economic and political interests rest.

The revolutionary movement in the Gulf area is directly tied to anti-Western elements like Iran. At the individual level, some are motivated by religious symbols or concepts, while others are moved by political or economic values. No one doubts the sincerity of the religious beliefs of Iran's leaders, but it is abundantly clear from a number of cases that they are prepared to cooperate with almost anyone in order to spread the revolution. Those who have in common with the Islamic revolutionaries the desire to extrude the West from the Gulf are often motivated by sublime motives. Leftists in the Gulf—and outside of it—are among this number.

In addition to the the political pressures of revolution, there is in and around the Gulf a political entente of anti-Western forces consisting of Iran in the Gulf, South Yemen and Ethiopia on the Red Sea, Syria, and Libya. All of the members of this alliance save

27

Iran are closely tied to the Soviet Union and all without exception use virulent, almost obsessive, anti-American rhetoric. There are strong indications that coordination and cooperation among these countries, which has been increasing for some time, will continue to manifest itself in political violence taking the forms of sabotage, subversion, and terrorism. The documented linkage of Iran to terrorist groups throughout (and beyond) the Middle East, groups targeting American interests or the interests of governments friendly to the United States is merely the top of a large iceberg, a complex and complementary set of relationships reflecting a careful and dangerous specialization of labor. These forces are not so much revolutionary as they are anti-Western, and the outcome of a putative triumph is unpredictable in terms of institutions, but quite predictable in terms of international political behavior.

Because of the importance of the region in world affairs and in the economies of the West, the Western political position in the Gulf is itself significant. Anything that drives a wedge between the Gulf governments and the United States (or the West generally) is contrary to Western interests in two ways—first, and most directly, because of its immediate effect on the credibility, influence, and role of the West; second, by weakening the Gulf governments, depriving them of greater Western support.

The Arab-Israeli conflict is one of the issues that undermines the American position in the Gulf. All the peoples of the Gulf, including those of Iran, identify with the Palestinians and support the Palestinian cause. (This is true even though Iran has received assistance from Israel in the former's war with Iraq.) While their prescriptions vary widely, virtually all see in the United States, the primary ally and supporter of Israel, their enemy. In many ways, manifest and subtle, the Arab-Israeli conflict has undermined the U.S. position in the Gulf. Although many pressing issues have attenuated to some extent the impact of the problem, there can be no doubt that it has damaged American standing. Popular pressures to distance the Gulf governments from the United States are an important threat to the protection of shared interests.

The credibility of the United States is also at stake. The history of close relations and the litany of security assurances provided by the United States government to Saudi Arabia constitute another test by which American behavior will undoubtedly be judged, and not just in the Gulf or the Middle East. Thus, how and how effectively the United States and other Western countries respond to political, economic, security, and other threats in the Gulf will inevitably affect their *political* credibility in and beyond the Middle East.

While it would be erroneous to see the Gulf as a primary theater for the superpower rivalry, the manifestations of that rivalry are certainly apparent. For a century, the Gulf has been dominated by Western powers, principally the United Kingdom. Although the United States decided not to try to replace Britain as the policeman of the Gulf (see above, Chapter I), there is little question that the United States was seen as the dominant outside power in the Gulf in the period following the British withdrawal, or that Iran was seen as an American surrogate in the Gulf. In order to secure ever more favorable treatment from the United States in arms transfer considerations, the shah intentionally painted Iraq as a Soviet surrogate. Certainly, Iraq did look to Moscow for arms, and ultimately even signed a treaty of friendship with the Soviet Union, but Iraq was in many respects more independent of Soviet policy than Iran was of American policy, at least as regards political and security issues. We have already noted that proximity alone confers some importance on the Gulf, in Soviet calculations. However, there is no evidence that Moscow was ever prepared to substantially or significantly increase the superpower rivalry in the Gulf. Lacking dependable friends there, and with a surfeit of enemies, to do so would have required the use of force and inevitably entailed a confrontation with the United States, which had much more entrenched interests. Thus, a direct rivalry was averted. Instead, the superpower conflict manifested itself initially in a Soviet attempt to weaken and destroy the security relationships with Gulf states, and principally those directed specifically against the Soviet Union.

The first phase of U.S.-Soviet rivalry was then indirect and extended. As the Central Treaty Organization (CENTO) and the Southeast Asia Treaty Organization (SEATO) eroded, the most important aspect of Soviet policy in the Gulf was achieved. Only secondary to it was the general political strategy of sowing instability and political turmoil in a region of growing importance to the United States, and even this intent was modulated by the need to prevent a greater recourse to the West on the part of the local states, something that occurred in Oman as a direct result of the "internal" conflict there.

The superpower rivalry in the Gulf has usually been indirect. While Soviet sources may depict the rulers of the Gulf states as reactionary, feudal, and so on, that has not stopped the Soviets from seizing immediately any occasion to upgrade diplomatic representation in the region. The only Soviet embassy among the Arab Gulf states (outside Iraq, of course) is in Kuwait, with which formal relations have existed for over 20 years. There is no inherent reason to consider the government in Kuwait, which is an emirate, any more or less "anachronistic" than those in the other Gulf states.

But the principal targets of Soviet policy are clearly the countries with the closest relationships to the West or the greatest value to the Soviets (often a denial value). Recent Soviet overtures toward Oman and the UAE, culminating in the establishment of mutual diplomatic recognition with the two states, reflect this pattern of Soviet activity.

The deposition of the shah of Iran was a great improvement in the Soviet position, not because the Islamic Republic is any great friend of the Soviet Union, but because the shah was so close to the United States and advanced much of U.S. policy. The shah also took an active role in opposing revolutionary forces and extremism in the Gulf. The Islamic Republic raises other problems for the Soviet Union (including the traditional Soviet paranoia concerning the "nationality question" within the Soviet Union) without question, but the problems are substantially less formidable than those posed by the shah. Moreover, despite the difficult straits into which the Tudeh Party has fallen in Iran, there are still hopes that Iran, or parts of Iran, can one day be dominated by its northern neighbor. Meanwhile, for all the well-advertised disagreements between the two countries, Iranian sponsorship of anti-American forces in the Gulf, in the Middle East, and even beyond, Iranian support for terrorist groups and movements given to extremist violence, Iranian pressure on the countries that are closest to the United States—these activities and their effectiveness are causing few sleepless nights in Moscow.

The Soviet invasion of Afghanistan, which was the immediate precipitating incident leading to the Carter Doctrine, and continued Soviet military operations in that country are also relevant to the Gulf. Whether these acts are seen as stepping stones toward the Gulf, or whether, instead, they relate much more to other Soviet perceptions and objectives, there is no question that they raised alarm in Western capitals and in the Gulf alike. Some of the loudest protests about Soviet activity in Afghanistan continue to come from the Gulf. Certainly, de facto absorption of Afghanistan into the Soviet empire would confer or does confer specific and tangible military benefits in terms of mobility.

Nor is the Soviet military presence in Afghanistan the only harbinger of the Soviet power in the area. Close ties with South Yemen have yielded the Soviet Union base rights in that country, and Ethiopia, too, operates as part of a geographically discontinuous but politically active and cooperative pro-Soviet alliance. Taken together, the two countries effectively transfer a powerful Soviet presence into the Red Sea, whose waters are important to the Gulf states as the only possible outlet for the petroleum trade should travel in the Gulf generally or through the Straits of Hormuz become impossible. Much more a part of the region than Afghanistan is Syria, as well. While Syria is not a Gulf country, it remains a major Arab power, and enjoys very close relations with the Soviet Union. Thousands of Soviet military advisors are present in Syria, which has received some of the most advanced Soviet military equipment outside the Soviet Union itself, materiel more advanced than that shipped to Warsaw Pact countries.

Gulf governments have shown themselves anything but unaware of the potential dangers of a proximate Soviet physical (as opposed to diplomatic) presence. Saudi Arabia took active and ultimately effective steps to persuade Somalia to move away from the Soviet Union and toward the United States. (The United States now has contingency facility agreements with Somalia.) And indeed, Saudi Arabia in particular has urged the United States to provide greater support for the Afghan insurgents struggling against the Soviet occupation, and this in spite of the close ties between Saudi Arabia and Pakistan, which is heavily burdened by the on-going battle for freedom in Afghanistan. For its part following the Afghan invasion, the United States, which has provided some support to the Afghan rebels, encouraged the Gulf countries to cooperate with the United States to form a strategic consensus. However, despite Gulf concern with the problem in Afghanistan, at least as prominent, and far more subject to public pressure, is the Arab-Israeli issue, an issue on which the United States, as principal supporter of Israel, is on the "wrong" side in Gulf eyes.

Economic Interests

The petroleum industry and the financial empire originally built upon it are the principal Western economic interests in the Gulf region. Even though the oil companies have been largely taken over by the oil producers, the commerce in oil represents a continuing investment of great magnitude for Western companies. Petroleum commerce is a significant factor in American business.

Of greater importance in the recent era has been the oil itself. Although the degree of Western dependence upon Gulf oil varies enormously from one Western country to another, approximately one-fifth to one-quarter of all petroleum consumed in the West derives from the Gulf. Moreover, this figure is misleading. In the event of a significant shortage, it is in the Gulf where a large shortfall could be made up. The quality of Gulf crude, its cost of extraction, and the existing logistical facilities provide production

31

quantity and flexibility simply unavailable elsewhere. Beyond production, the Gulf's reserves remain the bulk of all those known in the Free World.

The economic interests of the West are also financial. Saudi Arabia is today a financial colossus, and Saudi decisions carry great weight in international financial circles. The stability of the dollar and some other Western currencies is to a large extent a function of Saudi decisions on the form of its reserve holdings and the means of exchange for oil purchases.

Of course, Western interests are not merely a one-way street. The Gulf producers depend upon a sound Western economy. Neither producer nor consumer economies benefit from economic chaos, rampant inflation, or paralyzing recession. Oil producers and oil consumers are, after all, both part of the same international economy. Despite a long period of confrontation, the truth is clear: they are interdependent.

Security Interests

The bulk of Western security interests are related to the economic value of the Gulf. In that context, internal and regional security are related to conditions that assure the unimpeded flow of petroleum to the West. The same consideration mandates attention to external influences that may disrupt or impede the oil trade, whether directly through some form of coercive interdiction or indirectly through support to elements contributing to the instability and turmoil of the Gulf or its environs. Western powers, especially the United States, have become increasingly wary about the physical security of their personnel, facilities, equipment, resources, and services in the Gulf in recent years with the growth of political violence there. Finally, as a result of the emergence of the Red Sea alternative oil route, the connection between Gulf and Red Sea security has become increasingly strong.

The Iran-Iraq War

Certainly, the immediate security problem in the Gulf, and the most visible threat to conditions favorable to stable oil supply, is the Iran-Iraq war. This war endangers Western interests in several ways. First, the war has threatened to spread on several occasions. Iranian aircraft have overflown other Gulf countries, and have in

MAIN OIL MOVEMENTS BY SEA: 1984

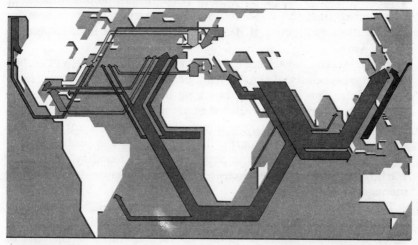

SOURCE: *BP Statistical Review of World Energy,* The British Petroleum Company, June 1985, p. 17.

fact bombed Kuwait. The escalatory potential of the war in terms of drawing in other participants has occasioned several crises alone. Second, though, both the belligerents have threatened and attempted to interrupt the oil trade in the Gulf. Iraq has attacked vessels calling at, en route to, or coming from Iranian ports. Iran, in turn, has attacked vessels of non-belligerents in transit to or from the ports of the other Gulf states. Third—although first chronologically—the previously off-limits oil infrastructure became a primary target for each country in the other at an early stage in the war. This put an early end to the hopes of some that "oil targets" would be spared, and since they have not been, the immunity of non-belligerent oil infrastructure in the event of spreading violence is anything but certain. Thinly veiled threats from Iran about attacks on Saudi targets have compounded these concerns.

The pattern of Iranian and Iraqi arms procurement and military development also endangers Gulf security. While the arms race between these two Gulf powers has continued for many years, they have been until recently unable to use their equipment beyond their borders in any effective manner. The war has led both to procure and employ surface-to-surface missiles (SSMs). While the missiles have not demonstrated any great accuracy, this quantum step poses dangers for the future, since the concentration of vital petroleum facilities on the Arab side of the Gulf could be held hostage by the presence of SSMs by either Iran or, as longer-range missiles become available, Iraq. A single barrage of SSMs, either as punishment or as an act against the West, could produce serious consequences for the Western economies if it hit certain sensitive installations in Saudi Arabia.

Moreover, the development of the military forces of the two belligerents, especially of that of Iraq, has been advanced appreciably by the war. The Iraqi army has long been big; its inventory was impressive before the war. But there is no substitute for combat as a training technique. Experts now believe that the Iraqi army has made very significant progress in overcoming the problems that have bedevilled it for years, problems of C^3, mobility, maneuver warfare, combined arms, logistics and other support, and battle management.

The fighting between Iran and Iraq has not itself been very disruptive of the oil flow. However, the constant political threat to the other Gulf states takes a number of forms. Iran has threatened them for assisting Iraq (mainly financially); Iraq has threatened them for not providing enough assistance in a battle the Iraqi leadership believes it is leading on behalf of the entire Arab world.

Internal Conflict, External Conflict, Western Security

The political turmoil of the Gulf was also generated, at least in part, by the results and implications of the 1973-1974 oil crises. The wealth of the Gulf and its demonstrated importance to the West have enhanced its value and attractiveness as a target, and they have also created conditions conducing to conflict in some particular cases. As the region has developed and emerged into a more active role as a 20th century political actor, several latent or less salient conflicts have taken on a new and more virulent form. Thus, the sectarian conflicts in the Gulf area between extremists and moderates and between Shi'as and Sunnis, as well as the ethnic conflict between Persian and Arab, have both been seriously exacerbated by the continuing Iran-Iraq war. The different population groups that make up the Gulf are now exploited as tools by Iran, in particular, creating in turn greater distrust and internal dissension.

While Iran has been notably unsuccessful in stirring up sectarian friction within its Gulf neighbors' polities to the point of effecting revolutions, rebellions, or widespread civil unrest, the periodic discovery of a plot or some other subversive action has very seriously increased tensions and spawned substantially greater levels of distrust than existed in the region heretofore. Moreover, inefficacy has

34

put no damper on the efforts; they continue. The Shi'a communities and Persian expatriates along the Gulf continue to experience subversive appeals from Iran.

The remaining local conflicts that are a legacy of the colonial period have also been exacerbated by the new problems experienced in the Gulf. For example, the border conflict between Iraq and Kuwait, which has generally been non-violent, has taken on a larger meaning against the background of the Iran-Iraq war. The limitations imposed by Iraq's tiny Gulf littoral have proven to be a major constraint on Iraq's freedom of action and maneuver. As a result, Iraq has insisted that Kuwait be more responsive to Iraq's security and economic requirements, especially in this time of crisis.

Iran's Ambitions

Iran's territorial designs must be considered another destabilizing factor. The Islamic Republic continues to claim Bahrain, and continues to occupy Arab islands in the Gulf. Beyond territorial ambitions, however, it is quite clear that the fanatic leadership of the Islamic Republic is bent upon creating a new, revolutionary, anti-western, and Iranian-dominated regime throughout the Gulf. Saudi Arabia's leadership of the Arab Gulf outside Iraq has made the kingdom an especially attractive target. Its close cooperation with the United States on security issues has only served to increase this attraction. Symbolically, any attack on Saudi Arabia serves several purposes. It is an attack on the United States. It is therefore an attack on the "tilt" of the conservative Gulf states toward the West. It is an attack on moderation. It is an attack on the remaining pillar and clear leader of the lower Gulf. It is an attack on political legitimacy, because the support and roots of the Saudi government are greater than those of most of the other Gulf states. Thus, a high priority has been placed on undermining the security of Saudi Arabia. Much of the range of the threat spectrum has been experienced, but the essential nature of the society is sufficiently stable to have been able to weather what has so far come from the storm.

Western Personnel and Facilities

A new development in the Gulf and elsewhere in the Middle East is the targeting of Westerners and their property located in the region. It is an important U.S. interest to protect its nationals and their property, an interest that was long taken for granted. American citizens, reflecting the international status and activity of the United States, are involved in commerce and a myriad of other activities throughout the world. They are present in large numbers in the Gulf as a result of the heavy economic interaction of the United States in that area. Terrorist attacks, abduction, and threats directed against the West have become commonplace in anarchic environments like Lebanon, but they have also noticeably increased in the Gulf. The bombing of the American and French embassies and of the facilities of an American defense contractor in Kuwait in December 1983 was the most spectacular case to date in a phenomenon that has serious implications for the American presence worldwide. It must be said that while the trend is evident, attacks on Americans or American property in the Gulf—and in this respect it is unlike the rest of the Middle East, Latin America, or even Europe, for that matter, where such attacks have become frequent— are still quite rare.

Direct Interdiction of Oil Supplies

While attacks on Americans and their property are low-intensity operations—generally, terrorist or terrorist-like in nature—physical interdiction of the flow of oil to Western consumers can be conceived as the result of a wide range of activities at various levels of the force spectrum. Systematic sabotage of pipelines, blocking the Strait of Hormuz, terrorist attacks on or mining of oil tankers, sabotage of the production or control infrastructure, physical threats to the producers or shippers, or overt military action by a Gulf power or an external power—any or several of these levels of force could result in a partial or complete interruption of the flow of oil. Clearly, it is an important American interest to prevent such a development.

Lower-intensity operations are generally assumed to be associated with internal threats, whether independent of or associated with external support. Military operations designed to interdict oil commerce, or resulting in such an interruption, could be the product of a Gulf conflict (as in the current Iran-Iraq war) or of Soviet military intervention. While the Gulf Arab oil producers might be able to take concerted action to protect the oil industry in most cases, they could not of course prevent Soviet military intervention or interdiction of the oil flow. In such a contingency the producers would have to look to the United States to protect the LOCs and SLOCs vital to the transport of petroleum to the West.

36

The Multi-Faceted Soviet Threat

Soviet military threats to Western interests in the Gulf could manifest themselves in a variety of ways. The preoccupation of American planners following the invasion of Afghanistan was a direct Soviet military thrust into the Gulf. The objective of such a move would presumably be occupation and control of the oil fields and facilities of the Gulf; or, at the very least, their denial to the West. Soviet forces enjoy a number of advantages over those of the United States in contemplating, planning, or carrying out military operations in the Gulf. While many have pointed—and with good reason—to the considerable logistic and topographical problems such a Soviet move would have to overcome, it is equally true that impediments to an effective American response would be at least as impressive. In any case, while the possibility of a Red Army push toward the Gulf must be considered, it is neither the only, nor certainly the most likely, alternative available to the Soviet Union to improve its position and dramatically weaken or endanger that of the West.

The Gulf states' definition of the Soviet threat has been summarized by Saudi Arabia's Chief of Intelligence, Prince Turki, in this way:

> What is the Soviet goal in the Middle East? . . . .
> The answer is simple: our oil. Iran has too
> many domestic problems, and its oil reserves
> are being quickly depleted. . . . . At this mo-
> ment, we do not expect an invasion, but we do
> expect the Soviets to use their power to ma-
> neuver themselves into a position to make ar-
> rangements for a guaranteed oil supply.[1]

The Soviet invasion of Afghanistan jolted the Gulf states' consciousness not just because of the proximity of the intervention, but because of the precedent it set. The Soviet Union had used a friendship pact as a pretext for military intervention. Both the PDRY and Iraq have such treaties with the Soviet Union. As Prince Turki described the problem:

> We can envisage an Iraqi scenario in which
> religious unrest among the Shi'ites and trouble

---

[1] David B. Tinnin, "The Saudis Awaken to Their Vulnerability," *Fortune*, March 10, 1980, p. 56.

37

with the Kurds lead to the downfall of the present regime. Then a group of dedicated Com-
munists seizes power and calls for Soviet
support. The next thing we know, Soviet troops
will be landing in Baghdad.[2]

The more the Gulf states conclude that the Soviet invasion of
Afghanistan was originally motivated to remedy a deteriorating
situation rather than a part of a new strategic advance, the more
persuasive the foregoing scenario is. Even though one may be in-
clined to discount the Iraqi scenario above, if what was considered
to be a very conservative, risk-adverse Soviet leadership was willing
to use force just to preserve a strategic position for future use, how
much more willing would a younger, more risk-accepting Soviet
leadership be prepared to take such action for a strategic prize as
valuable as the Gulf itself?

A military move limited to Iran would add substantial oil and
natural gas reserves to Soviet control, and, given the state of Western relations with the Iranian regime, would likely be unopposed
by the West. Alternatively, a quisling pro-Soviet regime could be
created in Iran following, say, on turmoil in the aftermath of the
death of Ayatollah Khomeini. Still another approach might be an
even more limited move into northwestern Iran, possible as a result
of anarchic conditions in an area adjacent to the Soviet Union that
could be called "important to its security." This contingency would
be easily accomplished by Soviet forces, practically unopposed in
the disordered state of Iran's defenses in that perimeter, and certainly well beyond the reach of American or other power to affect.

The net effect of all these Soviet military options, it should be
noted, is not to capture *any* of the Gulf oil resources or facilities.
However, the security effect is quite clearly to fundamentally alter
the political and military realities, such that thereafter *all* Gulf
petroleum exports would be easily subject to Soviet control from
points southwest of the intimidating mountains of northern Iran.
No significant impediment would any longer separate operating
Soviet forces from the Gulf, and the pulse of Soviet power would
clearly be felt throughout the Gulf. At the very least, this Soviet
stranglehold over NATO oil resources would force a reconsideration
of force allocations and strategy for non-nuclear conflict with the
Soviets in other theaters. And to pretend that these new realities
would not have political consequences in the Gulf would be folly of
the most extreme sort.

---

[2] *Ibid.*, p. 55.

The Ominous Trends in Physical Security

The physical security manifestations of this range of emerging security problems have already been witnessed—attacks on oil production, refining, storage, loading, and transport (including both pipelines and shipping); assassination attempts against political, religious, and business leaders; barricade-and-hostage situations; terrorist bombings of installations of symbolic or other importance; insurgencies; limited hostilities; and full-scale war. There appears to be a growing traffic in illegal papers and an increasing coordination among subversive intelligence operatives of Syria, Iran, and Libya, in particular. Whatever the motivations involved, whatever the immediate or ultimate targets, the implications for security of both the broader Western interests in regional stability and security and narrower interests in the security of installations and Western personnel and property are clear—and ominous.

Social Interests

The West and the Middle East have been linked since the beginnings of recorded history. For all the historical differences between the cultures of the Middle East—Persian, Turkish, Arab, Jewish, Berber, Kurdish, and others—and those of the West, the interaction between the two areas forms much of the fabric of the history of both. From Phoenician times 4,000 years ago, the peoples of the Middle East explored westward; and the religious origins of the vast bulk of the West lie in the Middle East. Europe discovered the greatness of ancient Greek civilization through the Arab world, and today all the peoples of the Middle East look to the West in turn for advances in technology and for their own socio-economic advancement.

What is called economic, political, or security cooperation (American business, the oil trade, coordination of positions on issues as diverse as terrorism or the Soviet invasion of Afghanistan, scientific and technical cooperation that depends upon the geographical or financial resources of the region—all aspects of our interests) rests, ultimately, upon social cooperation. This element of the relationship between the West and the Middle East is experiencing greater potential threat than at any time in the last millennium.

Still representative of a distinct minority, the forces of religious extremism, religious extremism in all faiths in the Middle East, are growing and challenging the very bases on which the social intercourse of diverse people within the region, and between the Middle

East and the West, depends. Although it is certainly true that extremism was growing prior to 1979 and was visible in every country of the Middle East, the Iranian revolution has infused a powerful and dangerous new momentum to the movement. Despite the religious differences between Shi'a Iran and the other countries of the region, what pass for the "victories" of the revolution over the United States (i.e., the humiliation of the American superpower) have been heady intoxicants for many who were frustrated, embittered, and demoralized before.

There is no doubt that religious extremism of any stripe constitutes a danger to the interaction of diverse societies. Just as it has within the West itself (such as during the religious wars), the fanatic and xenophobic element of this trend leads to acts that are incomprehensible and outrageous when seen from the point of view of social interdependence. Recent events (the attacks on Western installations in Kuwait, the hijackings of Western airplanes, attacks on individuals in the Levant—all acts that have also been attempted against existing institutions and leaders in the Gulf who are seen as "allied with" the West) leave little doubt that this trend poses a potent and imminent threat to Western interests in the Gulf.

III

THE THREAT PROFILE
IN THE GULF

**The threat to security in the Gulf takes
many forms from low-intensity internal
problems to full-scale war, and comes from
north, south, east, and west. While the Gulf
itself is a small area to defend, the threat
to the Gulf states arises along more than
12,500 km of exposed front. The most prominent targets—not necessarily for destruction—are the Gulf oil facilities, which are
at least as important for the West as for the
Gulf states.**

Introduction

In order to consider the present state of security and the most
appropriate and effective approaches to maintaining or enhancing
that security, this chapter describes and assesses the nature and
magnitude of several types of threat. Following this analysis, the
external threat from each of several directions is reviewed and
evaluated.

Security threats in the Persian/Arabian Gulf run the gamut from
low-intensity internal problems to full-scale war, such as the current
conflict between Iran and Iraq. Despite the apparent variety of
threat forms in the region, most have in fact already manifested
themselves at least once. Because the focus of this work is on external security, only those forms of internal threat linked to outside
support or sponsorship are addressed.

41

The profile of external threat considers the individual and the potential combined threat resources of Gulf and proximate countries in terms of military and other assets that could be employed to carry out the forms of threat identified in the first section of the chapter.

Security Threat Spectrum

Manipulative Mobilization

By the infelicitous term, "manipulative mobilization," we refer to the possibility that a country or force external to the Gulf, or at least external to the target in the Gulf, might be able to mobilize the populace of one of the Gulf states through the manipulation of important symbols or values.

Every society maintains a number of key values and is sensitive to a variety of symbols that tend to excite the passions of its members. Under these circumstances, loyalty to temporal governments is tried. Whether the bulk of the populace resists the appeals is determined by many considerations such as the nature of the appeals; the legitimacy and rootedness of the government; the salience of the values or symbols appealed to; the degree of conflict between those values and symbols, on the one hand, and the credibility of the government as a protector of such values and symbols, on the other; the homogeneity of society; and the responsiveness and reasonableness of government.

Economic development and the rapid expansion of secular education at home and opportunities for study abroad have thrust up whole new classes of Western-educated technocrats that increasingly dominate the bureaucracies of the GCC. The expansion and modernization of the armed forces of the Gulf states has meant the parallel expansion of the Western-educated or trained officers and non-commissioned officers (NCOs). Rapid economic development has profoundly altered the demographics of the Gulf states in the form of urban migrations (especially in Saudi Arabia) and the creation of a whole new class of urban workers who may or may not have the same ties to traditional Gulf leaders and roles.

Given the pace at which economic and social transformation has taken place in the Gulf in the last 20 years, it should come as no surprise that the Western educated technocrats and entrepreneurs are pressing hard for more modernization. Similarly, it should not be surprising to discover that many Western educated and trained military officers and NCOs are dissatisfied with the traditional royal family-oriented command structure. Nor should anyone be shocked that the burgeoning class of successful "commoner" entrepreneurs would like to have more of a say in the political decisions taken by the GCC governments, or that these new social groups resent excessive government corruption.

These pressures are continuously counterbalanced by the more traditional elements in society such as tribal and religious groups and disaffected elements from the traditional merchant families who have lost influence in ruling circles as the Gulf states' economies have shifted increasingly from construction and merchant activities to industrialization and financial services. Some of these groups have reacted to modernization (which they often perceive as Westernization) and the resulting social changes with growing hostility, sometimes choosing to attack the development process rather than seeking to benefit from it. They resent and fear the pace of development and recoil at what they consider to be massive corruption, conspicuous consumption, and the unravelling of the moral fabric of society.

However, the growth of tensions between religious and political conservatives, who are bent on preserving traditional family, social, and religious customs, and the "modernists," who believe the only alternative to radical leftist or ultraconservative reactions is to integrate the Gulf countries' changing populations into an industrialized society, does not in and of itself threaten the Gulf regimes for at least three reasons.

● First, disagreement on the pace of social change does not imply disloyalty or a questioning of the legitimacy of the current regimes.

● Second, these cleavages extend into the leadership. Thus the views of contending "constituencies" are represented by members of various royal families and senior officials within the bureaucracies and the armed forces. What counts is the extent to which the governments can regulate the pace of social and economic change by seeking broad structural solutions to internal problems rather than by relying on punitive internal security measures. This certainly appears to be what is taking place in Saudi Arabia, and there is substantial evidence that the Saudi approach is also being tried by others. Indeed, the "conservative"-vs-"modernist" continuum may supersede and reduce to some extent the traditional tribal and regional animosities that have posed a barrier to achieving more complete domestic cohesion within the GCC.

● Third, the drop in oil prices has led to an across-the board economic contraction in all the GCC countries. If the halcyon days of unlimited oil income strained the rather simple structures of the traditional Gulf governments and societies, leading to rampant corruption, indiscriminate acquisitiveness, and a heightened disdain for productive effort, this period of economic retrenchment might introduce an element of social stability as the development pace slows and an opportunity for political, social, and psychological adjustment. Despite the declines in oil revenues, however, the GCC countries collectively have the money and the educated elite to make more effective attempts to cope with social change than any other group of developing states. They are keenly studying the successes and failures of other nations, especially Iran under the Pahlevi dynasty. The process of social change is occurring late enough in the Gulf so that there are countless examples of how not to manage it.

When autonomous developments are the object of external manipulation they cease to be internal. Few external attacks are likely to occur without advance preparation that attempts to legitimize the enterprise by providing it with a domestic component as well. In a period of rapid social transformation it is not too difficult for external enemies, such as revolutionary Iran, to find a few citizens sympathetic to external ideological blandishments. Even though indigenous fifth columns may constitute infinitely small minorities, their potential for alignment with outside adversaries for subversive purposes makes them a serious security threat far out of proportion to their numbers.

In the case of the Gulf states, there are several values and symbols that can be manipulated by outside forces in order to reduce the legitimacy, and hence the long-term control, of local governments. These are Islam, Westernization, and the Palestinian issue. The first two are closely related, and even the third bears some important linkages to the first two.

External forces in the region have already attempted to use the universality of Islam to undermine the legitimacy and credibility of the governments on the Arab side of the Gulf. They have given support to extremist religious groups, such as the one that seized the Grand Mosque in Mecca in 1979, endeavoring to suggest that current national leaders in these countries are not sincerely practicing Islam or are not doing enough to protect the faith and the faithful. While such claims were used against the shah and are more effective in the case of secular governments, they have been common in the Gulf over the last several years. Dissidents try to mobilize unrest over alleged corruption, violations of Koranic proscriptions against alcohol, and the like.

Closely related is the effort to portray contemporary Gulf leaders as corrupted or co-opted by the West. The West is overwhelmingly Christian, just as the Gulf is overwhelmingly Muslim. Unlike the West, however, the Gulf's religious orientation is a predominant characteristic of life, and Muslims believe that compartmentalization of one's daily life and behavior into "religious," "political," "economic," "business," "family," and other categories is contrary to God's will, and that, in effect, their religion provides laws and precepts that apply with equal force to every aspect of life. Consequently, the influence of the West is seen by many as little different from an "invasion." Because the ruler in Islam is judged very heavily by how diligently he protects the faith and the faithful against inroads by non-Muslims, it is not difficult for dissidents to manipulate these attitudes to attack the legitimacy of governments in the Gulf.

While there is no basic anti-Western feeling per se in the Gulf, all traditional societies fear the destruction of the pillars of their society by the forces of social change. The Islamic societies of the Gulf are especially concerned by the inroads made by the secular West, because their practices often appear at odds with the teachings of Islam and the traditions of the region. In particular, the consumption of alcohol, the dress of both men and women which is considered immodest by regional standards, disrespect shown the religious institutions and practices of Islam, simple criminal behavior, and displays of intimacy—many of which have also been the object of great concern in the West as well—have led to a substantial fear on the part of many Muslims of the Gulf that their own values and traditions are in danger of being overwhelmed by those of the alien West.

The Palestinian issue has long concerned all Arabs—and many non-Arabs. While there is no agreed prescription, most Arabs believe that a monumental injustice was perpetrated against the Palestinian people in the late 1940s, and that no resolution to the Arab-Israeli problem is possible without resolving the Palestinian problem as well. They perceive the expansion of Israel beyond the territory allotted to it in 1947, and especially beyond its pre-June 1967 boundaries, as nothing short of an unacceptable, immoral, and illegal attack upon the Arab world, upon Islam, and therefore upon all Arabs and Muslims. The occupation and annexation of Arab East Jerusalem is seen as an especially provocative and morally unacceptable condition.

Under these circumstances, disruptive elements can exploit and have in fact exploited the ties of Gulf governments to the West, particularly the United States, as links to the primary supporter of Israel. While it is not possible to determine the level of salience of the Palestinian issue, it is quite clear that its universal appeal makes it a potent tool for mobilization of popular discontent when government becomes too closely identified with the forces supporting Israel or supportive of policies that are seen as contrary to the interests of the Palestinians.

There is no doubt that all the governments in the Gulf support the Palestine Liberation Organization (PLO) as the sole, legitimate representative of the Palestinian people. Nor is there any doubt that they support PLO claims against Israel, and often even against other Arab states. Such positions usually reflect real views, not merely political posturing. However, it is abundantly clear that the American position of total support for Israel, whatever the merits and reasons in terms of U.S. interests and perceptions, has seriously impeded closer security cooperation with the United States for the reasons given. More important, if conflict continues to grow in the Gulf and the Arab-Israeli problem endures, the resulting schism between the Gulf governments and the United States in security cooperation will be as predictable as it will be contrary to the interests of both.

The mobilization of the Gulf populations by external forces on any one or more of these three issue areas will therefore continue to be a principal danger to the governments. While it is evident that they will maintain something like their current postures in support of the PLO, postures often critical of the West, it is also certain that hostile forces will continue to use dissident elements to try to persuade the population that their governments are not protecting Islam and its institutions, are allowing excessive Western encroachments, and are betraying the Palestinians.

The threat of manipulative mobilization requires a certain set of regional conditions which, unfortunately, exists. But it also requires communication channels with and within the Gulf societies under attack. This communication involves propaganda disseminated through the airwaves, on cassette, and in printed and word-of-mouth form; the use of trained agitators; use of rumor and fear to manipulate the perception and assessment of actual events and developments; and networks to efficiently and effectively tie these elements together. It also requires certain credible communicators within the framework of the Islamic religious and Gulf cultural contexts. These elements are only partially available to the adversaries of the Gulf governments at this time; but they are being used more and more effectively over time.

The Islamic revolution in Iran and the rise of extremist religious sentiment in the Middle East have contributed to the credibility of Islam-based attacks on local governments. Support from hostile governments of secular or other orientation is funneled through strongly Islamic governments like that of Iran and Libya in order to enhance the credibility of this type of attack, and these two governments themselves have committed considerable resources to the discrediting of the Gulf countries' Islamic and Arab *bona fides*. Iran, in particular, has mounted a massive radio propaganda campaign against the Saudi government, a campaign that uses all three issues—Islam, Westernization, and the liberation of Palestine.

Mobilization of domestic dissidence has long been a staple of politics in the Third World—and not only in the Third World. The West uses Radio Free Europe and Radio Liberty, among other tools, and the Soviet Union and other communist countries have plethoric outlets for their propaganda. The purpose of all of these channels of communication is to encourage dissent. Whether it is by providing alternatives to the sterile "news" available in eastern Europe or by fabricating stories or showering Western audiences with ideological rhetoric, the attempt to mobilize opposition is a commonplace of international relations. Clearly, however, it is much more dangerous in the Third World where literacy is limited, where the roots of government are young and fragile, and where political maturity of systems and people are still developing.

Subversion

A common and growing problem in the Middle East is that of subversion, where hostile foreign governments procure or otherwise obtain the services of nationals or residents of the victimized state to mobilize opposition and violence, not merely political expression. In the Gulf polities which are very new, common political languages uniting the countries around the government and national symbols and institutions are only now developing. These are not nation-states, in any real sense of the word. And while it is true that there are in fact few true nation-states in the world, the youth of the Gulf countries means that nation-building is less far along there than almost anywhere in the Third World. The heterogeneity of the states of the Gulf provides a variety of minorities that may be receptive to the idea of overthrowing the government. These mi-

47

norities may be ethnic, religious, tribal, socio-economic, national, or political-ideological—but the addition of outside support will give them substantial potential for disruption far out of proportion to their size, particularly in the small, young, and fragile polities in the Gulf where technical competence and leadership are often spread very thinly.

The Problem of Expatriate Workers

In some respects the GCC countries' dependence on expatriate workers and advisors constitutes more of a potential problem than external attempts to exploit tensions resulting from rapid economic development and social change. The GCC countries have a combined population of about 13 million, of whom approximately five million are expatriate workers. The impact of expatriate labor in the Gulf countries is everywhere dramatic, but nowhere more so than in those where expatriates now outnumber the native population (Kuwait, Qatar, and the UAE). Expatriate personnel comprise more that 50 percent in five key economic sectors in Saudi Arabia: construction, electricity, finance, manufacturing, and trade.

Of particular relevance to internal security are Arab expatriates.[1] Most of the Arab migrants come from Yemen, Egypt, Jordan/Palestine, and the Sudan. While precise figures on inter-Arab labor migration are difficult to retrieve, the approximate level was estimated to be about three million in 1980.[2] The Arab expatriates share important elements of the same culture, especially the same language, with the indigenous Gulf populations. Therefore, barriers to communication are minimized by contrast with those between indigenes and South Koreans, Filipinos, Europeans, or Americans.

On the one hand, widespread contact between expatriate Arabs and the indigenous Gulf populations could facilitate social and psychological adjustments to outside influences and so reduce the disruptive side effects of intense, large-scale foreign presence. On the other hand, the very presence of large numbers of foreign workers can only complicate domestic politics by causing resentment and by tying events inside the GCC to events in the outside world.

---

[1] For discussion of the relationship of expatriates to external security, see Chapter IV below.

[2] Saad Eddin Ibrahim, "Oil, Migration and the New Arab Social Order," in Malcolm H. Kerr and El Sayed Yassin, eds., Rich and Poor States in the Middle East: Egypt and the New World Order (Boulder, Colo., and Cairo: Westview Press and the American University in Cairo Press, 1982), p. 291.

The most serious problem is the expatriates' potential involvement in political protest activities in alliance with dissident indigenous citizens. The large numbers of Palestinians in the Gulf countries and the popular sympathy with the Palestinian cause must be placed in the security context—viz., that one of the most serious problems in achieving strategic stability in the Gulf is the Arab-Israeli problem. This is only one illustration of the links between events beyond the Gulf and the presence of a large body of expatriate labor.

More than 600,000 Palestinians live in the Gulf states. This is a quarter of the Palestinian diaspora, more Palestinians than in Lebanon and Syria combined. The numbers, however, understate the real weight of this community, for its members occupy important positions in the GCC states whose local elites are still in formulation. Most importantly, Palestinians staff the state administrations. These circumstances have made the Palestinians the most influential expatriate community in the oil-rich Gulf states. This situation has far-reaching political implications. Not only do the Palestinians constitute between 10 and 20 percent of the labor force in most Gulf states, but they are also located in the middle and upper portions of the economic structure of the host countries. The Palestinians—particularly those in Kuwait—are the most politicized of all Arabs. With strong affiliations to the PLO, the Palestinian expatriate communities represent a subtle deterrent and an intimidating constraint on governmental behavior in the GCC.

Another expatriate threat derives from the potential takeover or domination of North Yemen by the South Yemeni-backed National Liberation Front, with both sharing the political orientation of the soi-disant Marxist, pro-Soviet PDRY. In that event, thousands of Yemenis in the GCC countries could constitute a potential "fifth column" at the service of the Soviet Union or its regional client.

The attack and seizure of the Grand Mosque in Mecca in November 1979 is an actual case that underscores the potential for expatriate involvement in political subversion. Fully 20 percent of the attackers (about 80 persons) were Yemenis, Egyptians, Iraqis, Moroccans, Pakistanis, and other non-Gulf nationals. The participation of expatriates in indigenous subversive movements means that some outsiders, by no means more than a tiny minority so far, are prepared to channel their political discontent locally. The foregoing example underscores that any social or political problem or grievance common to both expatriates and some members of the indigenous population can be a pretext for subversive action, particularly when encouraged or actively supported by external powers such as Libya, Iran, or the Soviet Union.

The growth of the expatriate communities has peaked as the construction boom in the Gulf has leveled off and the decline in oil prices has compelled a reduction in the pace of development spending. However, the dependence on expatriate personnel in just about every economic sector continues to be strong, so their numbers in proportion to the indigenous populations are not likely to decline noticeably. While member countries have successfully used the GCC framework to maintain coordinated supervision and control over their foreign communities, they are in no position to deport expatriates, especially Arab expatriates, wholesale.

Thus while the unique demographic structure in the GCC countries is a potential source of subversion, it also gives the oil-poor labor-exporting Arab countries a large stake in the continued prosperity and economic expansion of the GCC states. This is strong inducement for the governments of labor-exporting countries to support the political and social status quo within the GCC states and to oppose the activities of subversive movements within the Gulf.

Subversion is not new to the Gulf, but it has become a much more pressing problem with the growing political tensions and the growing schism between the traditional Arab states of the Gulf that seek change and progress at a steady but measured, evolutionary pace; and the militant revolutionism of Iran that seeks to eliminate all vestiges of the past in an orgy of destruction and violence such as that which Iran itself experienced and has taken pride in.

Terrorism/Isolated Violence

Terrorism and other acts of isolated violence are yet another dimension of the threat to the security of the Gulf states. In 1985 there were attempts to raise the specter of insurrection in Saudi Arabia through "bombings" claimed by the Islamic Jihad organization. By contrast, a spate of bombing attacks in Kuwait in December 1983 was both a "punishment" to France and the United States and an incitement to potentially dissident elements in Kuwait. These are all examples of terrorism and isolated violence. They are not part of a larger, systematic program or process of violence, even though they are intended in some cases (as in Saudi Arabia) to set the stage for such a process.

It is very difficult in highly regulated societies to mount attacks using physical violence. However, it is also impossible even in totalitarian countries such as the Soviet Union to eliminate *all* violence. The danger of terrorism and of isolated violence with political intent is less the physical or tangible cost than the political cost; it is not in the existence of terrorism, but in the image of impotence and vacillation that terrorist attacks can create; not in the eruption of isolated violence, but in the image of growing and ever-more-militant dissent that the violence suggests.

Symbolic Attack

Another type of threat is the direct attack by foreign forces on institutions or property that has symbolic importance. Symbolic targets are frequently government buildings such as royal palaces, government centers, and key ministries. They may also be official or quasi-governmental offices of institutions symbolically related to the regime and rulers, such as national airline offices and communications centers.

In the Saudi case, an attack on the cities of Mecca or Medina would also carry potent symbolism. The Saudi government takes pride in its role as protector of the holy places, and strikes against the cities or specific sites therein detract from Saudi credibility and prestige, suggesting the kingdom is unable to provide adequate security to the holiest sites in all the Islamic world.

The target may not be a mainstay of the country; it may possess no inherent importance whatsoever in terms of legitimacy of the government or its political or economic strength. However, it is targeted because of its location or of its linkage to other targets. It is a symbolic target. A series of attacks on American individuals and institutions in Lebanon after the spring of 1982 said little about the legitimacy of Lebanon or its weakness, since even the U.S. government with a relatively free hand in the country was unable to prevent these attacks. None can doubt their symbolic importance in terms of U.S. interests and credibility, and ultimately, their success both in that context and in forcing a complete change of security policy on the Lebanese government.

While the Gulf states do not have the quantities of symbolically important targets that many other countries have, neither do they have the manpower resources to adequately protect such targets as do exist in those countries.

Attack on Key Facilities

The primacy of the economic infrastructure of the Gulf states in their international role and domestic legitimacy makes of that infrastructure a key target for political as well as other objectives. A number of specific installations, notably the Ras Tanura complex, are for all intents and purposes important Western economic nodes. Attacks on these facilities could have the farthest-reaching political, economic, and security implications.

Attack on Key Locations

Because of limited LOCs and underdeveloped infrastructure in the Gulf area, there are key chokepoints that may also be targeted and that could effectively carry major shockwaves to the Gulf countries or to Western trading partners. Control of the Red Sea commerce can be effected easily by presence at a few key locations, and the Strait of Hormuz can also be largely controlled from a few key vantage points. Similarly, Gulf transportation nets, while far from developed, do provide a number of central points which if attacked could severely hamper movement in and through the area. While such attacks would not have anything near the political visibility (and hence value) of the others mentioned, they could quite significantly reduce the ability of the Gulf governments to respond to military contingencies.

Border Hostilities

Another limited type of military threat concerns border hostilities possibly arising from current boundary disputes, but more likely the visible manifestation of more far-reaching political hostility. It should be noted that the Iran-Iraq war, which has already lasted over five years—five years of almost inconceivable attrition on both sides—began as a series of Iranian provocations along the border. The resurfacing of Iran's claim on Bahrain and its continued occupation of Abu Musa and the Tumb Islands suggests that the Islamic Republic may not hesitate to advance and take action on territorial claims.

Border hostilities of a limited type—that is, not part of a general war between the two parties—pose little threat to regime security if they are terminated quickly. If they persist, as in the Iran-Iraq case, they can quickly sap the will and challenge the responsiveness of security forces and creativity of strategic thinkers. At present the Gulf countries face a number of potential border conflicts that could create, and in the past have created, a certain level of border hostilities.

52

Attack/Invasion

As violence in regional affairs grows and the Iran-Iraq war rages, the threat of full-scale armed conflict resulting from attack or invasion of the Arab Gulf states cannot be relegated to the category of "improbable." While the current Gulf war is certainly absorbing most of the resources and efforts of Iran and Iraq, the end of the war could usher in a new era—and new targets for these larger and very powerful armies. Moreover, continuing conflict in the Gulf raises the possibility that Soviet or other external adventurers may use that instability as a pretext for other movements that will threaten or breach the security of the Arab Gulf states.

Based on the recent past, a Soviet attack on the Gulf does indeed appear to be improbable. However, this assumes the stimulus for invasion derives from the Gulf itself. Somewhat less unlikely is a Soviet move resulting from the global rivalry with the United States—a tactical military move either in response to or in preemption of an American military action. For such a Soviet initiative—an attack in the form of an invasion, not merely an attack on key facilities, which is considered separately—the stakes would have to be high, indeed. Despite Soviet caution in the Gulf area, and the limited on assets there, the growth of Moscow's interest in the area is quite clear, and the move into Afghanistan, whether related to the Gulf (as some suggest) or not (which appears more likely), does provide the capabilities and perhaps the additional incentive for the Soviet Union to play a more active and aggressive role in the military equation in the Gulf.

Combinations

Finally, it is evident that several of these diverse military contingencies could co-occur, either in the same country (countries) or in different states. Border hostilities in southwestern Arabia might invite some kind of intervention in the northeast or along the Gulf coast, since an aggressor would choose a period when Saudi Arabia was preoccupied and, with divided forces, could not effectively respond to a second threat without the prospect of losses on both fronts. The same kind of possibilities apply with even more telling consequences to the smaller Arab Gulf states.

Not one of the Arab states of the Gulf, even Iraq, is adequately prepared to deal with a multi-front set of military contingencies. Yet, with the growing cooperation between countries such as Iran, Syria, South Yemen, and Ethiopia, and their recourse to insurgent, terrorist, subversive, and other low-profile threats as well as to large-scale armed provocations, such complex threats, whether coordinated or spontaneous, can no longer be taken lightly.

Threat Assessment[3]

The North

The principal threat to the Gulf system from the North remains a rather unlikely but catastrophic scenario—a Soviet land invasion striking out from existing Soviet air bases in Afghanistan and through Iran. Only in the event of instability in Iran, and possibly of Soviet incursions there in the aftermath of such instability, is such a contingency realistically even conceivable in terms of local precipitants. Nevertheless, such a military thrust is possible, and global rather than regional considerations could prompt the Soviet Union to take the military initiative to place NATO in an untenable position in Europe, forcing the choice to nuclearize a conflict or accept a new status quo.

A full-scale Soviet attack on the Gulf countries would certainly be purposeless if it did not either aim at the defeat and subsequent control of Saudi Arabia, at the control or destruction of Saudi oil facilities, or at the control of the SLOCs through which Gulf oil must move to the West. The Gulf does not possess sufficient inherent value to the Soviet Union to justify the potential military and political costs involved in an attack except in terms of its oil resources and Western dependence upon them.

A Soviet military thrust through part of Iran that left safe passage in the Gulf completely subject to Soviet control would also constitute a capital threat to Western and Gulf interests, even if the move did not actually reach all the way to the Gulf itself. Such a move could be justified by the Soviet security concern for its own territory if substantial disorders erupted in northern Iran near the extended Soviet border.

The possibility of Soviet airstrikes to accomplish political or military objectives in the Gulf cannot be ruled out, even though such strikes are highly unlikely in the near or intermediate term. The nearest Soviet bases are so distant that aircraft range in hi-lo-hi flight profiles would allow unrefueled strikes against Arab Gulf

---

[3] Summaries of equipment inventories of the countries discussed below are provided in the annual surveys of the International Institute of Strategic Studies, entitled *The Military Balance (Years)*.

littoral targets by only four active, modern aircraft in the Soviet inventory—the MiG-25, the Sukkhio-24, and the Tu-22 and Tu-26 (Backfire) bombers. The hi-lo-hi flight profile is reasonable only assuming no opposition. Lo-lo-lo profiles degrade range estimates with ordnance loads sufficiently that only the Tupolovs (bombers) could extend their coverage to Gulf targets.

Table 3.1 compares aircraft action radii based on mission for all major types of fixed-wing, combat aircraft in inventory of the Gulf states and for the principal Soviet and U.S. ground-based and carrier-based aircraft.

The Gulf

At this time, the most immediate and visible threats come from within the Gulf system. These threats involve both military contingencies arising from the Gulf war and those more likely in its aftermath.

The war has already led to belligerent attacks on non-belligerent vessels engaged in commerce. While air attacks on oil tankers have received the greatest notoriety, in fact ships involved in other types of trade have also been hit. In May 1985, Royal Saudi Air Force (RSAF) fighters had to protect shipping, and indeed shot down an Iranian aircraft. The perpetuation of the war poses the threat of continuation of Iranian and Iraqi attacks on merchant vessels and the consequent disruption of the oil flow.

But attacks on non-belligerent merchant vessels are far from the most dangerous contingency relating to the war. In the course of the conflict, the two parties have acquired new arms that change the complexion of the military threat in the Gulf. Both now have stand-off precision-guided munitions, and while neither has displayed any effective use of or tactical ingenuity in their employment, the presence of these missile systems adds a distinctly new and ominous element to the OBs. In the context of the war itself, Iran and Iraq can now threaten much more credibly the oil tankers and facilities that the other needs. Beyond the parameters of the war, however, Iran may also threaten to retaliate against key Saudi oil facilities should its leaders perceive the United States as aiding Iraq, should they experience American pressure on some issue of bilateral relations, or should they encounter American retaliation for terrorist attacks on U.S. citizens or property. While it is certainly true in principle that Iranian military forces could also attack Ras Tanura or other Saudi oil facilities, it is true *only* in principle due

TABLE 3.1

COMPARATIVE RADIUS OF ACTION OF RELEVANT COMBAT AIRCRAFT

Radius of Action (Nautical Miles)

System	Interception	Ground Attack (hi-lo-hi)	Ground Attack (lo-lo-lo)
A-6	—	700	
A-7	—	550	
A-10	—	400	250
F-104A	228	—	—
F-4E	429	869	782
F-5A	170	485	
F-5E	180	480	325
F-14A	178	500	
F-15A	286	786	571
F-16A	675	580	350
F-18A	>200		
F-111		800	
IL-28	—	600	—
Kfir	200	512	238
Kfir2C	288	700	351
KfirC7	419	640	
Lightning Mk 2	225		
MiG-17		300	
MiG-21F	260		
MiG-21MF	365	390	200
MiG-21SMT	440	470	236
MiG-23S (FLOGGER B)	325	380	160
MiG-27 (FLOGGER D)	380	580	310
MiG-23MS (FLOG. E)	550	560	296
MiG-23BM (FLOG. F)			
MiG-25A	593	1187	391
Mirage IIIE	156	325	160
Mirage V	173	350	218
Mirage F1C	365	593	348
Mirage F1BQ			
Mirage F1EQ			
Su-7		300	
Su-20		340	195
Su-24		970	200
Su-25		300	
Tu-16	—		
Tu-22	—	1500	
Tu-26	—	1900	900
Tu-28	—		

to the current inability of the Iranian military to project its force in a concentrated and accurate manner across the Gulf.

Following the present war, the military equation in the Gulf can be expected to change significantly. Iraq's ability to bring power to bear in the Gulf will increase immeasurably and immediately once its substantial and experienced military forces are no longer tied down by the war. Although Iraq has never won high marks for the capability of its military forces, and has been particularly weak in the areas of maneuver and command and control; most seasoned military observers believe the length of the Gulf war and the intensity of the experience at all levels of the Iraqi army have provided an invaluable and effective learning environment, and that, as a consequence, Iraq's military forces have improved markedly.

In the aftermath of the war, which has produced unprecedentedly strong ties between Iraq and the other Arab countries of the Gulf littoral, a deterioration of relations could occur as a result of oil production levels, political differences, ties with Iran, political objectives in the Gulf, or security planning there. Alternatively—but no less conflict-producing—an Iranian victory, whether delivered by military or political means, would engender a new political order in Iraq. The new regime would almost certainly conspire with Tehran on a military move toward the South.

Nor will Iraq alone benefit militarily from an end of the war. Iran too, for the first time since the revolutionary period, would have an opportunity to fully develop and organize its armed forces and paramilitary groups in a coherent and mutually reinforcing manner. The respite from conflict could afford the Islamic Republic the resources to rebuild the once-considerable land, air, and naval forces necessary to affect security throughout the Gulf, and to intimidate or endanger the smaller Arab Gulf states. The political decisions that would be required to recreate such formidable capabilities may not be in the offing, for they involve international relations as well as domestic considerations. But none can doubt the dedication of some of Iran's rulers to a complete alteration to the contemporary political order in the Gulf.

Direct military threats from the two major powers of the Gulf are not the only, nor even the most likely, threats to Gulf security emanating from those quarters. Instead, whether from Iran, Iraq, or both, the more probable challenges will come in the future (as they have in the past) from indirect attacks on the other Gulf states—creating and promoting insurgency, internal violence, opposition political movements, and terrorism. Although there is little base for these kinds of political violence at present, the real legitimacy of such movements is often incidental to the magnitude of the problems they can create, the leverage they can exert, and even to their success. To a certain extent, they create the conditions of their own success. By generating enough violence, they create dissatisfaction with the protection afforded by the government. By encouraging government overreaction, they lead to repression which does engender a certain legitimacy. And even if the campaign does not topple the government subjected to it, the pressure often leads that government into a different stance vis-a-vis the sponsor or third parties in order to create breathing space.

The monarchies of the Gulf appear anachronistic to Westerners, and often to the educated citizenry of the Gulf countries themselves. The "republican" model has long been the dominant one in world politics, despite the persistence of a number of monarchies in industrialized countries, both in Europe (the United Kingdom, Belgium, the Netherlands, Spain) and elsewhere (Japan). But institutional trappings have little to do with political efficiency, and republican forms are no more nor less amenable to repression than their monarchical counterparts. The Soviet Union is a republic in form, and the inhuman atrocities carried out in the name of the people in Cambodia or those we have witnessed in Equatorial Guinea and Uganda were no less despicable because the government purported to be a republic rather than a monarchy. The climate of liberty in the Gulf is distinctly superior to that available in most developing countries, and people of the Arab Gulf states as a group have enjoyed the fruits of both stability and security at the national and individual levels.

Figure 3.1 summarizes principal Arab Gulf country targets by type of attack from Iran within the typology provided above. Iraq is excluded as a target, and may indeed become the staging point for the attack, depending upon the outcome of the Gulf war.

Table 3.2 and Map 3.1 give indications of distances from existing Iraqi and Iranian air bases to targets in the Gulf.

The South

The southern threat picture differs sharply from the threat within the Gulf. There are no major Indian Ocean powers. The largest navies with forces deployed in the Indian Ocean are external to the Gulf and Indian Ocean area (although the Indian Navy has the largest forces in the Indian Ocean). Since the revolution in Iran, the United States has maintained sizable forces in the region either as a result of crises or as an indication of continuing concern and a symbol of American over-the-horizon presence.

FIGURE 3.1

IRAN ATTACK: GULF COUNTRY TARGETS AND TYPES OF ATTACK

TYPES OF IRANIAN ATTACK

TARGET	Terrorism/ Internal Violence	Symbolic	Key Facilities	Key Locations	Attack/ Invasion
BAHRAIN					
Manama	X	X	X		X
Sitrah			X		
KUWAIT					
Kuwait City	X	X	X	X	X
Mina Abdallah			X		
OMAN					
Goat Island			X	X	X
al-Khassab			X	X	X
Masirah	X	X	X		
Muscat	X	X	X	X	X
Seeb			X		X
QATAR					
Doha		X	X		
SAUDI ARABIA					
Dammam	X		X	X	X
Dhahran	X	X	X	X	X
Jubayl	X		X	X	X
KKMC		X	X		
Mecca	X	X			
Ras Tanura	X		X	X	X
Riyadh	X	X	X	X	
UNITED ARAB EMIRATES					
Abu Dhabi		X	X	X	X
Dubai			X	X	X
Sharjah			X		

FIGURE 3.2

IRAQ ATTACK: GULF COUNTRY TARGETS AND TYPES OF ATTACK

TYPES OF IRAQI ATTACK

TARGET	Terrorism/ Internal Violence	Symbolic	Key Facilities	Key Locations	Attack/ Invasion
BAHRAIN	IV	*			*
KUWAIT		X	X	X	X
OMAN	IV				
QATAR	IV				
SAUDI ARABIA	IV				
Dhahran		X	X	X	X
Jubayl			X	X	X
KKMC		X	X		X
Ras Tanura			X	X	X
Riyadh		X	X	X	X
U. ARAB EMIRATES	IV				

Note: IV=Internal Violence. *=as surrogate of Iran. Terrorism is not anticipated as an Iraqi tactic, except as a surrogate of Iran.

TABLE 3.2
DISTANCES (NAUTICAL MILES) FROM IRAN/IRAQ AIR BASES TO GULF TARGETS

TARGET	Ahwaz	Abadan	Ban. Abbas	Bushire	Diz.	Shir.	Basra 1*	Basra 2+	Nasir.
Kuwait	122	60	NA	148	176	239	76	NA	139
Mina Abd.	139	77	NA	139	200	230	93	NA	159
KKMC	213	168	NA	339	262	176	NA	156	143
Dhahran	308	260	157	159	363	236	282	NA	356
Dammam	330	250	157	156	356	224	276	NA	352
Jubayl	263	225	182	131	322	219	236	NA	295
Ras Tan.	324	240	328	143	349	213	261	NA	339
Riyadh	413	350	NA	339	NA	427	NA	348	387
Manama	321	270	310	161	380	224	300	NA	367
Sitrah	330	275	308	165	385	226	302	NA	368
Doha	389	NA	NA	222	455	427	372	NA	NA
Abu Dhabi	NA	NA	195	326	NA	323	503	NA	NA
Dubai	NA	NA	128	321	NA	126	508	NA	NA
Sharjah	NA	NA	119	321	NA	122	513	NA	NA
Seeb	NA	NA	235	504	NA	467	NA	NA	NA
al-Khassab	NA	NA	62	328	NA	282	575	NA	NA
Goat Island	NA	NA	57	331	NA	283	591	NA	NA
Muscat	NA	NA	249	521	NA	482	NA	NA	NA
Masirah	NA	NA	415	NA	NA	634	NA	NA	NA

MAP 3.1
DISTANCES FROM IRAN/IRAQ AIR BASES TO GULF TARGETS

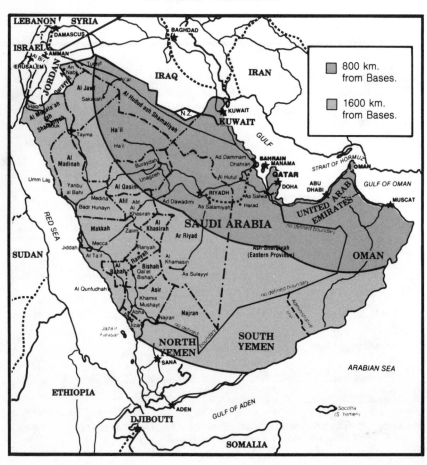

For some years the growing Soviet naval presence in the Indian Ocean occasioned concern, even though it appears that Soviet naval forces were deployed in the area largely in response to potential threat to the Soviet heartland of U.S. ballistic missile submarines. Moscow and Washington even held talks on naval limitations in the Indian Ocean, but without agreement. A number of naval experts believed, however, that these talks had substantial potential for accord. The changes in the region following the Iranian revolution were as responsible as any other element for putting the talks on the shelf.

Both superpowers have bases in the Indian Ocean area. The United States maintains a naval base at Diego Garcia, and has contingency basing agreements with Kenya, Oman, and Somalia; the Soviets have rights in Aden and on the South Yemeni island of Socotra, just off the Peninsula (see Map 3.2).

• Diego Garcia is about 3,000 miles from the Gulf, but it can now accommodate strategic bombers and has become a primary location for pre-positioned equipment.

• Kenyan and Somali facilities are also too distant from the Gulf to be directly valuable. Like Diego Garcia, their primary value is as rear supply/support facilities, and it is in the value of their airfields that these bases may prove themselves. Staging from Diego Garcia, Kenya, or even Somalia to the Gulf would be virtually impossible, given the range limitations on most equipment.

• The agreements with Oman are clearly the most valuable accords in terms of the ability of the United States to provide military force for Gulf contingencies. The Gulf lies within easy reach of Oman, which is situated comfortably outside the Gulf—a highly desirable situation in terms of the safety of U.S. operating air forces. The United States is improving the airfield on Masirah Island.

• Socotra is much closer to the Gulf than Diego Garcia, but is still a small facility of limited naval value. Fewer than 2,000 Soviet armed forces personnel, principally naval forces, are stationed in South Yemen.

• Overall, the United States has substantially improved its ability to mount military operations from the Indian Ocean into the Gulf area, but neither superpower can feel it has sufficient permanently based power to project significant force into the area over long periods. For both the United States and the Soviet Union, Indian

MAP 3.2
U.S.-SOVIET FACILITIES IN THE INDIAN OCEAN

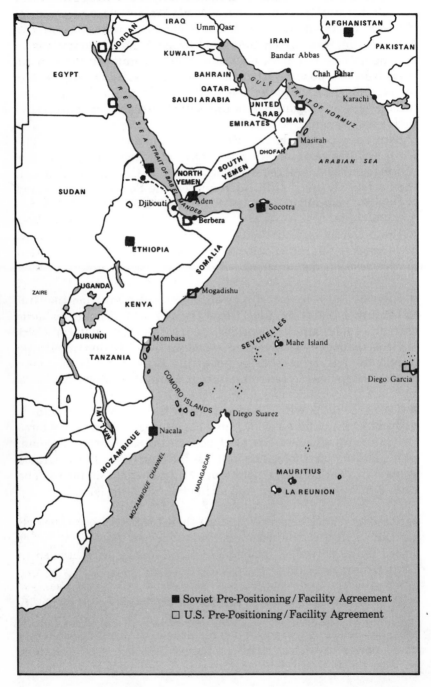

Ocean-staged operations are naval operations. However, U.S. carrier-based airpower in the area means that the United States can bring to bear overwhelming air superiority in any engagement in the lower Gulf. (While it is not germane to consideration of the Indian Ocean area, the proximity of Soviet territory raises important questions about the northern Gulf, but only in theory, because home-based Soviet strike aircraft cannot reach primary Gulf targets if faced with any opposition.)[4]

Table 3.3 and Map 3.3 illustrate distances from potential or actual hostile air bases in the Indian Ocean area to targets in Oman and Saudi Arabia.

The Red Sea

The Red Sea's importance has grown markedly even as the Gulf's has diminished. While the oil of the Gulf is now a smaller proportion of the total world oil consumed, the Red Sea, which had languished during the oil decade, has taken on added value as an alternative to the Gulf for the shipping of oil from the Peninsula. Although the diminution of the role of Gulf oil therefore also affects the Red Sea in theory, it does not in practice simply because the Red Sea is a newcomer as a major SLOC in post-1974 oil shipping.[5] The Red Sea assumed additional significance in 1985, with the completion of the line connecting Iraqi oil shipments to the main Saudi pipeline to Yanbu.

The Red Sea is no longer the safe shipping lane it once was, however. Whereas its shores were once lined with Western colonies and pro-Western states, this is no longer the case. The British colonial area of Aden is now the Marxist PDRY. The former Mutawakelite Kingdom of Yemen, now the Yemen Arab Republic (YAR or North Yemen), is unstable and vacillating between the pressures of South Yemen and those of Saudi Arabia. The Ethiopian Empire

---

[4] Available range estimates of the SU-24 suggest that it could in fact reach the northern Gulf from bases on the Soviet-Iranian border, but only if by flying ideal flight profiles. Opposition must be assumed—even if only from carrier-based U.S. airpower. Moreover, the SU-24 would fly well beyond any friendly air cover—another assurance that evasive measures, which consume valuable fuel, would be required.
[5] The Red Sea was used for oil shipments before 1967, when the Suez Canal was closed as a result of naval activity there. The canal did not open again until 1975. In the meantime, the development of supertankers altered the nature of petroleum shipping, and the canal could not accommodate the larger supertankers even after it re-opened. Therefore, while oil was shipped through the Red Sea after the Suez Canal re-opened, the bulk of oil shipped to Europe was carried by pipelines or supertankers using other routes.

TABLE 3.3
DISTANCES (NAUTICAL MILES) FROM
INDIAN OCEAN BASES TO
GULF STATE TARGETS

TARGETS	Aden	'Ataq	Bayhan al-Qisab	al-Ghayda	al-Mukallah	Tarim
Jidda	574	—	—	—	—	—
Khamis Mushayt	—	322	270	—	417	383
Shararuh	—	152	159	300	196	122
Ta'if	548	—	—	—	—	—
Salalah	—	—	—	120	311	—
Thumrayt	—	—	—	139	337	—

MAP 3.3
DISTANCES FROM INDIAN OCEAN BASES
TO GULF STATE TARGETS

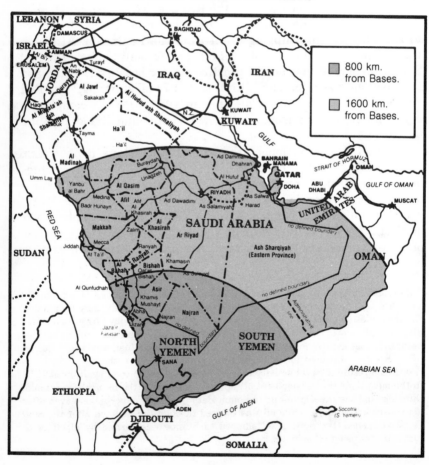

has given way to a pro-Soviet state, and Sudan, under pressure between Libya and Ethiopia, is anything but stable. The Soviet navy has a facility at Dahlak Island in the Red Sea.

The Red Sea threat to the Gulf is manifested in several ways. First, there is a considerable threat to the Red Sea as an alternative to the Gulf as a shipping lane. Second, while no Red Sea country is in a position to assault the Gulf itself, several could attack Gulf littoral states, specifically Saudi Arabia or Oman, whether in the form of border hostilities or as an all-out military offensive. Despite the Soviet bases nearby, neither the Red Sea nor the Indian Ocean is a likely source of Soviet attack on the Gulf.

The principal naval powers of the Red Sea are France, with its base in independent Djibouti; Egypt; and Israel, the capabilities of whose forces in the Red Sea (based in Eilat) have improved dramatically since the October 1973 war. Of these three, only Israel is hostile to the moderate Arab Gulf states. Israel can control the shipping of the waterway with its small but competent forces. However, Israeli forces in the Red Sea are not likely to be used except in an Arab-Israeli context.

So narrow a body of water is the Red Sea, and so very vulnerable are its outlets, that it does not require a major naval power to interdict shipping there. South Yemen, with its position on Bab el Mandeb, or Ethiopia, with its extended Red Sea coast, could disrupt Red sea shipping very easily. The Bab el Mandeb mouth of the Red Sea could be threatened from either naval vessels or shore positions in South Yemen. The South Yemeni navy has improved considerably in recent years, and while it is still quite small it could certainly create problems in the Bab el Mandeb area. Despite the limitations on the naval capability of Ethiopia, the Ethiopian Air Force could also come into play over the Red Sea, certainly a mismatch for any commercial tanker traffic in the area.

Red Sea-originated military operations against Gulf countries can affect only Oman and Saudi Arabia. The key Red Sea country in this case is South Yemen, which has mounted campaigns against both Oman *and* Saudi Arabia in the past. However, Ethiopia, too, could support its cross-Red Sea ally,[6] South Yemen, principally in the air. (South Yemen has in fact supported Ethiopia in military

---

[6] Ethiopia, Libya, and South Yemen formed an alliance in August 1981. However, in the aftermath of the latest coup in South Yemen, which began January 12, 1986, and as a result of of continued Ethiopian support for the ousted government of Ali Nasser Mohammed, the two countries are undergoing political and diplomatic strain in their traditionally close relationship. Whether these tensions will endure will probably not become apparent for some time.

operations against the Eritrean Liberation front.) Finally, if the Yemens ever agree to unite, the presence in Saudi Arabia of over one million Yemenis would constitute a potential internal security threat. Indeed, Saudi Arabia and North Yemen have had a long history of fractious border relations, primarily due to smuggling from Yemen, and these troubles, far from abating, continue to produce border skirmishes.

South Yemen has an army about two-thirds the size of Saudi Arabia's, and substantially smaller and less capable air and naval arms. Oman's ground forces are smaller than those of South Yemen. Because primary Omani and Saudi targets are largely out of reach of South Yemen's air power, and because Saudi forces have improved much more than those of South Yemen, it is unlikely that the latter on its own constitutes a direct military threat to the survival of either the Omani or the Saudi governments. It may conduct border operations with some success, however, and could increase its support of dissidents in Oman and Saudi Arabia. South Yemen's primary threat comes in the context of a multi-front conflict or conflicts for Oman or Saudi Arabia. (See below.)

Figures 3.3 and 3.4 describe possible targets in Oman and Saudi Arabia of threats emanating from the Red Sea states of South Yemen (whether directly or through North Yemen) and Ethiopia.

Table 3.4 and Map 3.4 present distances from Red Sea air bases to Gulf country targets.

The Regional Threat Picture

The regional threat to the Gulf includes individual threats posed by Israel or Syria; and various combinations of threats discussed individually above.

—Israel

Having bombed the Iraqi nuclear reactor near Baghdad, staged a dramatic raid on Entebbe, Uganda, and struck the PLO headquarters in Tunis over 2,000 km away from Tel Aviv, none can doubt that the strategic reach of Israel easily extends to Saudi Arabia. In fact, Israeli overflights of Saudi territory have been frequent, and sometimes these overflights have been accompanied by symbolic gestures such as dropping aircraft equipment on Saudi airfields, breaking the sound barrier, and the like. While Israel can clearly reach the Gulf—e.g., the raid against Iraq—a *sustained*

FIGURE 3.3

SOUTH YEMENI ATTACK: GULF COUNTRY TARGETS AND TYPES OF ATTACK

TARGET	TYPES OF SOUTH YEMENI ATTACK				
	Terrorism/ Internal Violence	Symbolic	Key Facilities	Key Locations	Attack/ Invasion
SAUDI ARABIA					
Jidda	X				X
Khamis Mushayt		X	X		X
Mecca/Medina	X				
Shararuh			X		X
Ta'if				X	
OMAN					
Salalah	X	X	X	X	X
Thumrayt			X		X

FIGURE 3.4

ETHIOPIAN ATTACK: GULF COUNTRY TARGETS AND TYPES OF ATTACK

TARGET	TYPES OF ETHIOPIAN ATTACK			
	Symbolic	Key Facilities	Key Locations	Attack/ Invasion
Jidda	X	X	X	X
Khamis Mushayt		X		
Shararuh		X		
Ta'if		X	X	X

TABLE 3.4

DISTANCES (NAUTICAL MILES) FROM
RED SEA AIR BASES TO GULF STATE TARGETS

Target	Ethiopia Massawa	North Yemen San'a	Sa'dah
Jidda	348	517	365
Khamis Mushayt	250	193	97
Shararuh	452	202	198
Ta'if	343	—	—

MAP 3.4
DISTANCES FROM RED SEA AIR BASES
TO GULF STATE TARGETS

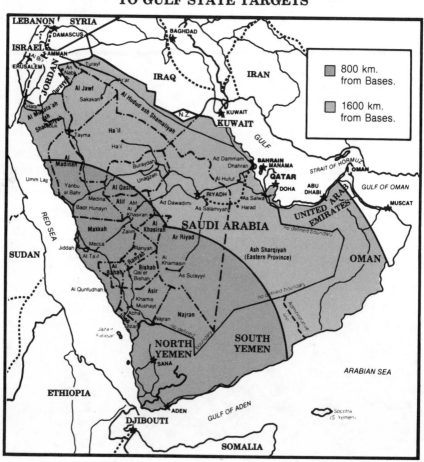

68

attack on Gulf targets is beyond Israeli capabilities. Thus, Saudi Arabia is effectively the only Gulf country threatened by Israel.

Israel clearly has no territorial designs per se on Saudi Arabia nor any compelling interest in changing its government, since any conceivable Saudi government will maintain something very close to the present policies of the kingdom as regards the Middle East conflict. Thus, for political as well as military reasons the Israeli threat can be seen as limited to specific strikes, whether to "punish" the kingdom, to warn its leaders, to disengage the oil embargo threat, or to affect Saudi-American relations. Targets for these kinds of strikes are limited to those accessible by air rather than ground forces. The most likely such targets would include principal military bases, major industrial developments, and oil facilities. These are summarized in Figure 3.5 below.

Table 3.5 and Map 3.5 depict the distances from representative Israeli air bases to targets in Saudi Arabia. Practically speaking, all such strikes beyond the two proximate targets (Tabuk and Yanbu) would require aerial refueling. However, Israel is the only country in the region with extensive experience in in-flight refueling under crisis or combat conditions.

FIGURE 3.5

ISRAELI ATTACK: GULF COUNTRY TARGETS AND TYPES OF ATTACK

TARGET	TYPES OF ISRAELI ATTACK	
	Symbolic	Key Facilities
Jidda	X	X
Oil Target	X	X
Riyadh	X	X
Tabuk	X	X
Yanbu	X	X

TABLE 3.5

DISTANCES (NAUTICAL MILES) FROM ISRAELI BASES TO GULF COUNTRY TARGETS

TARGET	Israeli Air Base
Jidda	539
Ras Tanura	843
Riyadh	674
Tabuk	111
Yanbu	345

MAP 3.5
DISTANCES FROM ISRAELI BASES TO GULF STATE TARGETS

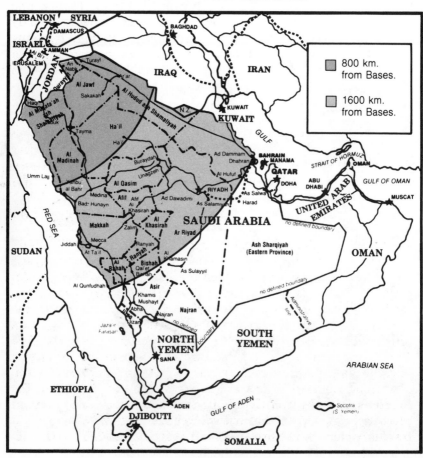

—Syria

Syria has not openly threatened military action against any of the GCC states. The country's posture in the relations of the region is unique and complex. On the one hand, Syria has been careful to avoid steps that might involve it in a war with Israel: attacks on Israel never try to penetrate the Golan, where Israel and Syria have shared a de facto peaceful border for many years (except in regional wars); Syria has reached gentlemen's agreements with Israel on its deployments in Lebanon and on Israeli overflights of Lebanon. On the other hand, no Arab country has been more heavily or effectively involved in regional destabilization than Syria.

Syria claims to have but two demands in the Arab-Israeli context: return of the Golan Heights to Syria, and a resolution of the Palestinian problem that is endorsed by the PLO. Syrian leaders do not believe—probably correctly—that any action short of war can now sever the Golan Heights from Israel. They tend to oppose any movement toward peace that appears unlikely to succeed in achieving their objective, and nothing on the horizon is very likely to see the Golan Heights returned to Syria. In a sense, cooperation with Libya, Iran, South Yemen, and Ethiopia would be mandated by the need for fundamental change in (destabilization of) the region prerequisite to obtaining Syria's goals; but it is certainly far from clear that this is the logic behind such cooperation.

Apart from their demands specific to the regional conflict, Syrian leaders appear also to seek recognition and treatment as the key Arab power. Yet, for the United States and other parties interested in pursuing any lead toward peace, active cooperation with Syria effectively means scuttling the peace process, a process to which Syria is adamantly opposed for a variety of reasons, including those already noted.

The Syrian military threat is practically limited to the lower end of the threat spectrum—manipulative mobilization, subversion, and terrorism/isolated violence—at the present time, since Syria is separated from the Gulf countries by Jordan and Iraq. Because no important Gulf targets are within range of Syrian air power, the GCC countries can realistically rule out the possibility of a Syrian conventional military attack. The only means by which Syria could gain direct access to the Gulf states would be a change of regime in either Iraq or Jordan, both primary political adversaries of Syria.

A regime change in Iraq could come about as a result of the country's defeat by Iran, Syria's ally, in the Gulf war, or by internal processes, e.g., a coup that ousted Saddam Hussein. However, an Iranian victory is not probable, and short of that almost any domestic political change in Iraq is not likely to alter Iraqi-Syrian relations, which reflect a natural and inevitable conflict of geopolitical interests.

Nor is there any apparent margin for rapprochement between Jordan and Syria as long as King Hussein and Hafez al-Assad remain in power. They have burned the bridges of reconciliation. Some prominent Israeli leaders have proposed that Jordan is properly or should become a Palestinian state. Syria maintains an influence on some Palestinian elements who feel the same way. The likelihood of such a change is very remote at best in the foreseeable future. The replacement of moderate Jordan by an ally of Syria in its current posture would hardly be helpful to planning Gulf security. Jordan has taken an active if low-silhouette role in assisting the smaller Gulf countries in their security planning, and the Hashemite Kingdom's geographical presence separates Syria from the Arabian Peninsula, an insulation that reduces what is already a significant Syrian influence there.[7] Jordan's attempts to develop some initiative in the Middle East peace process, while they have certainly not been welcomed by Israel or many others, reflect the continuing Jordanian concern with regional as well as national security. The Syrian response has been a wave of terrorism directed against Jordanian (and some mainline PLO) officials and the Jordanian airline.

Thus, Syria is restricted to indirect and low-intensity threats, hardly a novel tool for Syria, which has used terrorism and implied threats of violence often, and which maintains extensive contact with and supports numerous extremist groups. Some leftist groups, including some Palestinian groups, that have occupied the attention of Gulf internal security personnel and organizations are closely tied to the Syrian regime.

Combinations

As we shall point out below, Saudi capabilities to deal with many of the contingencies we have discussed here have improved markedly over the last five years. Saudi Arabia has a modest deterrent in its F-15s, although their deterrent value is significantly degraded by limitations on their ability to strike ground targets in Iran—or in an Iranian-dominated Iraq. (The kingdom's F-15s do not have

---

[7] See W. Andrew Terrell, Jr., "Jordan and the Defense of the Gulf," *Middle East Insight*, March-April 1985, pp. 34-41; and Anthony H. Cordesman, *Jordanian Arms and Middle East Balance* (Washington, D.C.: Middle East Institute, 1983).

bomb racks. However, these racks are available, and certainly it is in the Saudi interest to acquire them in the near future.) Given available LOCs necessary to support an attacker, the RSAF is currently able to prevent sustained ground or naval invasion, as long as air control and battle management support from U.S.-assisted assets such as the Airborne Warning and Control Systems (AWACS) operate effectively.

The same cannot be said about the more vulnerable smaller Gulf states whose land and manpower reserves are simply insufficient bases on which to build adequate defenses, much less deterrents. The only hope for these states lies in cooperation with Saudi Arabia.

A problem that continues to trouble Saudi planners and that remains beyond the country's capabilities is the potential of coordinated hostile attack, possibly combined with internal action. As to the latter point, the kingdom's principal adversaries have all been extensively involved with subversion and terrorism. It would be surprising if any military attack scenario did not include a significant role for subversion and internal violence. These are internal security issues beyond the purview of the present examination.

Even a few years ago, coordinated external attacks would have been much more improbable that they are today. Although an Iranian attack related to the Gulf war is unlikely to be carried out with the support of diversionary attacks on other parts of the kingdom, military contingencies outside the context of the Gulf war may well take place on a multi-front basis. The close political relationship of pro-Soviet radical states—Libya, Syria, South Yemen, and Ethiopia—remains a source of concern. Should Ethiopia, South Yemen, and Iran carry out coordinated attacks on Saudi Arabia, Saudi defenses would be over-taxed. The kingdom's frontline aircraft, F-15s, are simply too few and consequently either too vulnerable or too widely dispersed to be able to protect the western, southern, and eastern fronts simultaneously. Because of the enormous distances between east and west in Saudi Arabia, only Riyadh can serve as a reserve and redeployment center. Moreover, because of heavy maintenance loads, the existing 5 AWACS aircraft in the east are too few to provide round-the-clock coverage (Saudi Arabia has requested additional AWACS from the United States). *No* adequate battle management system exists for the western or southern fronts, and any partial diversion of existing AWACS assets in the east would simply destroy the more critical Gulf early warning capability without creating any compensatory advantage in the south and west.

Of the other GCC countries, only Oman must consider the possibility of a two-front conflict. In theory, South Yemen and Iran could coordinate attacks against the Sultanate. However, this possibility is remote, because neither South Yemen nor Iran has more than a marginal capability to inflict significant damage on Oman at present, and, in contrast to the Saudi case, the pay-off from a coordinated attack on Oman would scarcely justify the political costs or military risks.

IV

SECURITY RESOURCES OF THE GULF COUNTRIES

The GCC is a new phenomenon, and security planning resources in the Gulf naturally reflect the pre-GCC condition: equipment is not inter-operable, and coordination of defense planning is only beginning. Key to the viability of the GCC as a security system is Saudi Arabia, with the largest and most capable armed forces and the greatest strategic depth of any of the GCC states.

Introduction

The Context of Gulf Security

In order to appreciate the security problems confronting the members of the GCC, some definition of security is required that identifies the source, type, and vehicle of threats. Absent a clear picture of what kind of security is required, against whom, and by what means, no useful evaluation of the Gulf states' political and military resources (i.e., capabilities, skills, and sources of support) can be made.

Events since the October War of 1973 and the "Oil Shock" of 1974 have underscored the declining utility of many conventional distinctions made with respect to security problems in the Gulf. In the 1980s, traditional reference points such as "internal" and "external" or "regional" and "extra-regional" are useful but no longer adequate analytical dichotomies. Instead, they are part of a broad continuum upon which interactions affecting the security of the Gulf states occur *within* and *between* regions *across* a broad spectrum of security issues, for at least two reasons. First, traditional sources of conflict such as disputes over water or tribal grazing rights, or the location of boundaries, may remain potential *occasions* for inter-state conflict but they are not likely to trigger a conflict that can threaten the political stability of the Gulf *as long as they do not involve parties with radically divergent concepts of what domestic legitimacy and national order ought to be.* When such fundamental conflicts do arise, the specific bilateral dispute (e.g., the Shatt al-Arab question between Iran and Iraq) does not constitute what is really at issue, but only the *occasion* or *arena* of conflict in which an entire array of issues including the legitimacy of the contending regimes themselves is at stake.

The second reason for the blurring of traditional distinctions among conflict cases arises from the fact that challenges to the Gulf states' security generally involve three problems:

• the control of strategic geographical locations and resources;

• issues that directly affect the interests of the superpowers; or

• issues that affect the interests of regional powers engaged in interstate conflict.

Each of these conflict areas involves the Gulf states, collectively or individually, in political and security issues beyond their borders. Each of them provides significant incentives for regional and global powers to involve themselves in the affairs of the Gulf states on an unprecedented scale. When any source of conflict exhibits any of these criteria and involves parties ideologically hostile to one another (i.e., who have radically different conceptions of what domestic legitimacy and national order ought to be), it can affect not only the Gulf states' security against external threats, but can expose their domestic social and political stability to severe external pressures.

The GCC countries are more experienced in and capable of dealing with problems relating strictly to internal security. Relatively new are the requirements for external defense, often against external threats aimed at domestic stability. The problem is that some of the more threatening external sources of conflict involve issues and actors beyond the Gulf states' borders over which they have relatively little influence. While these threats can most effectively be deflected by marshaling and enhancing the political and military resources available to the GCC countries, the problem is more complicated than it may first appear.

Political Constraints on Military Resources

Obviously, the resources available to the Gulf states are partly defined by the configuration of external threats confronting them. Equally obvious, the Gulf states must be concerned with threats operating on multiple fronts. What is far less evident is that planned utilization of military and political resources to meet certain types of external threats from one direction imposes very serious constraints on the use of these same resources to defend the Gulf against the threats. In some extreme cases (discussed below), the very existence or acquisition of the military resources needed for Gulf defense (including the necessary political cohesion of the member states) creates new threats from other directions, constrains their use in Gulf defense, or degrades their utility altogether. The most prominent example of the latter condition is the spillover effects of the Arab-Israeli conflict on Gulf security issues.

Framework for Analysis

The multi-front nature of the threats operating at the internal, peninsular, regional, and global levels often imposes severe constraints on the way existing military and political resources can be used—or whether they can be used for Gulf defense at all. What underlies the multi-front nature of the Gulf security is the threat of external manipulation or exploitation of domestic or intra-GCC political conditions that constrain the use of what assets are available for meeting external attacks. More benign, but certainly no less important, are the potential local repercussions from political or military events within the region or beyond. Security management in the Gulf countries must address the threats discussed in Chapter III, but is constrained by the following six problems:

1. Socio-economic change limiting the GCC's ability to mobilize indigenous manpower for defense of the Gulf. The by-products of social change define, condition, and constrain the mix of political and military resources employed for external security purposes.

77

2. Traditional disputes and distrust that can adversely affect efforts to plan for and create a truly effective and integrated GCC force structure.

3. The geographic size of the area to be defended, its linkage to other regions and their problems, and the concentration of military resources contrasted with the dispersion of targets tax the integrative capabilities of the GCC and its political cohesion as much as they challenge GCC military capabilities. At the very least they pose serious constraints on the effectiveness with which the Gulf states can deploy the military resources at their disposal.

4. Changes in regional distributions of power determine the extent to which the GCC member states can utilize the political resources at their disposal, and so avoid drawing on military resources with which they have relatively less experience. These also have slowed the pace at which the GCC states have been able to move toward creating an integrated Gulf Defense Command.

5. The superpower balance in the region defines the extent to which the GCC can rely on its own resources for its defense without the need to call upon external allies whose intervention could create as many problems as it solves.

6. Economic factors associated with the price of crude oil affect the capacity of the oil-rich Gulf states to support a regional political system that enhances their political power and the GCC's internal and external security.

Each of these dimensions implies a different mix of political and military resources needed to meet particular threats emanating from multiple fronts: (1) within the territory controlled by the GCC member states; (2) the Arabian Peninsula; (3) the Middle East and the Horn of Africa; and (4) a global strategic level which refers primarily to the projection of superpower conflicts into the region. The most immediate areas of concern in terms of resource evaluation are the spillover effects from regional conflicts and changes in regional distributions of power. Changes in these areas can suddenly redefine the external threats confronting the Gulf states and the resource requirements to meet them.

The implications of these six problems are particularly important when addressing questions of force structuring and security assistance discussed below. In the context of the range of threats we have discussed in the previous chapter, they provide an appreciation of one of the most important parameters of defense planning in the Gulf—that collectively and individually they are incapable of deciding major regional issues on their own by projecting military power. Each one of these security issue areas requires further discussion.

An Overview of Gulf Security Management Problems

Socio-Economic Change

The fact that no Gulf state can expand its armed forces without drawing extensively on new social classes or groups outside the traditional elite for its officers and NCOs is crucial to understanding the fundamentals of effectively addressing Gulf security problems. While the GCC states have become quite experienced and effective at handling many internal security threats, external defense confronts the Gulf rulers with an entirely new enterprise which centers on the building of modern armed forces in a way that does not undermine their political system in the process. This imposes a serious constraint on the human resources that can be drawn upon to fill the ranks of a modern force structure. And, in fact, only one of the Gulf states—Saudi Arabia—is seriously broadening its recruitment base, especially in the air force.

The Impact of Social Change

All of the Gulf countries are confronted with managing the social change that has accompanied the rapid acquisition of oil wealth in the context of political structures still in their formative state. One consequence is that rapid economic development and social change have had a profound impact on the capacity of the Gulf states to mobilize indigenous manpower for military purposes. The most serious constraint is the trade-off the Gulf states face in increasing their military effectiveness against external attack while maintaining control over the loyalties of their newly expanded militaries as they become staffed by new social elements thrust up by rapid economic development and social change.

The GCC governments are attempting to adapt political and social institutions that are generally patriarchal in nature to increasingly politicized publics whose ties to the traditional leaderships are weakening. This process involves creating broader forums for popular representation (such as consultative assemblies) while modernizing governmental organizations and "professionalizing" the bureaucracies. All of the GCC countries have experienced a rate of social transformation and modernization that has no parallel in history. The oil wealth and the resultant economic expansion have forced a gradual redefinition of many social norms, religious customs and patterns of social behavior. This has created a class problem with traditional social groups having to make way for rising technocratic and entrepreneurial groups whose skills and expertise (and social prestige) can only increase as the Gulf economies become more complex in the process of diversification. Rapid economic growth and industrialization have long since exhausted the limited supply of skilled indigenous personnel and have produced enormous inflows of foreign labor.

As the GCC economies have expanded and become more sophisticated, pressures have increased to modernize not only government bureaucracies, but the structure of military establishments as well. These developments have necessitated substantial reliance on foreign experts, new social classes, and other groups outside the traditional ruling establishment—"new groups" which may lack the traditional mix of family, economic, and political ties to the leadership.

External defense based on the development of modern air, sea, and land forces in a way that strengthens rather than undermines their political systems presents the Gulf rulers with an entirely new enterprise for which there is very little precedent to guide them. The sheer novelty of modern warfare requires a mastery of organizational and technical skills with which the traditional pools of military manpower—Bedouin tribesmen—have no experience. While various Gulf rulers may continue to show preference for taking recruits from the Bedouin portions of their societies, the indigenous population with the necessary skills are the urban and modern elements with less intimate ties to the leadership. Moreover, there is a culturally based disdain among Bedouin recruits for combat support and combat service support tasks-operations without which a modern army cannot function. Other cultural characteristics associated with tribal recruits, such as an aversion to manual labor and a disregard for the tools and maintenance procedures associated with the servicing of modern weapons systems, appear to suffuse the entire weapons absorption and military modernization process.[1]

---

[1] See Anthony Pascal, Michael Kennedy, and Steven Rosen, *Men and Arms in the Middle East: The Human Factor in Military Modernization* (Santa Monica: Rand, June 1979), p. 42.

These problems are complicated by the fact that oil wealth and rapid modernization in civilian sectors compete with military recruitment and present those trained in the military with high-paying alternatives for advancement in civilian life. Military careers have lower relative prestige in the Gulf than civilian occupations open to most of the indigenous citizens, which has obvious negative implications for recruitment in these countries. The interaction effects of a rapidly expanding civilian economy and the simultaneous introduction of sophisticated weapons systems into these countries' armed forces have only worsened the Gulf states' manpower problems.

While military modernization programs have yielded skilled operators and limited numbers of indigenous support personnel, the introduction of new weapons has been accompanied by a large and growing polyglot community of foreigners to support them. Meanwhile, the Gulf states have been reluctant to make a concerted effort to develop a class of indigenous military technicians akin to the homafars in Iran. Such local technical experts would have to be drawn from the more educated, urbanized elements of their populations whose ties (and therefore commitments) to the leadership are weaker. The fact that the homafars ultimately rose against the shah of Iran probably has reinforced the GCC rulers' aversion to training a similar cadre of indigenous military experts.[2]

We have discussed above some of the problems of expatriate workers in terms of internal security and the ability of foreign states to exploit internal differences. Expatriate workers in the defense sector present other problems as well. Whether indigenous personnel will perform capably, or even bravely, is unknown, but this is a question that at least is in some ways indirectly, as well as directly in others, subject to the policies and foresight of the Gulf states themselves. Whether foreign personnel remain "when the balloon goes up" is another matter altogether, and not one as responsive to national policies. Will the United States encourage the departure of its nationals in the event of a conflict in the Gulf or on the Peninsula? Can the United States tolerate, from the point of view

---

[2] The homafars were non-commissioned officers in the Imperial Iranian Army. They were drawn largely from the urban middle classes and were highly trained specialists who filled a variety of technical positions. After they received education and technical training from the government, they did not enjoy privileges commensurate with those of the officer corps. Thus, unlike the officers, who owed their positions to the shah and who therefore were loyal to the monarchy, the homafars were anti-shah. As the shah's position began to deteriorate in 1979, the homafars became the vanguard of the movement that eventually toppled him. See William Hickman, *Ravaged and Reborn: The Iranian Army* (Washington, D.C.: Brookings, 1982), pp. 5-6.

of public policy, the active participation of American nationals on one side in a regional conflict? Those same Western nationals who offer some insurance against too powerful a military taking a hand in domestic politics and are therefore balm to internal security planners, may also leave Gulf forces in the lurch in the event military forces must face a major military contingency.

In trying to develop modern armed forces capable of defending their countries against external regional threats without undermining their political system in the process, the Gulf rulers have made haste slowly. This has involved a series of tradeoffs between effective military modernization, on the one hand, and internal control, on the other. For example, promotion in the officer corps continues to be based on personal loyalty as well as (in some cases more than) on competence, especially in the smaller Gulf states where family members often dominate all forces. Reliance on expatriates (particularly Jordanians and Pakistanis) and seconded foreign personnel to fill key officer as well as advisory positions, especially in the smaller sheikhdoms, does more than compensate for shortages of local technical expertise. In some instances, these expatriates also serve as sources of intelligence and control. The purchase of high technology weapons systems may further strain shortages of indigenous skilled manpower, but modern weapons, regardless of their suitability, tend to raise the status and satisfaction of military officers. Modern weapons depend far more heavily than traditional Bedouin forces on logistics and support. This enables the GCC rulers to maintain more control over their forces by controlling access to ammunition and spare parts. They also control the salaries, and therefore presumably the loyalties, of the large expatriate communities which accompany the introduction of the new weapons.

Control at the expense of military effectiveness is also exercised through highly centralized decision-making structures. Consequently, there is a tendency for middle level officials to reject decision-making responsibility and to pass even small matters up to higher commanders who then become burdened with decisions on issues about which they lack necessary information. LOCs tend to be vertical, not horizontal. This characteristic may impede performance on the battlefield, but has had the effect of curbing the potential threat to the Gulf regimes by making coordination across military units more difficult. It can be argued that even the battlefield cost is limited by the fact that vertical decision-making and communication are typical of most of the Middle East and therefore likely to characterize the attacker as well as the Gulf defender.

A reliable and definitive assessment of the degree to which the

GCC rulers still fear their own militaries or the extent to which the militaries are a real threat is impossible to make. However, things are changing slowly in favor of improved military effectiveness, particularly since the beginning of the Iran-Iraq war. Whether this is an indicator that the Gulf rulers perceive themselves more secure with respect to their militaries or a function of the greater proximity of threat as evidenced by actual externally supported attacks (air attacks, assassination attempts, and bombings in Kuwait, the Iranian-supported coup attempt in Bahrain, the tanker war, subversion during the Hajj in Saudi Arabia, and threats against several of the countries) is unclear. On close examination the political legitimacy of the Gulf regimes appears to be one of their strongest assets. Further, there is no reason to presume an inevitable relationship between an increase in Gulf military capabilities and the threat of a military takeover.[3] These issues are discussed in detail below.

Traditional Disputes

The elites in the six GCC states have been engaged in territorial and other disputes with each other well into the twentieth century. Bahrain and Qatar, for example, remain at loggerheads over the possession of the Hawar Island. The Al-Khalifas of Bahrain also claim Zubarah, a northwestern coastal strip on the Qatari Peninsula, a claim which is both historical and tribal in nature. While Saudi Arabia and Kuwait have no strategic differences, they are still arguing over who has sovereignty over the islands of Umm al-Maradem and Qarwa. This issue remains a sore spot and (apart from Iranian pressure) may have affected Kuwait's decision to refrain from signing a bilateral security agreement with Saudi Arabia in 1982.

More fractious are the dynastic rivalries within the UAE. The discovery of oil has both inflamed and ameliorated intra-UAE rivalries and tensions. The residual conflicts that are by-products of

---

[3] If there is a serious threat of a backlash to rapid military modernization, it is from indigenous Gulf nationals'—civilian and military alike—reaction to the cultural abrasiveness of foreign advisers, arms sales profiteering (again mainly by foreign advisers), personal excess of some in the military sector, and internal rivalry for position and wealth. This raises the risk of having the expansion and modernization of Gulf militaries viewed by their own citizens, especially by the students and the growing middle class, as a form of repression, waste, and corruption or as serving Western rather than Gulf interests.

the evolution of the system of states of the Arab Gulf remain within the GCC, albeit in attenuated form.

Intra-UAE rivalries are also reflected in what might be called a "micro" arms race between Abu Dhabi, on the one hand, and Dubai and Ras al-Khaimah, on the other. While UAE forces were nominally "unified" in May 1976, each emirate has continued to expand its own forces as de facto "national" forces, even through they have been designated "regional commands." Indeed, Abu Dhabi's forces are larger than those of the UAE. The development of independent force structures has exacerbated the proliferation of equipment types, contributing to training and logistical problems.

The distrust that lingers from such disputes can compound the manpower and force structuring problems the GCC states face in trying to expand their armed forces, and may affect the political resources available to the member countries either individually or collectively. The problem is most apparent in the proliferation of different systems within the same class of weapons (e.g., combat aircraft) across the armed forces of the various member states. The proliferation of weapons types creates serious problems in achieving effective operability in an integrated GCC force structure.

On balance, expressions of intra-GCC differences make it more difficult to plan a truly integrated GCC defense force, just as intra-NATO squabbles, e.g., between Greece and Turkey or Iceland and the UK, complicate the Western Alliance's planning. However, such problems are not in and of themselves a threat to intra-GCC security, if for no other reason than they are not as susceptible to external manipulation as some of the problems already discussed. Indeed, traditional rivalries that are not officially resolved should diminish steadily in the 1980s in response to population growth, labor mobility, and urbanization. Furthermore, Gulf leaders look increasingly for advice and for many decisions to a new class of Western-trained civilian and military technocrats whose attitude in these traditional rivalries is at best indifferent. Although the influence of this class of technocrats is still fairly limited in most Gulf states, their members are generally able to understand the geopolitical pressures and the implications of social and demographic trends in the region in a broader and more modern sense than are the Gulf's more senior elite members.

Military Geography and Linkage

The two most immediate and serious regional threats to the Gulf states' security are clearly the spillover effects of the Iran-Iraq war and the Arab-Israeli conflict in general and an activist Israeli defense and foreign policy in particular. It was regional conflict (the war between Iran and Iraq) that was the catalyst for the activation of the GCC, which posed a direct internal threat to the member states, and raised the prospect of escalation and outside power involvement. These conflicts constrain the integrative capabilities of the GCC and its potential cohesiveness as much as they challenge the Gulf states' military capabilities directly.

The Iran-Iraq War and the Northern Gulf

A continued stalemate in which neither Iran nor Iraq is able to achieve a decisive victory would appear to be the optimal short-term outcome with respect to the Gulf states' security concerns. Yet, even the stalemate that has largely prevailed since 1983 has severely constrained the cohesiveness of the GCC states and their potential for acting as a unified bloc in matters of defense policy. Alternative outcomes of the war offer the prospect of intensifying some of the social constraints already operating on the utilization of domestic human resources in the armed forces. Nor has the current stalemate insulated the Gulf states from the war itself. An improvement in Iran's military fortunes in 1982 was followed by political pressure on the Gulf states which weakened the GCC's efforts to strengthen their collective defense. Iran exerted particularly intense pressure on Kuwait and the UAE in the wake of its military victories over Iraq to check Abu Dhabi's move toward closer defense cooperation. Iranian pressure helped prevent Kuwait from joining the other GCC states in signing bilateral security agreements with Saudi Arabia following the Iranian-supported coup attempt in Bahrain in 1981. Iranian pressure prompted Kuwait and the UAE to advocate mediation in the Iran-Iraq war and to limit their support for Iraq.

In December 1983, Kuwait experienced a series of Iranian-inspired bombings including truck bomb attacks on the American and French embassies in Kuwait. In May 1985 Kuwait's ruler, Sheikh Jabbar al-Ahmed Al-Sabah, narrowly escaped an assassination attempt. These events are not a reflection of internal tension. Rather, they appear to be the work of the radical Muslim group, al-Dawa, which has close ties to Iran and is bent on the overthrow of the government of Iraq.

A victory for either side, however, is less important than the conditions of victory. Of particular importance would be the forces and resources at the disposal of each side that would be available for commitment to the Peninsula and the southern Gulf. Equally important would be the incentives or disincentives the victorious government might have to commit these forces for hostile action against the Gulf states. It is not hard to conceive a scenario in which both the victor and vanquished are too exhausted and too preoccupied with internal recovery or with staving off internal collapse to apply any pressure southward.

However, an Iranian victory that left Iran only slightly less exhausted than Iraq would have more threatening implications for the Gulf states than a victory by Iraq—now seen as impossible—under similar conditions. Iraq is not run by a revolutionary government still ideologically hostile to the continuing existence of the regimes of the Gulf states. Iran is. A victory by Khomeini's forces would, at the very least, unleash unsettling political forces on the Peninsula. It would provide a new burst of revolutionary elan and renewed incentive to Khomeini sympathizers in the Gulf to redouble their efforts to extend the Iranian revolution southward. An increase in Iranian subversion against the GCC states would be a foregone conclusion.

A more decisive Iranian victory could mean the collapse of the Ba'th regime in Baghdad and its replacement by a government that would have to show some deference to Tehran's policy preferences. More dire possibilities include the collapse of the Iraqi government and the creation of a Shi'a state in southern Iraq aligned with Iran, with Turkey perhaps dominating northern Iraq; or even a Shi'a-dominated Iraqi government controlled by Iran. Iranian troops, their morale boosted by victory, would be in a position to move into the region north of Kuwait unchecked by the Iraqi Army and to extend the Iranian revolution southward. A still worse scenario envisions a possible alliance tying Iraq and Syria to Iran, thereby isolating the Gulf countries from the Fertile Crescent and shifting the balance of power in the Middle East in favor of revolutionary, anti-Western forces.

A weakened or defeated Iran would not necessarily improve the Gulf states' security posture. An Iraqi "victory," such as was anticipated by most observers in the fall of 1980, undoubtedly would have fragmented Iran's ethnically diverse population and could have led to the disintegration of the Iranian army as a coherent fighting force. Iraq would have become the strongest state in the Gulf. An aggrandized Iraq and a weakened, fragmented Iran would certainly contribute to checking Shi'a revolutionary penetration of the Arabian Peninsula and the southern Gulf. But an Iraqi victory would surely have been followed by a renewed Iraqi drive for leadership of the eastern Arab world while Egypt remained relatively isolated and relegated to the sidelines of inter-Arab politics. A revival of Iraq-sponsored pan-Arabism backed by a strong Iraqi army could easily become a destabilizing influence in the Gulf.

The internal disintegration of one or both of the combatants under the pressures of continued warfare would be no cause for relaxation, since the ensuing anarchy from any such collapse could spread southward. Indeed, a civil war in Iran (possibly aggravated by internal competition among various political factions over succession to Khomeini) would have repercussions throughout the Gulf, especially if the Soviet Union intervened to stabilize its border.

The problem is that any of the foregoing outcomes would intensify pressures to expand the Gulf states' armed forces at least to the extent of filling current units to full strength. But intensified recruitment and stepped-up training efforts invite greater dependence on the same sources of manpower that are often the most attractive targets of external subversion.

The Arab-Israeli Conflict

An equally serious and more enduring problem continues to be the potential linkage between the Arab-Israeli conflict and the Gulf. The very existence of this conflict constrains the ability of the GCC states in general, and of Saudi Arabia in particular, to acquire the advanced weaponry and training needed to create an effective deterrent against future aggression from Iran, a new Iraqi government under Iranian control, or other extremist forces. Further constraints are introduced by Israel's treatment of acquisition of new weapon systems by the GCC or the upgrading of current GCC systems for the purposes of Gulf security, as hostile threats to the Jewish state. In view of Israel's doctrine favoring preemptive attack, this interpretation puts existing GCC (mainly Saudi) forces unnecessarily at risk. It confronts the Gulf states with the prospect of having to field military engagements that exceed their military capabilities or interests and lie outside the military missions (i.e., Gulf defense) for which they were created. This problem has serious implications for GCC internal security as well.

The linkage between the Arab-Israeli conflict and constraints on the utilization of military resources for Gulf security can involve something less intense than the outbreak of a fifth round between Israel and a coalition of Arab states. Israel's raid on the Osirak nuclear reactor near Baghdad in June 1981 demonstrates that Israel will not hesitate to involve the GCC countries if it deems it necessary to forestall a perceived threat from a regional state. Israel violated both Saudi and Jordanian airspace en route to bombing the nuclear reactor in Baghdad. Repeated Israeli overflights of Saudi Arabia's air base at Tabuk (not to mention repeated violations of Jordanian and Iraqi airspace) have dramatically underscored the weakness of GCC air surveillance and air defense capabilities.[4]

The Arab-Israeli conflict has dramatically affected GCC defensive capabilities in the Gulf. Because of the threat of an Israeli preemptive attack, Saudi Arabia concentrated a considerable portion of its radars and sensors to cover the northwest corner of the kingdom. The Iran-Iraq war revealed that so many radars and sensors had been oriented toward the threat from Israel that coverage of the Gulf was woefully inadequate.

Some have suggested that Saudi acquisition of sophisticated weapons systems such as the F-15 and the AWACS have linked Saudi Arabia, and, by implication, the other Gulf states to the Arab-Israeli conflict. The rationale is that these weapons give the Gulf states the capability to target Israel in the event of another full-scale Arab-Israeli war. In this concept, both the F-15s and AWACS will rank high on Israeli target lists, and their very presence in Saudi Arabia makes an Israeli preemptive strike highly probable. These arguments are not very persuasive when subjected to close scrutiny, since these advanced weapons are capable of providing a one-front defense that covers the Gulf. Neither the F-15 nor the AWACS is deployed near the Arab-Israeli theater.

Israel's insistence on linking Saudi acquisition of sophisticated weapons to the Arab-Israeli conflict creates a paradoxical security dilemma for the GCC states. Saudi Arabia's acquisition of sophisticated extended-range fighter aircraft, an airborne warning and control system and the need to integrate such weapons in a centralized C^3I to cover all the GCC states provides an effective deterrence to regional disputes, and so promotes stability in the Gulf and on the Peninsula. In fact it was the U.S. decision to provide AWACS as part of a general air defense enhancement package that gave the Saudi government the necessary capability vis-a-vis Iran and Iraq to make credible its military linkages with the smaller Gulf states while avoiding issues of sovereignty and patriotic credibility that inevitably would be associated with any formal U.S.

---

[4] Accounts of such overflights are contained in the Foreign Broadcast Information Service, Middle East and Africa, *Daily Report*, November 1981, and January 4, 1982, p. E-1. See also Henry Bradsher, "Israel Practiced Raids on Saudi Air Base," *Washington Star*, March 27, 1978. The Israeli Air Force continued to overfly Tabuk regularly through November 1981. These demonstration flights finally provoked a Saudi military response and a formal Saudi protest to the United States.

basing structure on the Peninsula. An effective and credible Saudi air defense system must be able to guard against sudden air raids or saturation attacks on a 24-hour basis and to offer broad coverage over a wide area which extends to other members of the GCC. Absent such capabilities it cannot function either as an effective deterrent or as an effective defense. However, the more effective the GCC becomes in meeting its air defense needs, the more insistent Israel will become in linking an effective GCC air defense capability to its conflict with the surrounding Arab states.

Tensions from the Arab-Israeli conflict may affect the Gulf in the form of another projection of Israeli power, either along the Red Sea or southeast toward Syria and Iraq stemming from activities of major Palestinian groups displaced from Lebanon if these groups sought to turn Jordan or one or more Gulf states into a substitute base of operations. Alternatively, Israel might arrogate for itself the role of "protecting" the West's oil supplies transiting the Red Sea in response to increasing instability in Sudan or the operations of Palestinian splinter groups unaffiliated with any of the mainstream Palestinian organizations in the Red Sea.

Any projections of Israeli power that violate the sovereignty of the Gulf states put these countries on the horns of a dilemma. Failure to defend against such Israeli intrusions as repeated violations of airspace (especially in connection with an Israeli air attack on an Arab country) or temporary border crossings on the ground, can create internal discontent, especially among the officer corps (an officer corps' professional self-esteem is not a trivial matter). Yet mounting a determined military defense against Israeli military penetrations risks exceeding the capabilities of the GCC's armed forces. Either alternative risks humiliating the military, and the political repercussions of such experiences have often been far-reaching. The spillover effects from these and other regional conflicts underscore the point that the most serious challenge to achieving strategic stability in the Gulf lies in achieving an enduring peace settlement between Israel and its Arab neighbors.

Changes in Regional Distribution of Power

The disparities of power in the Gulf have forced all the Arab Gulf states except Iraq to pay close attention to the overall balance of power in the region and to adjust their policies accordingly. The evolution of the GCC's defense policy has been subjected to these concerns. Developments such as a union between North and South Yemen, or a regime change in Syria that aligns it with Egypt,

Jordan, and Iraq against Iran, can alter drastically the security picture of the GCC countries. The Gulf countries' sensitivities to changes in regional power balances are illustrated in Kuwait's decision to postpone accepting Saudi proposals for an integrated Gulf Defense Command until the Iran-Iraq war is over and the distribution of power in the Gulf is clarified. The evolution of the GCC's role has been subject to these concerns.

It is a commonplace in the Arab world that fragmentation among Arab states has been costlier than war. Nowhere is the danger of such divisiveness felt more acutely than in the Gulf, underscoring the degree to which regional conflicts and their impact on local and regional distributions of power have important implications and consequences for one of the principal political strategies of the GCC countries, namely attempting to forge and maintain inter-Arab consensus on major political issues. Changes in regional distributions of power can affect the foreign or defense policy positions of the Gulf countries on issues of particularly high salience to the United States (e.g., a settlement of the Arab-Israeli conflict, international cooperation on combating terrorism, blunting Soviet attempts to expand its influence into the region).

The GCC states do not have the raw power to effectively decide regional political issues. They can, however, avoid taking positions on issues that threaten to split the Arab world into two antagonistic factions, and so reduce the GCC's influence with one of them. Usually the "outgroup" is the more militant. Such divisions not only reduce GCC regional influence, but expose the Gulf countries, collectively or individually, to unfriendly pressures from one of the rival caucuses.

One clear example of this political strategy at work and the constraints under which it operates is the GCC countries' perceived sense of threat in response to the Egyptian-Israeli peace agreement at Camp David and to U.S. pressure to support that agreement. None of the GCC countries opposes peace with Israel. Indeed, all GCC leaders have made it clear that they believe a final resolution of the Arab-Israeli conflict would have a strong stabilizing influence on the Gulf. Egypt, however, secured what the GCC states regarded as a comparatively unimportant gain, the Sinai, at the expense of a collective Arab effort to secure some form of Palestinian self-determination. GCC adherence to the Camp David agreements would have meant endorsing an accord no one believed could solve the core problem, and endorsing it against virtually the Arab world, provoking the active opposition of Syria and Iraq, and possibly isolating the Gulf states even from Jordan. Given the Gulf states' dependence on expatriate labor, and their political and security vulnerability, any posture that is or might be construed as anti-Palestinian would lead to serious internal unrest and would almost certainly alienate a very large number of younger Gulf citizens who passionately support the Palestinian cause.[5] In addition, part of the legitimacy of the GCC governments in general and the legitimacy of the Saudi regime (as custodians of the holy places in Mecca and Medina), in particular, derives from the ruling families' commitment to the defense of Islam. Accepting the Camp David agreements would have meant accepting Israeli occupation of even Arab Jerusalem and of the third holiest Muslim shrine. This position could only have alienated the more conservative religious elements who were already becoming hostile to what they perceived as the threatening social and political by-products of government-sponsored rapid economic growth.[6]

Egypt's option—to move toward a separate peace and thereby isolate itself from the Arab mainstream—cut the Gulf states off from one of the few Arab military powers that could provide emergency military assistance if necessary. However, in helping to maintain a residual of Arab consensus on the Palestinian issue, the Gulf states managed to insulate their societies as much as possible from the destabilizing ripple effects of Egypt's action. Cooperative relations with Iraq (which the GCC came to view increasingly as a critical buffer following the revolution in Iran and the Soviet Union's invasion of Afghanistan) and even with Syria were strengthened.

Recent Power Shifts: The Re-emergence of Syria

The re-emergence of Syria as a strong power center in the Arab Levant is a function of both the decline of Arab oil money and of Syria's political victory over Israel in Lebanon. The latter event was a potent political and psychological reminder (for Arab and Israeli societies alike) of Syria's ability to affect the course of regional developments.

This perception of a change in the regional distribution of power—

---

[5] Regional preoccupation with the Palestinian problem tends to glamorize the Palestinian cause in the classroom as well as in the media. The demography of the Arab world, in which half the population is under 15 years of age, assists in magnifying this phenomenon.

[6] These reasons were not the only cause for rejection of the Camp David accords. Even more important throughout the Arab world was the conviction that the agreements, as drafted, did not respond to the requirements to achieve some acceptable kind of Palestinian political expression.

of Syria's growing importance in Arab politics—illustrates how such change can work both for and against the interests of GCC security. Assad's role in securing the release of American hostages in a hijacked airliner (TWA flight 847) in July 1985 contributes to a growing awareness that he is one of the few leaders in the Middle East who can deliver on a promise.

Syria's signals to Washington through the media that Damascus would favor an improvement of relations with the United States could open new possibilities and pose new problems for the GCC and for U.S. interests in the region. On the one hand, better relations would probably ease the concerns of the Gulf states about local security issues. On the other hand, closer ties between the United States and Syria can only extend so far, in view of the divergent positions of the two countries on issues salient to both. Greater attentiveness to Syria could also undermine the existing close ties between the United States and Egypt, which is hostile toward Syria. It could trigger a strong negative reaction from Israel, which considers Syria to be its most dangerous enemy, and might therefore produce far-reaching political and other responses designed to disrupt a U.S.-Syrian rapprochement.

Similarly, while Assad himself seems to have no illusions about Soviet interests in the region or beyond, his interpretation of the alignment of Syrian and Soviet interests has led to an effective working relationship. Syria depends exclusively on the Soviet Union for its weaponry and military assistance. Damascus does not appear to be in a position to radically alter its relations with the Soviet Union analogous to Anwar Sadat's expulsion of Soviet advisers and technicians from Egypt in 1972. There is simply no other country that could quickly replace the volume of weaponry the Soviets provide Syria or the intensity of security support provided by the Soviet Union and its East European "allies." Thus an expansion of Syrian power and influence in inter-Arab politics expands the number of opportunities for the Soviet Union to involve itself in the region. Syria's emergence as the dominant military power in the Arab Levant and simultaneous Israeli "suggestions" that the Palestinian problem could be settled in Jordan increase pressure on Jordan to seek additional arms to compensate for the growth in Syrian and Israeli military forces. Close American political and military ties to Israel and unprecedented American responsiveness to Israeli opposition to almost any assistance to Arab states have made the United States reluctant to provide Jordan with the weapons systems the Jordanians believe they need to defend the Hashemite Kingdom against external military threats. Since Jordan functions as a buffer that helps secure the Gulf's western flank, insulates it from the

Levant and even greater Syrian influence, and participates actively in supporting the internal security of the smaller Gulf states, Syria's expanding military capabilities and American reluctance to provide arms to Jordan cannot be very reassuring to the GCC. A fundamental change in Jordan, which—given the circumstances we have described—cannot be excluded, would clearly have a telling and unfavorable impact on GCC security.

The resuscitation of the Arab-Israeli peace process by King Hussein and PLO Chairman Yasser Arafat in late 1984 and early 1985 created a major dilemma for the Gulf countries. Despite the agreement of the PLO to the principle of territory-for-peace (the essence of the February 11, 1985 Amman accord), political divisions in Israel and the opposition there to return of the West Bank, or even to talking with the PLO, persuaded many that the search for peace was chimeric at this juncture. On the one hand, then, the Gulf states stood to benefit significantly from a settlement, which would offer them much greater latitude in the development of Gulf defense and cooperation with the West. On the other hand, given the predominant perception that the attempt was unlikely to succeed and the certainty that the opposition (particularly that of Syria and of the rejectionist Palestinians) would stop at nothing to block fruition of the process, involvement in the initiative was a very high-risk option for the Gulf states, one that would in fact complicate their security problems.

While the interests of the Gulf governments have long been vulnerable to instability in the area, including instability emanating from the continued stalemate in the Arab-Israeli arena, their aggressive endorsement of an abortive initiative that had little prospect for success would only expose them to domestic resentment, and provide countries like Iran with a credible and effective propaganda tool for use against their own populations. Consequently, although the Gulf states refrained from condemning the initiative and in fact were mildly supportive, they concluded it would be imprudent to go further until the odds for success looked more promising. Yet, it is predictable that if the peace process does fail, many will place at least part of the blame on the Arab moderates who did not provide the necessary support. The probability of this reciprocal finger-pointing suggests that failure of the peace process could lead to a deterioration in U.S. relations with the Gulf countries, including Saudi Arabia, which is nothing dramatic but a development nonetheless adverse to mutual cooperation.

The foregoing discussion underscores the gross asymmetry that exists concerning the GCC states with respect to prevailing distributions of power in the region. They cannot easily change regional power balances in their favor, but changes in regional power balances can have a decisive impact on the type and severity of the external security problems they face. The only indigenous political resource the Gulf states have to deflect external pressures that emerge from such changes is prudent diplomacy that seeks to maintain an inter-Arab consensus on sensitive political issues, and avoids isolating them from regional and global allies. If there is any predictability in this behavior it is that the GCC states will pursue a foreign policy or favor a regional alignment that is perceived to be the most effective in achieving one of two objectives: either (1) it insulates the Gulf from the spillover effects of regional or superpower conflicts; or (2) it insulates their societies as effectively as possible from external subversion and penetration.

When regional power balances become fluid and their definition is unclear, as in the case of the Iran-Iraq struggle in the northern Gulf, efforts toward increased integration of GCC military forces may be effected in the direction of inertia. This is a subtle constraint, but a real one which must concern the United States.

The Superpower Balance in the Region

The possible consolidation of the Soviet Union's control of Afghanistan presents new but not insurmountable military problems to the GCC countries. However, such a consolidation could easily create a climate in which the Gulf states, including Iran, move to adjust their security policies to take account of Soviet regional power. In the absence of any effective American response to neutralize this type of Soviet expansion, the Gulf states could conclude that it is more prudent to accommodate an adversary in close proximity than to rely solely on a distant and doubtful ally.

The Soviet use of military force in Afghanistan introduced the note of urgency that eventually led to the activation of the GCC. This was accompanied by the unaccustomed vigor of the U.S. response, including force deployments. American indecision and inaction in other cases, combined with unwavering support for Israel, have raised doubts in the minds of the GCC leaders about the effectiveness and constancy of U.S. commitments to defend the Gulf. This erosion of confidence in the value of U.S. commitments and the continued presence of Soviet forces in Afghanistan rule out the possibility of any formal alliance between the GCC per se and the United States. It was the formal foreign presence of British and American bases in the Gulf in the early 1960s that helped shift the focus of pro-Nasser Arab nationalist forces to the Gulf. The elimination of these forms of "imperialism" from the Gulf became the rallying cry of radical nationalist groups. Since they viewed the Gulf governments as clients of the West, a change in the leadership of these governments was considered a necessary part of the radicals' regional strategy. Given this recent history and the fate of the 1958 Baghdad Pact, any formal alliance between the GCC and the West would expose the constituent Gulf states to additional external subversion from both Islamic fundamentalist groups supported by Iran and radical secular Arab nationalists backed by Syria, Libya, and the PDRY, all of whom, in turn, would probably be supported by the Soviet Union in this campaign.

The hurdles facing formal or open collective alignment with the United States do not necessarily obtain at the bilateral level, where individual Gulf states' needs may outweigh the interests of the regional organization. As we have already noted, the United States has contingency arrangements with one GCC member, a relaxed accord with another on facility support for MIDEASTFOR, and extensive formal and informal cooperation with the GCC's largest and most critical country, Saudi Arabia. In addition, specific crises have led to talks on the other forms of bilateral contingency cooperation, and Saudi Arabia has indicated its willingness to permit U.S. use of bases in the kingdom in the event of a Soviet attack or of a major crisis in the Gulf.

The foregoing discussion helps to explain why principal organizational objectives of the GCC are to insure their own internal and external security *and* to avoid dependence on any external power. Yet these goals illuminate a very serious dilemma for the member states. Very few external military attacks are likely to occur without being preceded or unaccompanied by the ideological window dressing that provides them with a domestic component as well. Large quantities of sophisticated weapons alone do not address the domestic security problems resulting from external penetration and support of domestic security problems resulting from external penetration and support of domestic dissidents, while the logistical and training problems involved in trying to absorb large quantities of new weapons may render the GCC forces ineffective in dealing with external attack. The issue is one of quality, not quantity.

Economic Factors Associated with the Price of Crude Oil

Economic issues illuminate most clearly the configuration of political, military, and social resources upon which the GCC states can draw to enhance their own security. Rapid and large swings in the price of oil not only affect the Gulf governments' national incomes, but their ability to engage in "checkbook diplomacy" to influence allies and adversaries alike. Large decreases in oil prices diminish the ability of Gulf states such as Saudi Arabia and Kuwait to play influential roles in international finance, and undermine the basis for stability in the Arab world.

Oil Wealth and the Asymmetry of Power

Structural conditions affecting the price of oil can have a decisive impact on the security position of the GCC member states, because oil and the results of oil commerce make the Gulf states an attractive target, because income from oil largely determines the configuration of both political and military resources available for the member states' protection, and because oil wealth has created some paradoxical asymmetries in the political power of this bloc of states.

The economic and strategic foundations of GCC political power tend to give these countries, as a bloc, more political influence with the industrialized world than within the Middle East. None of the Middle Eastern states' economies is big enough or industrialized enough to depend upon supplies of imported oil as much as the United States, Western Europe, and Japan.[7]

Domestically, the power of the GCC governments rests on a combination of the stability of established institutions and the political legitimacy of the traditional elites. Oil wealth and its increasingly egalitarian distribution have been used to strengthen this indigenous power base. Notwithstanding the dramatic social changes alluded to earlier that are the by-products of the development process "fueled" by the income from oil, the governmental institutions of most the GCC states exhibit a degree of stability and durability uncommon in the developing world.

The member states, however, cannot be treated as undifferentiated units within the GCC collectivity. The GCC has no political or military viability without Saudi Arabia. Saudi Arabia is the least threatened of the GCC states in terms of internal security. The kingdom's massive land area provides the GCC with the only strategic depth it has. It is the only member with a military capability sufficiently large and modern to act as the backbone for any integrated GCC defense forces. Saudi Arabia is in the best position to subsidize the poorer GCC members in the building of any GCC joint

---

[7] A number of Middle East states do depend on oil imports for most or all of their fuel. Their attitude is often that the oil belongs to the entire "Arab nation."

defense system. Finally, Saudi Arabia is the only GCC member that has provided monetary aid to the West. This has enhanced its political strength in Western capitals and the significance of its strategic importance in ways other GCC members cannot duplicate. Further, Saudi diplomacy is undoubtedly the most sophisticated and most effectively managed in the Gulf area. The kingdom's control over the key Islamic holy places confers upon it broader prestige and political influence in regional affairs that the other GCC members do not command.

In many respects, then, the regional power of the GCC in general derives from its constituent states' geostrategic and financial importance to the West; however, this is mainly based on the dominant position of Saudi Arabia within the GCC, and on Saudi Arabia's ability to significantly influence the great powers, particularly the United States.

At the regional level, the political power of the oil-rich states in general and of Saudi Arabia in particular derives principally from the influence this oil wealth confers both through the actual and potential financial transfers to other governments and through the regional visibility and leadership the sheer volume of transactions has conferred. The economies of oil-poor countries like Jordan, Syria, and Lebanon were sustained by these direct subsidies and by

TABLE 4.1

OIL REVENUES FOR
THE MAJOR ARAB OIL PRODUCERS
($ U.S. billions)
1973–1983

	73	74	75	76	77	78	79	80	81	82	83
ALGERIA	1.0	4.1	4.1	4.5	4.8	4.8	4.8	—	10.6	9.8	9.0
KUWAIT	1.7	8.8	6.3	—	7.3	8.8	16.4	18.4	15.9	9.6	10.8
LIBYA	2.2	6.4	6.4	—	8.5	—	—	22.2	15.4	12.2	9.8
QATAR	.5	1.8	1.9	2.1	2.2	2.1	3.6	5.4	4.7	6.6	4.0
SAUDI AR	4.3	30.6	27.2	34.2	40.1	34.5	58.0	98.0	88.7	56.0	36.0
UAE	.9	6.6	6.9	7.9	9.1	8.0	12.1	18.3	12.9	9.4	7.2

97

the flow of remittances from expatriates working in the GCC countries.

Table 4.1 displays the oil revenues of the major Arab oil producers between 1973 and 1983.[8] The peak revenue year for most of these countries was 1980. From 1980 to 1983 Saudi Arabia's oil revenues declined from $98.0 billion to $36.0 billion or by 63.3 percent, a decline that accelerated in 1985 as Saudi Arabia absorbed the brunt of the cutbacks mandated by OPEC production ceilings. The UAE's oil income in the same period declined from $18.3 billion to $7.2 billion, which amounts to a 61 percent drop. Kuwait's oil revenues dropped 41.3 percent from $18.4 billion to $10.8 billion. Iraq's oil income in the same period (not shown in Table 4.1) declined roughly 81 percent from $26.14 billion to $4.96 billion. This drop is attributable to disruptions caused by Iraq's war with Iran as well as to the drop in oil prices. These figures indicate Iraq's diminishing ability to finance the war from its own resources. Iraq's political difficulties are likely to be compounded by the reality of declining incomes in the GCC states, whose prior support for the Iraqi war effort is conservatively estimated at between $30 billion to $40 billion for the period from 1980 to 1984. Revolutionary Iran, in contrast, continues to appear better able psychologically and financially to absorb the high cost of the war.[9] As in the case of other oil producers, Iran has also experienced a precipitous decline in its oil revenues in early 1986. However, the Saudi decision to boost the kingdom's output from just over 2 MBD to 4.5 MBD, which accelerated the present decline, is aimed largely at restoring discipline within OPEC and likely to be reversed once that objective has been met. This would promise relief for Iran as well.

The decline in oil prices is not an episodic phenomenon, but attributable to systemic forces, which will probably keep world demand for OPEC oil relatively weak (compared to 1979-1980) until the 1990s. Rapid increases in oil prices in the 1970s spurred production in non-OPEC countries while simultaneously forcing the

---

[8] Source: U.S. Central Intelligence Agency, National Foreign Assessment Center, *International Energy Statistical Review*, various years.

[9] See David R. Francis, "Iran's Resilient Economy Takes the Costs of Iraqi War in Stride," *The Christian Science Monitor*, July 11, 1985, p. 19. The war's costs in hard currency to Iran are estimated at between $3 billion to $4 billion a year, while Iran's oil revenues were about $1 billion a month. For example, in the Iranian year ending in March 21, 1985, oil sales averaged about 2.2 million barrels per day, yielding estimated revenues of between $15 billion to $16 billion. Deep cuts in oil prices in late 1985 did not prevent Iran from launching a major military offensive in February 1986. See also Loren Jenkins, "Iran-Iraq War May Hinge on Economics," *The Washington Post*, March 16, 1986, p. A-25.

industrialized world to take serious measures to conserve energy. The result is that OPEC production declined by about 42 percent from 1979 to 1984—down from 31.5 MBD to 18.3 MBD—while non-OPEC production increased by nearly 25 percent. OPEC's share of the non-communist world's oil production has declined from over 63 percent in 1979 to around 33 percent in 1985.

The burden of maintaining price stability within OPEC has fallen almost entirely on Saudi Arabia. While other OPEC members have exceeded their production quotas when they experienced cash flow problems, Saudi Arabia has produced below its quota. By mid-1985 Saudi Arabia was pumping only 2.5 MBD, which was almost 50 percent below its 4.353 MBD quota and only a fraction of the 10 MBD produced in 1979. Saudi Arabia could not have continued this policy indefinitely, since the decline in revenues threatened to destabilize its economy with spillover effects in other GCC states and into the Arab world beyond. Even in the face of Saudi restraint, oil prices were continuing their downward trend.

The Political Implications of Falling Oil Prices

Declining oil prices have already begun to undermine the economic basis for stability throughout the Arab world and beyond. The economies of oil-poor countries such as Jordan, Lebanon, and Syria were sustained by direct subsidies from Saudi Arabia and other oil-rich Gulf states as well as by a flow of remittances from workers in the Gulf. One result is that over the past two years Syria and Libya, as well as Islamic fundamentalist groups, have seized the political initiative from Saudi Arabia and the other oil-producing states in the Gulf. The Egyptian cabinet minister, Usama al-Baz, expressed the fear in early 1985 that by cutting back financial aid to Sudan in 1984, Saudi Arabia may have made Sudan dangerously vulnerable to internal upheaval as well as to a takeover by Libya's Muammar Qaddafi. Syria's ascendancy in the Levant and the Arab paralysis on a consensus position on negotiating a final settlement with Israel are attributed partly to the decline in political leverage of the conservative, oil-rich Gulf states that has accompanied the fall in their oil incomes.

The systemic consequences of the decline in oil incomes are much more fundamental. The deluge of petrodollars in the 1970s created a new dichotomy in the Middle East. The wealthy Arab oil-producing countries of the Gulf (plus Libya) became net labor importers, while Egypt and the oil-poor Arab countries such as Syria, Jordan, Lebanon, and others became net labor exporters. The rapid rise of oil wealth and the transnational manpower migration in the Middle East became the most clearly observable manifestation of the development of what in now referred to as the "new Arab social order."

The decline in oil revenues means fewer jobs for Egyptian, Syrian, Lebanese, Jordanian, Palestinian, and other expatriate Arab workers in the Gulf states, because less oil is being produced. Other consequences include growing competition between indigenous citizens and expatriates for white-collar jobs in some of the Gulf countries, a competition that is exacerbated by the growth of educated classes in the GCC. Countries like Jordan and Egypt, in particular, face tougher economic times as thousands of their citizens who were working in the Gulf return. Not only will these governments find themselves bereft of an important source of foreign exchange earnings; even more important, the decline in labor emigration will increase domestic social pressures associated with higher unemployment rates among the middle class, whose skills and expertise cannot always be absorbed into the domestic economies.

The general economic contraction has already affected many countries that have been the beneficiaries of oil wealth. The budgets of Jordan, Syria, and Egypt have been hurt by the drops in income of Saudi Arabia and Kuwait. Jordan received only about half of the aid from the Gulf states in 1983 that it did in 1982, a decline from $1.2 billion to $670 million. Syria, too, is receiving less than half of the $1.8 billion annual subsidy it was promised by the Gulf states in 1978. Kuwait's annual subsidy to Syria, Jordan, and the PLO was cut from $561 million in 1984 to $340 million in 1985. The $340 million, originally earmarked for the period beginning July 1985 to July 1986, was suspended, however, on the grounds that previous subsidies had been misused.

The cancellation of this aid would not be worth mentioning except that it illustrates the potential danger to the internal security of the oil-rich countries from violent backlashes by outside groups who are accustomed to receiving what they may consider to be their "fair share" of Arab oil largesse. The suspension of the subsidies, recommended by the Kuwaiti National Assembly's financial and economic affairs committee, is noteworthy because the committee's recommendation is thought to have triggered two bomb explosions in two seaside cafes in Kuwait on July 11, 1985, that killed eight people and injured 88. The shadowy Muslim guerrilla group, the Arab Revolutionary Brigades, claimed responsibility for the bomb blasts and demanded that Kuwaiti authorities "give up their policies hostile to Arab and Palestinian nationals."[10]

---

[10] *The Los Angeles Times*, July 18, 1985, p. 22.

As oil prices and revenues have continued their decline, political tensions between the GCC countries, particularly Saudi Arabia, on the one hand, and Iran, on the other, have escalated. Since 1982, Iran has used its oil policy to wage economic warfare against Saudi Arabia and to create an OPEC-wide struggle for markets, revenues, and influence. This struggle [11] eventually split OPEC in January 1983 and may be expected to continue for the foreseeable future. For the GCC, these problems may be only a harbinger of what is to come. Iran, supported by Libya and Algeria, is pressing for a sharp cut in OPEC's current production of 16 MBD in order to dry up the world oil surplus and so raise the price of oil. This proposal creates a serious dilemma for Saudi Arabia and the GCC oil-producing states. On the one hand, acquiescing to the position of the "price hawks" means the abdication of Saudi leadership of OPEC to Iran. It would also require further contractions of revenue in the short term, thereby creating more destabilizing domestic tensions. On the other hand, adopting a more aggressive oil sales policy to increase revenue, and so cushion their domestic economies from the worst effects of further economic contraction, will inevitably divert revenues from poorer, but militarily and politically more powerful, oil producers such as neighboring Iran and Iraq.

Iraq will have to increase its output in order to continue the war with Iran, and so will have to compete for a larger share of the oil market. A major Iraqi military set-back, especially one that threatens Iraq's important relationship with Kuwait, would intensify pressure on the GCC states for war recovery aid and additional political support. GCC failure to provide financial aid will only assure an undermining of Iraq's capability to act as a buffer against Iran, which in turn can only increase the Iranian threat to the constituent countries' security. Moreover, Iraq will have additional incentives to take possession of the Kuwaiti islands of Bubiyan and Warbah near its small seacoast in order to improve its naval position in the Gulf.

Rapid and drastic reductions in the domestic budgets of the GCC states could also create internal strains. Governments are slashing domestic spending in response to declining revenues. Bankruptcies are running at an all-time high, and salaries and benefits of government bureaucrats are being cut. Indigenous businessmen are facing economic difficulties, while record numbers of expatriate personnel are forced to leave. How much can oil-rich Gulf governments reduce domestic spending without political consequences?

---

[11] The struggle also reflects the inherent and deep conflict between large reserves-low population countries and large reserves-high population countries.

The economic contraction in the Gulf has been accompanied by a surge in Islamic fundamentalism, discussed above. Expressions of the resurgence of Islamic fundamentalism may reflect a variety of frustrations and causes that are likely to become more manifest during periods of economic retrenchment. Acts of subversion and terrorism by Shi'a militants probably reflect continuing Iranian hostility toward the GCC in general and to Saudi Arabia in particular. If the Iranian-supported Shi'as in Lebanon gain control of the Shi'a community there, this new Shi'a stronghold can be expected to be used as a base for additional attacks on moderate Arab governments in the Gulf and elsewhere. The growing expressions of fundamentalism of the indigenous middle classes and tribal Sunnis in the Gulf may also represent a quest for more rapid political participation and a more equitable sharing of income. Nativist fundamentalism also provides a medium of protest against the rulers' policies of large-scale importation of foreigners, which is regarded as a threat to the socio-cultural integrity of Gulf societies. By contrast, the fundamentalism of some expatriate workers may be a protest movement against both local leaders and their indigenous subjects. External exploitation notwithstanding, expressions of an indigenous Shi'a resurgence in the Gulf reflect to some degree the perception of a politically underprivileged status of the Shi'a minorities there.

The Trade-Offs in Gulf Security Policy

Absent the external exploitation of domestic tensions, the GCC governments appear quite capable of managing and ameliorating them. The problem remains, however, that these sorts of domestic tensions are susceptible to external manipulation. To the extent that events beyond the GCC's borders—revolution in Iran, another Arab defeat by Israel, rapidly falling oil prices—reverberate through the GCC states' domestic environments, the Gulf states cannot be completely in control of their security. To the extent that countries beyond their borders have the incentive and the ability to meddle in the GCC states' internal affairs, domestic tensions assume a much more ominous threat potential than otherwise would be the case.

The ubiquitous links between external events and domestic repercussions reduce Gulf security policies to a series of balancing acts between equally unattractive outcomes and trade-offs. Within the GCC, government deference to technocrats and entrepreneurs who favor more economic development risks the creation of a backlash from traditional religious, tribal, and social groups. In trying to reduce domestic tensions by assuring a more egalitarian distribution of national wealth, a reduction of discriminatory practices against indigenous minorities, and a diminution of elite privileges, Gulf leaders risk alienating powerful social and political elements of the indigenous population. In seeking to create more participatory political institutions that satisfy the more liberal "modernizing" elements of their society, the same leaders risk establishing political alternatives to their own rule.

Beyond their borders, the GCC governments must maneuver among an equally unpleasant set of dilemmas. If they concentrate on building their armed forces to defend against external threats, the leadership risks creating a well-armed internal threat to its control. Yet a clear demonstration of the military's inability to defeat external attack invites a loss of legitimacy and possibly a *coup d'etat*. In seeking to rely on external support against foreign threats, the Gulf states may increase the probability of becoming the targets of hostile action from these same foreign sources, especially on issues that associate them with close American support for Israel. In seeking to insulate their societies from the political cross-currents traversing the Middle East by supporting a consensus position on critical regional issues (such as a final settlement with Israel or oil production and pricing policy), the GCC countries risk weakening their bonds to an external ally such as the United States, one of the few countries able and willing to project military power into the region on their behalf in case of an emergency. It is to a discussion of the resources available to managing this complex security picture that we now turn.

Security Resources—Introduction

The human and material resources required to contain the threats described in Chapter III under the conditions delineated above could tax the capabilities of a superpower. The anxiety of Gulf security officials, when they cast their eyes beyond their borders, is understandable. Meeting external threats is far more difficult than managing internal problems if only because strictly internal problems are not new. Internal security rests on traditional foundations. It involves doing things that Gulf leaders have been adept at doing for some time; and their internal security forces have shown themselves capable of handling threats to domestic security.

External defense, by contrast, confronts the Gulf rulers with an entirely new enterprise, since it centers on the development of

modern armed forces in a way that such development does not
destroy their political system in the process. It is a task in which
they can turn to few useful precedents. A precedent they are unlikely to overlook, however, is the overthrow of the shah of Iran.
With this recent event clearly in mind, GCC leaders are eminently
aware that security against external attack (including defense
against external penetration and subversion) involves a political as
well as a military component, with primacy being given to the
political element. Each of these components will be examined in
turn.

Political Resources of the GCC

The problems of external defense and the creation of modern
military forces did not pose any serious challenges to the Gulf states
until the 1960s (at the earliest) for at least three reasons. One was
the presence of the British, who had provided for external defense
of the Arab littoral for over a century, and who did not finally
withdraw from the Gulf until 1971. Another was that the close
political linkage of Saudi Arabia and the lower Gulf states to the
rest of the Arab world did not begin until the 1960s, when the focus
of various Arab nationalist movements began to shift toward the
Gulf in their efforts to rid the Middle East of the remaining bastions
of Western presence. A third was the local belief that regional states
could provide adequate protection.

One of the earliest expressions of the integration of the Peninsula
with the rest of the Arab world was the Iraqi threat against Kuwait.
On that occasion, the Gulf countries relied on Egyptian pressure to
compel Iraq to back down. Even earlier, Gulf states agreed with
Egypt's opposition to the Omani sultan in the Buraimi Oasis affair.
Later, Egyptian President Gamal Abdel Nasser used Egyptian military forces in North Yemen between 1962 and 1967 to support the
republican regime there against the traditional leader's forces
backed by Saudi Arabia. Until the late 1950s and early 1960s, one
of the most important resources upon which the Gulf states relied
for their external defense was their geographical isolation from the
political cross-currents shaking the rest of the Arab world and the
Middle East. Maintaining a form of insularity from the spillover
effects of global and regional conflicts has remained the primary
object that defines the political strategy of the Gulf countries. The
principal resource that has helped that strategy work has been the
oil income of the Gulf countries.

The Political Strategy of the GCC

Because the forces of external adversaries are expected to be larger than the forces the GCC members will be able to muster in their own defense, the first line of defense of the Gulf states is a political strategy aimed at achieving three objectives:

1. The maintenance of an Arab consensus on regional issues (such as the Palestinian problem) to avoid the splintering of the Arab world into antagonistic rival blocs. Failing this, then...

2. The insulation of the Gulf from the spillover effects of regional or superpower conflicts, which could isolate them from regional or global allies. Where this is not sufficient, then...

3. The insulation of their societies as much as possible from external subversion and penetration generated by regional or global conflicts.

In practice the Gulf states pursue all three of these objectives simultaneously in their defense and foreign policies. The strategy is based on the recognition of internal vulnerability to external pressures. Consequently, this strategy manifests a built-in bias against decisive political action. Saudi and other GCC leaders sometimes remain passive in the face of initiatives that they in fact oppose.

National Political Resources of the GCC

The two most important political resources upon which Gulf leaders can draw to enhance their governments' security are (1) the political legitimacy of their rule and (2) their oil wealth, which can be used to buy allies and influence rivals. The interaction effect of the two resources may produce an unexpectedly resilient institutional stability that is less susceptible to external subversion and is capable of successfully managing the social change that is now taking place in the region. However, like other resources, these are not inexhaustible and must be managed carefully if they are to continue to stand the leadership in good stead.

Despite the multiple array of external threats and internal vulnerabilities discussed earlier, the political resources available to the GCC are not insignificant. Collectively, they provide considerable potential for the Gulf states to become a regional power capable of pursuing an active and influential diplomatic role within the Afro-Asian bloc, and toward the industrialized world, while reducing their vulnerability to external subversion.

The Political Legitimacy of Current Institutions

Political legitimacy refers to a widespread belief among the population that the prevailing political institutions and social order are the appropriate ones for society. Absent the resource of legitimacy, no quantity of new weapons or military spending can provide very much security for very long.

Despite the transformation brought on by oil wealth, the Gulf states are still largely governed along traditional patriarchal lines. Although the system of governance is clearly authoritarian, this quality is tempered by time-honored effective procedures for consultation among the political, religious, and tribal elites. One should not be deceived by institutions. Government in the "monarchies" of the Gulf is often more humane and responsive to social interests than many so-called "democracies" in Latin America, Africa, Asia, and even Europe, not to mention those of the Middle East. Moreover, this style of leadership, tempered by consultation with the "elders" of society, has been the traditional pattern of political rule throughout the region. As such, it probably remains acceptable to the majority of the indigenous populations in the Gulf. In a sense the Sa'uds, the Sabahs, and al-Thanis, the Qasimis, the al-Nahyans, the Maktums, and the al-Khalifas embody the legitimacy of the existing government and institutions. Thus, the internal power of the Gulf states' leaders derives from institutional stability and the legitimacy of the leadership roles of the royal families' positions in society.

The strength of existing institutions is based on a social order that may undergo fundamental shifts as a result of the process of social change in which the Gulf states now find themselves. The Gulf's oil wealth and rapid economic development have transformed nomadic, peasant, and village societies into new cultures oriented toward a market economy in which more than half the population now lives in cities of over 10,000.[12] The mean age of the native population of the Gulf states is estimated to be between 15 and 16. Something like two-thirds of the populations of what were once

---

[12] Cordesman, *The Gulf and the Search for Strategic Stability: Saudi Arabia, The Military Balance, and Trends in the Arab-Israeli Military Balance* (Boulder, Colo.: Westview, 1984), p. 70.

village- and tribal-oriented societies no longer live within 50 miles of their birthplaces. Education and modern communications have further eroded the foundations of traditional society because they were introduced long before the Gulf states could develop any concept of how modernization could change society without destroying its cultural identity. The Gulf states' legal and political processes have been destabilized by these and other changes, but nobody has a clear idea of what alternatives will best meet the needs of these newly transformed societies. Yet, despite this transformation, traditional kinship remains the basis for social life and an important foundation upon which current institutions and the political legitimacy continue to rest. The fact that no viable alternatives to the prevailing social and political order have emerged provides a window of opportunity to GCC elites to ensure that revolutionary change does not arise. This can be accomplished by incremental political changes based on the social and political institutions which have retained their legitimacy through the tradition of kinship ties.

The same consideration holds for the changing social character of the military elites in the Gulf. In effect the Gulf military elites constitute a new class. It is a mixture of the "traditional" elements, with tribal or familial ties to the leadership, and "new" elements, who usually lack such ties but who have had more exposure to outside education, technology, and lifestyles. In this regard, no Gulf military force, with the possible exception of Iraq, is a fully known quantity. These forces are staffed by the changing sub-elements of their respective societies, which as yet display very uncertain ideological and political alignments. To the extent that they may have developed a political consciousness, it appears to consist of little more than a mixture of nationalism and resentment—resentment of change, of the role of foreign advisers, and of corruption and waste. Adherence to any particular ideology is not in evidence. If this assessment is accurate, their political loyalties and commitments are at least as malleable by the leadership they serve as by anybody else. Thus, there is no inevitable relationship between the improvement of Gulf military capabilities and the probability of a military *coup*.

The traditional leadership has functioned as a sheet anchor of social stability and psychological continuity during a quarter century of massive social trauma. They not only provide the heads of state and the political elites of the Gulf, but, in varying degrees, are well represented in leading managerial, administrative, and economic activities of all the Gulf states. This integration of elite members in society is most prominent in Saudi Arabia, but family connections are equally important in the other Gulf states where the core of the political and business elite always consists of members of the traditional elites.

Legitimacy in the Arab and Islamic worlds remains largely a function of the ruler's position with respect to trends in Arab nationalist and Islamic thought. The widely shared values of Arab nationalism and Islam have generated certain specific, widely shared interests. These have included, first and foremost, either the liberation of Palestine, or, more recently, a politically acceptable peace with Israel. The latter implies the creation of a national home for the Palestinian people on the West Bank and the Gaza Strip, Arab control over the Muslim holy places in Jerusalem, and the return to Syria of at least part of the Golan Heights. These interests include the development of inter-Arab solidarity on regional issues, although not necessarily political unity, so that Arabs will be able to protect their petroleum wealth and emerge collectively as a major world power. They include non-alignment with, and non-submission to, the superpowers. They also include the expectation of the Arab elites' commitment to economic and social development and a more equal distribution of wealth and power.

Strong public expressions and actions of commitment to these interests by the Gulf leaders help to forestall the erosion of their political legitimacy in times of sòcial change. It is the political legitimacy of the Gulf regimes in the eyes of their own populations that enabled them to withstand the pan-Arab attacks by Gamal Abdel Nasser and more radical Arab nationalists in the 1960s; and it is their political legitimacy today that is their most effective weapon against the Islamic fundamentalist attacks from Ayatollah Khomeini's revolutionary regime in Tehran.[13] This illustrates once again how external powers can cause internal conflict. There is no valid way of measuring whether the political legitimacy of the GCC regimes is increasing or decreasing. But policies or decisions that appear to be at odds with the widely shared interests of Arabism and Islam will most certainly undermine this political resource.

The homogeneity of the Gulf states' political institutions means

---

[13] The results of the Kuwaiti election in February 1985 were significant in this regard in that they registered the defeat of two of the leading Muslim fundamentalist candidates, leaving only two others in Kuwait's National Assembly to represent this trend. At the same time, these elections also returned the Arab Nationalist Movement to seats, along with reformists who previously have created major problems for the leadership elites.

an absence of competing (and potentially antagonistic) institutional structures and political cultures within the same polity. Whatever strains and disagreements the constituent members of the GCC face, they are not saddled with the additional burden of trying to bridge totally different systems of government (e.g., personalized rule versus constitutional monarchy versus republic) and competing political cultures.

Institutional homogeneity is accompanied by something that may be rare in the Third World—an incipient loyal opposition among members of the Gulf intelligentsia, high-level government officials, businessmen, and professionals. It is not, and for the most part does not appear to catalyze, real "opposition" in the literal sense; instead, it is a loose grouping for underlying but largely unfocused discontent. It is not organized, although Iranian elements and state organs have been trying to organize and invigorate it. The attempt to mobilize this latent discontent provides interesting insights into its nature. Unifying themes, and those that Iran has tried to exploit, have been issues over which Gulf citizens have felt great frustration and with which they have identified most passionately. Preeminent among these issues have been regional problems like Jerusalem, Lebanon, Afghanistan, and Palestine. To date, Iran's efforts to hold Saudi Arabia and the Gulf sheikhdoms responsible for these problems have been largely unsuccessful, in part because the Iranians offer no real acceptable alternative, in part because the GCC governments too have had strong and outspoken policies on these issues, and in part because there is a widespread understanding that there is, practically speaking, little the GCC governments can do to affect the course of events in these areas. To the extent domestic issues are a focal point of concern, Gulf intellectuals emphasize the need to focus on a popular base for political support; stress the importance of promoting education, public health, communication, and personal freedom; and call for a return to the *shura*, the Islamic practice of consultative democracy, which would, they argue, provide a point of departure for political modernization that is an integral part of the current institutional framework and prevailing political traditions. The legitimacy of the *shura* as a political concept is accepted both by the ruling elites and the indigenous populations.

This kind of enlightened, loyal opposition can serve as an indispensable counterweight against the two sources of subversive opposition that can act as an indigenous fifth column for external penetration—the Islamic fundamentalists (abetted by Iran) and the secular Arab nationalist-leftists (backed by Libya, Syria, the PDRY, or the Soviet Union).

Income from Oil Revenues

To the extent that the Gulf's petroleum riches have been used to uphold the foregoing list of widely shared values and interests, it is a resource that reinforces the political legitimacy of the Gulf states, particularly as the governments take the necessary steps to assure that some of the oil earnings percolate down to the less privileged elements of society. In this respect oil wealth may provide a strong foundation for lasting security.

Internally, the tribal tradition of buying loyalty has been reinforced by efforts of the oil-rich GCC governments to redistribute part of the oil income to their populations. The diffusion of oil revenues appears to have helped create new classes of technocrats and entrepreneurs whose interests and political orientation seem to be in accord with those of the traditional elites. The participation of members of the ruling elites in the managerial, administrative, and economic activities of their societies undoubtedly creates parallel and overlapping interests among individual family members, on the one hand, and the ascending technocratic and entrepreneurial groups within their societies, on the other. This has begun to result in the increasing participation of these groups in the public life of the Gulf states. If this trend gains momentum, incremental political change that accommodates these new groups' interests can be an additional source of strength to the incumbent governments.[14] The growth of technocratic groups within the Gulf states' bureaucracies offers the potential of effectively accelerating political modernization and of addressing the issues of expatriate labor and ethnic minorities.

Externally, oil wealth has been useful in more than just subsidizing a conservative counterweight in the Arab world (the conservative monarchies plus Egypt and Iraq) against extremist autocracies such as Libya, Syria, and Iran. It has contributed to creating a much more pragmatic genre of Arab nationalism. The new Arabism is characterized by the recognition of the primacy of *raison d'etat* as a fact of life in Arab politics. It emphasizes Arab solidarity as opposed to Arab unity, and economic cooperation based on mutual interests and the maintenance of the political *status quo*. Its principal instruments are diplomatic and financial in service of the political and strategic *status quo*. It generally operates at the

---

[14] For example, some observers believe that the rapid growth of technocratic government brought on by the oil wealth has actually enhanced the stability of Saudi Arabia and strengthened the legitimacy of the royal family.

level of governments and avoids the mobilization of mass populations to achieve its objectives.

This conservative brand of Arabism stands in marked contrast to the Nasserist type of Arab nationalism which focused on the political mobilization of mass populations and stressed the themes of anti-colonialism, non-alignment, republicanism, and socialism, all of which tended to denigrate the legitimacy of the Arab state system and the state-building process. It sought, instead, to channel sentiments of political allegiance from the individual state to a broader human and social collectivity.

The cumulative effect of an oil-powered, pragmatic form of Arab nationalism has been the transformation of the institutional and normative dimensions of Arab politics in ways that strengthen the Gulf states and contribute to their legitimacy domestically as well as in the inter-Arab political arena. Between 1970 and 1979 the growth of inter-Arab institutions was almost one and a half times the number of those established in the preceding 20 years. The three years from 1974 to 1976, after the oil embargo and the most dramatic increases in oil prices, witnessed an unprecedented institutional proliferation. Out of 63 organizations founded between 1970 and 1979, 41 (64.7 percent) were established in those three years.[15]

Perhaps more significant than the quantitative expansion of inter-Arab institutions was the increasing role of economic organizations such as joint economic ventures. For example, before 1970 there were eight inter-Arab economic organizations representing 18 percent of all existing organizations. This percentage jumped to 56 percent of all organizations founded after 1970.[16]

These institutional developments clearly reflect the influence of the oil-producing countries. Another indicator is that after 1970, the locale of the new inter-Arab organizations was usually in an oil-producing country, rather than the "traditional" capital of Arabism, Cairo. What is perhaps most important is that even with the decline in oil revenues, the kind of regional institutional and normative changes that have occurred since 1970 are not likely to reverse themselves abruptly. Therefore, the direction of political change at the systemic level can be expected, on balance, to contribute to the security posture of the GCC states at least for the immediate future. The longer-term prognosis, to the extent that it is predictable, appears less optimistic. If the decline in oil prices and revenues continues apace, the resulting constraints discussed

---

[15] Ali Hillal Dessouki, "The New Arab Political Order," in Kerr and Yasin, eds., *Rich*, pp. 323-324.
[16] Ibid., p. 326.

could seriously erode the oil-exporting Gulf states' capacity to maintain a regional political system that enhances their external and internal security.

Military Resources of the GCC

A cursory examination of the Gulf states' manpower and weapons inventories suggests that they have the military resources to constitute a potentially powerful military bloc and one of strategic importance to the West. Their military resources can be understood more clearly when set against a crucial set of missions they must perform if they are going to be effective in their external security role. This assumes the member states can integrate their separate, small, and disparate national forces into a larger interdependent military structure. Ideally, the five smaller GCC states must join with Saudi Arabia in a force structure that:

- preserves their sovereignty and independence;

- provides effective regional air and naval defense of all their respective oil facilities;

- deters aggression by Iran and Iraq;

- defends against amphibious or armored raids;

- maintains their internal security without external intervention; and

- develops the capability to support the over-the-horizon reinforcement by the United States to deal with "worst-case" contingencies.[17]

Whatever the available resource base, this mission profile must be tied to a coherent military strategy in order to provide an effective defense against external threats.

The Military Strategy of the GCC

Any military strategy the Gulf states may choose to follow must be cognizant of the following parameters:

[17] These criteria are suggested by Cordesman, *The Gulf*, pp. 568-569.

- In any sustained invasion of the Peninsula, external powers' forces will be larger than GCC forces.

- The strategic depth the Peninsula affords the Gulf states is more of an illusion that a reality, since the only targets that would justify an external overland attack are located along the Gulf littoral. However, the Peninsula's geography reduces the overland military threat by channelizing such attacks to narrow routes at each of the Peninsula's northern corners. Moreover, in the short term the effective utilization of the Gulf oil facilities *would* require control of interior space where related activities and facilities are located.

- The more probable (although not necessarily the most threatening) form of attack against the major producer, Saudi Arabia, and some others is likely to be air and seaborne attacks that are designed to harass or to intimidate. These attacks can overcome both geographical barriers and the inflexibility of overland assault.

Presumably military strategy is an extension of political strategy in that it seeks to insulate the Gulf from regional and superpower conflicts. In that sense, it is a preventive strategy. Beyond defense of shipping in the Gulf and the Red Sea, it does not require any projection of GCC military power. Given the plethora of political and military factors that constrain the use of their resources in their own defense, the first priority of a Gulf military strategy is to make air and seaborne harassing attacks too costly to be worth undertaking. Harassing attacks aim less at damaging facilities than at embarrassing, intimidating, and coercing the governments of the Peninsular oil states. The internal political repercussions from harassing attacks, if successful, could undermine the political strength and the legitimacy of the target government.

Military Resources of the GCC

Despite the combinations of factors that constrain the GCC states in the utilization of their resources to improve their security, they have the potential to effectively defend themselves and the Gulf from regional external threats without having to fall back on external allies except in the "worst case."

Geography

Except in Kuwait's case, one of the most valuable military resources is the factor of geography. The desert expanses and seas limit the ability of the Gulf states' most ominous potential opponents

113

to use their superior land forces against key strategic targets. Geography confers a special strategic importance upon air power and sea and air mobility in the region. The GCC states are at an advantage over their regional rivals in developing these capabilities. They have the money to afford the best available equipment and the Western training and support for it. They are equal to the task of developing the relatively limited numbers of trained manpower needed to operate an effective air force. Air power serves as an effective "equalizer" against more populous adversaries. It at least loosens some of the constraints imposed on military modernization in terms of recruitment and retention of adequate numbers of personnel. Since service in the air force is relatively "clean" and prestigious relative to the ground forces, the concentration on developing air power at least reduces the cultural barriers to acquiring necessary support and logistic skills.

Geography itself is an equalizer since it means the conservative Gulf states do not need to build large land armies. Sustained overland attacks from Iran or Iraq are channelized along narrow axes at the northern edges of the Peninsula, and will most likely originate from the region just north of Kuwait.[18] Unless they are confined to shallow border penetrations, geography and the region's roads would require the invading army to move through Kuwait. This would involve considerable combat in built-up, urban areas. Urban warfare tends to make all armies equal, since street fighting depends on the infantry and heavy weapons units, not on artillery and armored forces. As the Iran-Iraq war has already demonstrated, fighting in urban areas can go on for weeks with virtually no resupply. This sort of warfare depends on the will, morale, and tenacity of the individual soldier, and not on the high command, stocks of sophisticated weapons, or high technology. This is the sort of warfare where the qualities of the tribal recruits could stand the defenders in good stead.

Geography works to the advantage of the GCC in the south as well, providing protection to Saudi Arabia and Oman from North and South Yemen. North Yemen can move against the southwestern part of Saudi Arabia, but only along two land routes that cross very rough and easily defensible terrain. South Yemen lacks any major communications routes with Saudi Arabia and is not located near any strategically important Saudi objective. South Yemen's land

---

[18] Iraq has western land routes to Saudi Arabia which bypass Kuwait through Al-Najaf and Raflah, but these routes would put Iraqi forces in Saudi Arabia at a point far away from any major military objective. In addition, they are not expected to be able to support a major military operation through the late 1980s.

routes to Oman are equally limited and are defended by an impressive array of barriers constructed during the Dhofar rebellion. Cumulatively, geography enables the Gulf states to concentrate their priorities on the area defense of their airspace and surrounding waters. This involves concentrating their resources on the joint development of their air power and secondarily on the joint development of a navy optimized for coastal defense. This type of concentration will enable the GCC states to better defend key oil facilities and related strategic targets.

Money

The Gulf states' oil wealth has already been discussed in the context of a political resource, but is a vital military resource as well. In addition to buying weapons, training, and military infrastructure, it can serve as a "force multiplier" by:

● financing the purchase of compatible weapons systems for potential regional allies such as Jordan and Egypt whose forces could be deployed for the purposes of Gulf defense in "worst-case" situations (Jordan is already a military shield for Saudi Arabia. Egypt's military capabilities will become increasingly important to the GCC in the 1980s to protect Saudi Arabia's new oil export facilities at Yanbu and pipeline routes to the Gulf if the military balance in the Horn of Africa and the southern Red Sea shifts in favor of Ethiopia.);

● facilitating the realignment of states in the region whose militaries depend upon the Soviet Union as their principal source for arms, by financing their conversion to Western equipment (Saudi subsidies contributed to Anwar Sadat's decision to break with the Soviet Union in 1972, and helped to "wean" Somalia's Siad Barre away from his alignment with the Soviet Union in 1977.); and

● promoting coordinated military planning, force complementarity, and expanded shared combat support structures.

The potential for this last function can be seen in the formation of the Arab Military Industries Organization (AMIO) in 1975. The project was expected to do more than promote the merging of Gulf oil money with Egyptian production capabilities; it was originally intended to be the foundation for coordinated Gulf-Egyptian military planning, force complementarity, and—most significantly—

115

shared Saudi-Egyptian combat force structures. However, this special relationship was dealt a devastating setback from which it has yet to recover when Egypt opted to go it alone by embarking on the Camp David program. Yet, there is no permanent barrier to this sort of collaboration being resumed when the political climate favors it.

Gulf oil wealth enables the GCC countries to recruit Arab officers as cadres and advisors to compensate for local shortages of trained military manpower and for assistance in the upgrading of indigenous military capabilities. Despite the danger already discussed, the ability of Oman and some of the other smaller GCC states to draw on such assistance from Jordan has been particularly important in this regard.

Manpower

In a perverse sense the weaknesses and constraints imposed upon the Gulf states by demographic factors are also a resource to the extent that they impede the effectiveness of the forces of Iraq, Iran, and the two Yemens as well as other Arab armies. These weaknesses pose far more serious constraints in the context of power projection than they do for the strictly defensive missions which are the priority of the GCC forces. No Gulf country, including Iraq and Iran, is able to sustain prolonged military operations on the ground far from its borders. Even Iran and Iraq cannot support most of their combat units for long distances into hostile territory because of maintenance problems, inadequate combat and combat service support, lack of logistic equipment, and inadequate C^3I. A key question is: how hostile must the environment be to allow these factors to operate to the requisite degree?

Meanwhile, the GCC states have the opportunity to minimize these problems as they move from a collection of disparate national military organizations to a coordinated command and force structure. A more closely integrated GCC command (including C^3I) and force structure will enable the GCC countries to reduce the effects of the social, economic, and cultural constraints upon the mobilization of their indigenous manpower for military purposes. This type of integration should have a particularly salutary impact on the quality and effectiveness of essential combat support services.

Modern military forces are subject to strict economies and diseconomies of scale. A small national military manpower base is inefficient no matter how well trained its personnel because the required cadre of essential combat support services cannot be re-

116

duced below a given level and still permit the nation to maintain an effective force. Bahrain, Kuwait, Qatar, and the UAE all face critical diseconomies of scale and are separately spending large amounts of money on forces too small to be effective. These problems are compounded by the UAE's recent history of maintaining separate "national" force elements. An integrated combat services organization, for example, could support all the weapons systems the six members have in common. This would vastly improve the effectiveness of the GCC's air power for Gulf defense.

Another potential manpower asset might be the existence of a cadre of "officer princes" serving in the respective member states' armed forces, especially the air forces. Assuming they are seriously dedicated to their military careers, they are an important resource beyond their obvious function of ensuring civilian (government) control over the military by their occupation of key assignments. They can, by their example, help with morale and retention problems and instill a sense of commitment to the government in those who serve under their command. In any military showdown, the ultimate resource necessary to the Gulf states will be skillful and competent commanders, who can inspire those whom they command, as well as tenacity and a stake in defending the national patrimony on the part of those who follow them.

Equipment

Notwithstanding the various factors that constrain the development of an effective GCC defense force, the total active manpower and the quantity of modern weapons at their disposal suggests that the conservative Gulf states have the *potential* to effectively blunt any regional threat that confronts them, with the possible exception of a multi-front attack on Saudi Arabia. The major problems attending the design of a GCC force structure that can use weapons on hand more effectively for external defense are discussed in the next chapter.

Even a cursory review of the military balance in the Gulf in terms of major combat units and their equipment suggests that the GCC forces have or have on order a sufficient array of weapons to meet just about any realistic external conventional contingency. Until very recently, however, the member states purchased their major weapons systems with little regard to coordinating these acquisitions with one another.[19] However, assuming the member states can

---

[19] To date, the closest coordination of weapons purchases appears to have been between Qatar and Kuwait with respect to Qatar's purchase of Mirage F-1 fighters.

work out a politically acceptable "division of labor" for their common defense, weapons acquisition, training, and support packages can be much more effectively rationalized and the equipment purchases optimized for joint operations. Future purchases can also be made with a more discerning eye to the strengths and weaknesses of the human elements in their military establishments.

The process of military modernization addresses the distinction between weapons systems that require increased operator competence and higher operator skills levels, on the one hand, and highly sophisticated but very simple-to-operate weapons that reduce the influence of human skills in military operations, on the other.[20] The closer battlefield technologies evolve toward the mythical "automated battlefield" with push-button "fire-and-forget" weapons, the less individual competence and initiative will count. Such weapons would help to compensate for some of the factors that constrain the mobilization of Gulf manpower discussed earlier. Examples of such weapons are the second-generation anti-tank missiles (TOW, Dragon, Milan) which, once properly programmed, come much closer to truly automatic guidance than the weapons they replace. The eventual introduction of a third generation of such weapons (Aerospatiale ACCP, Honeywell AT-4) presumably will continue this evolution and so act as an "equalizer" between armies of unequal skill. To the extent that such weapons favor the defense, they will definitely enhance the capabilities of GCC forces.

However, for many systems the demands on operator skills and competence are increasing, not decreasing. Such systems augment the advantage of technically sophisticated military forces and widen any gaps of inequality between forces of unequal skill. In this respect, the GCC as a whole—at least as far as the Gulf front is concerned—can make more effective use of what it already has by utilizing force multipliers such as the AWACS or similar downward looking airborne radars to coordinate the assets already available rather than by acquiring additional types of highly sophisticated aircraft.

Conclusions

The foregoing discussion has stressed the potential strategic resource base at the disposal of the GCC states for their collective

---

[20] The emphasis here is on the skills required to operate various weapons on the battlefield. Such weapons may, however, impose more rigorous supply and maintenance demands on combat support systems.

defense. The focus has been on the development of capabilities that can emerge from this resource base despite the multiplicity of constraints, discussed earlier, that militate against its most effective exploitation. The general conclusion is that there is no insurmountable barrier to the GCC states' forging an effective collective security system centered on the military infrastructure developed by Saudi Arabia in the 1970s, an integrated C^3I to support a collaborative command structure, and an integrated force structure that promotes the rationalization of military facilities as well as inter-operability and standardization of equipment and procurement procedures. The concentration on the development of an effective air force centered on sensor and battlefield management systems like the Saudi AWACS appears to be the most promising avenue for GCC cooperation. It is to a discussion of some of the operational problems associated with positioning Gulf security capabilities in these directions that we now turn.

V

GAPS AND PROBLEMS
IN GULF SECURITY

**The most serious of the GCC's political, so-
cial, military, and economic problems apply more to the smaller members than to
Saudi Arabia or Oman, but they limit the
capabilities of the organization to form a
cohesive, effective multilateral deterrent.
The principal problems for the key to the
GCC, Saudi Arabia, are not overall equipment shortfalls but its need for certain specific technologies and its continued
dependence on expatriate manpower in
support roles.**

Introduction

The combination of resources and constraints described in the
previous chapters provides a useful context for evaluating the problems and gaps in the GCC's efforts to build an effective security
regime for the Gulf. The cumulative active manpower in the GCC
constituent members' armed forces and the quantities of combat
aircraft and armored fighting vehicles, contrasted with potential
external threats in the region, suggests that the GCC, with Saudi
Arabia acting as a "senior partner," has the potential capability to
check any regional threats. The focus of this chapter is on the
problems involved in transforming potential into actual capabilities.
Problems and gaps fall into four categories:

- *Political* problems stem from (1) the unwillingness of suppliers to provide necessary equipment on a necessary and timely basis; and (2) the asymmetry of the distribution of power within the GCC and from the structure of national force elements (in the smaller countries), which in some cases reflects the purposes of internal security and control, not external defense.

- *Social* problems vary greatly in their applicability to the different GCC states, but include the personal basis upon which loyalties and commitments are made; and status issues at various levels, which impede adequate leadership and cooperation; and aversion to manual labor. These problems hinder the effective mobilization of the GCC's manpower potential for defense.

- *Military* problems are mainly macro-level problems of lack of inter-operability within and between components of the same or other GCC forces; the questionable reliability of foreign officers, advisors, and technicians should a war occur; and the absence of a synthesizing strategy to adapt both the imported military technology and their own social institutions in order to effectively use their new equipment.

- *Economic* problems currently center on the decline in the price of oil, the resulting drop in income to the oil-exporting GCC states, and the shift in the international oil market from one favoring the sellers to one favoring the buyers. These factors constrain the GCC's ability to finance any ambitious military modernization programs.

These problem areas are discussed in light of the security demands imposed by external threats. The GCC must be able to stop (or at least delay) an overland invasion from the north; deflect harassing border attacks from North and South Yemen; interdict harassing air and coastal strikes aimed particularly at air fields (Israel) and key oil production facilities from the north (Iraq) and east (Iraq and Iran); and prevent infiltration of saboteurs and subversive elements from Iran or hostile Arab countries. Some capability must also exist to deal with more than one of these threats concurrently. The foregoing requirements generally call for coordination and inter-operability among national force elements in being, on the one hand, and for acquisition of limited but specific types of new technologies, on the other. They do not require large-scale or extensive acquisition of new weapons systems.

Only Bahrain and Qatar, the two countries with the smallest armed forces, have any history of significant military cooperation with Saudi Arabia. Kuwait may encounter serious political problems with both Iraq and Iran if it attempts to expand its military cooperation with other GCC states. The UAE's legacy of internal competition raises real questions about its ability to integrate its forces in any GCC-wide framework. In addition, there remain some UAE fears of Oman's influence over the large number of Omani troops serving in the UAE's armed forces. In short, the member states are still in the process of reaching agreement on the most appropriate form of defense cooperation. Consequently, much of the progress achieved in GCC cooperation appears to have been more in reaction to trends in the Iran-Iraq war or to Iranian-sponsored internal subversion than to the development of productive working relationships among the member states resulting from the creation of the GCC or from any consensus on the form of GCC cooperation in external defense matters.

Political Problems

Apples and Oranges, Planes and Tanks

Perspective on the political problems of transforming potential capabilities into actual combat effectiveness can be gained from an "apples-and-oranges" comparison of the GCC with NATO. The very fact that the two multinational organizations are not really equivalents obscures some important parallels in as well as some contrasts relevant to evaluation of GCC security problems. These lessons can be seen by comparing NATO at the time of its formation in 1949 with the GCC today. The political barriers to achieving effective inter-operability within the GCC can be better appreciated when it is remembered how limited NATO's progress has been in these areas over 35 years. Concern for national interests has been a constant stumbling block to the major European NATO members' being able to agree on a common tactical fighter for the 1990s.

First and foremost, the power differentials in NATO are not nearly as extreme as they are among the GCC states. This has important implications for the politics of security in the Gulf and the effective structuring of a viable GCC security apparatus. When NATO was first formed in 1949, the European members were still prostrate from World War II and could not mount anything like a credible defense against the Soviet Union without the participation of the United States. Given its near monopoly of economic and military resources in the first decade of NATO's history, it is no wonder that American domination of the alliance was almost total.

Had the determination to cooperate or the military capabilities of NATO been the yardstick for measuring NATO's potential, the organization would have quickly expired. Instead, it was for some time the military dynamism of NATO's backbone, the United States, that carried the organization, and it is no exaggeration to say that NATO thrived at least as much because of U.S. military progress that *carried* NATO as because of the subsequent resuscitation of European defense capabilities (a resuscitation stimulated in no small measure by the United States, as well).

Today, however, NATO consists of one superpower and three or four second-tier powers (depending upon how France's "associate" status is characterized) plus a collection of smaller states. With the postwar recovery of the European allies, defense responsibility in NATO is spread across the United States and the larger European powers. The postwar recovery of Europe facilitated more autonomous defense preparations by the larger European powers to the point where France was able to step largely outside NATO's integrated command structure. The loss, however, of any of the three major European powers to the Soviet bloc or the neutralization of Germany would be a devastating blow to the remaining NATO members, including the United States, since all the remaining allies would be relatively weaker. Strategically, this weakened condition probably could not be compensated for by additional contributions from the larger member states. The relative contribution to NATO by the larger members is one reason the United States shares the leadership of the alliance with the European "big three." However, if the U.S. commitment to NATO diminished appreciably, the remaining members have the capability (if not the resolve) to assume more of the defense burden themselves (something the French have advocated for years), or even to reorganize themselves in a viable European security pact.

By contrast, the GCC consists of one of the three major Gulf powers, Saudi Arabia, and a collection of mostly diminutive countries—Oman and four quasi city-states. The disappearance of one of the latter (especially one of the UAE sheikhdoms) might not appreciably weaken Saudi Arabia or seriously erode its strategic position in the Gulf. However, the loss of Saudi Arabia would render the GCC totally non-viable. None of the other GCC members can provide effectively for its own external defense outside the GCC framework now or in the future.

This important structural difference implies that the organization of GCC-wide security—particularly as it may concern an effective C^3I—must be centered on Saudi Arabia. However, it also means that the preservation of the constituent members' sovereignty plays a more prominent role in the organization of the GCC's security apparatus than in NATO's for two reasons.

• First, given the disproportionate contribution of Saudi Arabia to GCC defense, any rationalization of the division of labor among the other constituent members is bound to magnify their subordinate status, and inflame political sensitivities among these countries' leaders (the competition for "status" within the GCC via rapid purchase of "prestige" weapons—as, for example between Kuwait and the UAE—has already been mentioned). The subordinate status of the five smaller GCC members will only be magnified by a formal agreement on coordinating and integrating Gulf defense efforts. Hence there exist factions within these governments that resist the idea of any formal agreement. The other GCC members are aware that Saudi Arabia will come to their aid, to the extent that it is able, in the event of an external crisis without any agreement on integrating and coordinating their defense efforts. The counter-argument sometimes heard is that absent the organizational and C^3I infrastructure that enables forces to cooperate with one another, unilateral Saudi assistance in times of crisis may be too little, too late.

• Second, the evolution of the GCC into an effective lower Gulf defensive alliance will inevitably mean the substantial dependence of the smaller Gulf states on Saudi Arabia. Exertions of Saudi leadership may often be construed by members of the smaller Gulf states' elites as veiled efforts at Saudi "hegemony." This is a particularly delicate matter where intra-GCC coordination on internal security is concerned. Efforts at greater cooperation in this area have already produced scattered complaints about legitimizing an already significant Saudi role in the internal affairs of its neighbors. Much of the cooperation that has occurred in this area came about in response to clear-cut subversive attempts, such as the Iranian-sponsored *coup d'etat* in Bahrain in December 1981, rather than as a natural accretion of GCC powers. The completion of the causeway linking Saudi Arabia and Bahrain certainly introduces a new factor into the relationship and must be seen as at least a potential diminution of Bahraini autonomy.

A second useful contrast between NATO and the GCC concerns intra-alliance cooperation. At the macro level, the problems the GCC faces in building an effective external defense center on the fact that the member states have not designed their forces to co-operate with one another, so that they now have little or no inter-operability. This, too, is a problem confronted by a young NATO, and even now problems of achieving greater rationalization, standardization, and inter-operability in NATO are significant. More significant, the national force elements of NATO are organized primarily for external defense. By contrast, forces of the smaller countries have been structured in response to the most pressing threats of an earlier era—to safeguard internal security and to preserve government control of the military. Thus, the problems of rationalization of missions and inter-operability of forces are intensified by the fact that some GCC countries have followed a policy of segmentation with respect to their own military forces, creating organizational cleavages that leave components ill equipped or trained to work with one another, let alone with the armed forces of other members. These problems are only now being addressed.

The organizational cleavages reflect a concern for political control over military establishments. The creation of a dual military structure in Saudi Arabia where responsibilities for national defense are divided between the Saudi Arabian National Guard (SANG) and the Royal Saudi Army (RSA), and the retention of the original "national" components—disguised as "regional commands"—of the UAE's Federal Union Defense Force (UDF) are two very different manifestations of this problem.

A related problem is GCC government reluctance to move vigorously toward adoption of technological and organizational means of communication between air and ground forces despite the obvious necessity to rely on combined arms operations—especially close air support—to offset other attacker advantages in actual combat. Again, as in NATO, the GCC governments for reasons of national sovereignty and rivalry have been hesitant about placing significant defense assets—e.g., aircraft and air defense missile batteries, in the case of the GCC—under a unified command in spite of the manifest advantages. Kuwait, for example, took such a step in the summer of 1984, but more as a result of the Iran-Iraq war (mainly from Iranian air attacks on Kuwait) than from commitment to forging greater integration among GCC forces.

The Politics of Supplier Relations

The pattern of weapons purchases by the GCC states reflects important political problems only some of which are subject to GCC control. On the one hand, GCC states seek to maintain some independence from supplier control. On the other hand, and in recent years more decisively, external suppliers' politics have forced at times an unwanted diversification of supply sources on GCC members. Constraints on the availability of delivery timing of specific systems have had a significantly adverse impact on the defense planning in some cases, particularly in Saudi Arabia, where planning for specific packages of performance characteristics (systems capabilities) against specific needs has advanced much further than in the other GCC states. Multiple suppliers may curb internal military threats by making coordination more difficult and assure that loss of a supplier will not bring modernization efforts to a standstill. Neither Saudi Arabia nor the other GCC governments is oblivious to the importance of optimizing weapons procurement to provide effective capabilities. This enterprise, however, involves considerable advance planning which must assume that the weapons will be available from the preferred supplier. It further assumes that the training and advice provided by the foreign supplier are primarily concerned with helping the recipient government's armed forces obtain the maximum capability from what is provided. Those assumptions have not always held in the past, especially with respect to the Gulf states' purchase of major weapons systems from the United States. Therefore, GCC governments have found it prudent to "hedge their bets" on supply sources for big ticket items like aircraft, armored fighting vehicles, anti-aircraft missile systems, and the like.

A current example of the "hedging" policy concerns the GCC's procurement of an effective interceptor aircraft. A logical candidate for such a mission would be the Northrop F-20 Tigershark. Not only does this fighter possess state-of-the-art avionics; it has almost zero launch-delay time, which means it can scramble faster and meet intruders farther out from their intended targets than any other fighter including the F-15C. Moreover, the F-20 is relatively easy to maintain, and its acquisition by a number of GCC states would be eminently sensible in view of the severe shortages of skilled manpower. It is the successor to the F-5E, so GCC pilots should be able to transition to it with less difficulty than, say, to the Mirage 2000 or the Tornado Air Defense Variant (ADV). The latter two aircraft are inferior to the F-20 in terms of their target acquisition and fire control radars as well as in the ability to scramble on short notice.

The F-20 has scant chance of being selected, however, for several reasons:

• One area the new interceptor must be deployed is at Saudi Arabia's northwestern base at Tabuk, since by agreement with the United States Saudi Arabia's F-15s cannot be deployed there. The

127

F-20's mission would be to intercept intruder aircraft that penetrate Saudi airspace, but, given the Tabuk base location, such aircraft would realistically be Israeli. The United States, out of deference to Israeli pressure, is not likely to sell the F-20 to Saudi Arabia without a provision that the Saudis agree not to deploy the F-20 at Tabuk, which would leave the impression of Saudi collusion with Israel to leave that quadrant undefended, undermining Saudi Arabia's political influence within the GCC, weakening its leadership position in that organization, and weakening its political legitimacy in the eyes of important domestic constituencies (including the armed forces).

• Even with an agreement not to base the F-20 at Tabuk, few observers believe the U.S. Administration could secure Congressional approval of the F-20 sale, and certainly not without a great political controversy that would tend to damage U.S.-Saudi relations.

• Some of the Gulf governments would find negotiations with the United States for acquisition of F-20s politically difficult because of U.S. policies elsewhere in the Middle East and inevitable charges that the United States was endeavoring to obtain a choke-hold on Gulf air defense.

Therefore, the more likely candidates to fill this role are the French Mirage 2000 and the British Tornado ADV.[1] More probable, there will be no common interceptor.

The tempo of further GCC cooperation in joint defense matters is likely to be governed by the extent such cooperation is perceived to strengthen the member governments' internal security. For example, as noted earlier, initial efforts at joint defense cooperation began with agreements and intelligence sharing for internal security purposes. The benefits of closer cooperation in intelligence sharing became evident as a result of the role such efforts played in foiling the *coup* attempt in Bahrain in December 1981.[2] In the

---

[1] Oman has ordered or will soon order the Tornado ADV. Saudi Arabia, having encountered political obstacles in its attempts to purchase additional F-15s, is reportedly seeking modifications to the Tornado with the intention of acquiring· a multi-role combat aircraft.

[2] The *coup* conspirators, using GCC passports, had been able to move rather easily among the GCC states. The Bahraini government was alerted to the coup by a tip from airport officials in Dubai. In the months following the coup attempt, Saudi Arabia signed bilateral internal security agreements with four of its five GCC allies.

aftermath of the Bahraini *coup* attempt, renewed interest was shown in a joint military command for the GCC states and the formation of a GCC rapid deployment force. Within a year plans were finalized to establish a strong defense council and to improve the standardization, integration, and inter-operability of security systems and the monitoring of terrorist and radical movements among Gulf countries. Considerable progress was also made on studies of joint air and maritime surveillance, a unified high command, cooperative training, and standardization of equipment.

Social Problems

Traditional Gulf armies were personal armies having direct, personal contact with the tribal leader. While no Gulf state retains a "traditional" army or air force in this sense, notions of loyalty and allegiance are still widely understood in such personal terms in the Gulf. Thus, within the UAE, loyalty to the federal concept has yet to take root beyond the palaces and offices of the upper echelons of government. Even as in the early days of American independence, some leaders of the constituent states in the UAE continue to regard their armies as extensions of their authority and therefore are reluctant to hand over control of those armies to a unified federal command.

A parallel problem may exist among the GCC states to the extent that the members states' armed forces are viewed by the leadership elites and the more traditional Bedouin units within these military establishments as at least national armies if not quasi-personal military forces. To the extent that this perception prevails among the senior officer corps, it is likely to impede organizational changes to promote coordination and integration of GCC forces in such activities as cross basing, joint planning and joint training and support for the systems they have in common, and a joint air defense network.

To these "macro-level" problems are added the difficulties that are endemic in the social structure of developing states. The most important are attitudinal predispositions reinforced by education and social organization that combine to inhibit the emergence of technical sophistication in troops and modern management practices in military leadership.

One of the most obvious problem areas is simply a lack of suitably educated indigenous personnel. Shortages of educated and technically skilled manpower reflect a history of past educational shortcomings, a lack of education rather than inappropriate educational

129

practices. The problem afflicts virtually all military forces in the Gulf.

This demographic shortage is exacerbated by education systems that are in flux, notably at the pre-university level. In this respect, a clear distinction must be made among Gulf countries. In Saudi Arabia, especially in urban areas, and in a few schools in Bahrain and Kuwait, education has been modernized and secularized. In the vast majority of schools elsewhere in the Gulf, and even in Saudi Arabia outside the city, progress in this direction is uneven at best. In the latter case, acquisition of knowledge comes through repeated drill, not analysis. The stress on rote learning in such educational settings promotes mastery of routine tasks, but does not develop the ability to see cause-and-effect and ends-means relationships. In the military, this outlook is sufficient for training recruits on systems in which operation and maintenance is based on repetitive steps, such as the TOW anti-tank missile systems. But memorizing set procedures does not promote flexibility, innovative thinking, or the ability to adapt to new or unforeseen situations such as those that might arise in actual combat. A pre-secular educational system reinforces culturally instilled habits and perspective. Religion, language, and culture rather than mathematics, science and social studies have relatively greater emphasis in primary schools, and, in many of the Gulf states, even in secondary schools.[3] This concentration can only inhibit the development of mechanical aptitudes that are essential in maintenance and logistics operations.

In the poorer or more traditional households of the Gulf, children grow up with little exposure to the mechanical artifacts of modern society. In the middle class of wealthier families, where the products of industrial society may abound, the ingrained disdain for manual labor also militates against the development of mechanical aptitudes.

Although the social stigma attached to manual labor and the prejudice against hands-on activities are declining, they continue to have severe consequences for the improvement of the human element in Gulf military forces. Clerical, mercantile, and administrative operations command higher prestige in traditional Muslim societies than occupations requiring technical expertise. Consequently, even those people who have completed technical training programs, such as engineers, chemists, journeyman mechanics, and the like, often seek to leave the field, laboratory, or workshop to become managers. The negative attitude towards hands-on activities also leads to an unwillingness on the part of officers and NCOs to

---

[3] Pascal, Kennedy, and Rosen, *Men*, pp. 34-35.

directly involve themselves in training, logistics, and maintenance activities that are regarded as "manual labor." Once again, these attitudes are more typical in the smaller states, but are being steadily supplanted by new views in Saudi Arabia where engineering, for example, has become a "status" occupation.

Social distance between superior and subordinates in many societies makes the former distrustful and contemptuous toward initiative from the latter. In the Gulf military environment, this problem is found especially among NCOs, but the lack of social distance has perhaps been more of a problem in Saudi Arabia, where the proper degree of respect for superior officers has often been wanting, resulting in poor discipline.

Traditionalism in Gulf society—where leaders' decisions go unchallenged simply because they occupy elevated positions in an institutional hierarchy—leadership insecurity, and weakness in bureaucracic staffing have produced chronic over-centralization of decision-making ánd management. Over-centralization of command encourages middle-level personnel to reject decision-making responsibility and to pass even small matters up to higher commanders, who then become burdened with decisions on issues about which they lack the necessary information. This phenomenon has contributed in turn to a lack of the kind of inter-service cooperation and coordination that is absolutely essential to mounting any sort of combined arms operation. This problem is worsened wherever aristocratic vestiges and prerogatives still exist. In such instances, the propensity to monopolize decision-making power and the resistance to delegating authority are probably even stronger than elsewhere.

These social predispositions sustain the practice of nepotism or "politicization" of the promotion process. While the more blatant ascriptive criteria, such as birth, for assignment and promotion may have eroded, they have often been replaced by political loyalty rather than merit. A leader appoints the most faithful candidate, who frequently has ties to the same family, town, or sect as the governing group. This is particularly prevalent in the smaller sheikhdoms, where family members may dominate the military forces. One consequence is the possibility of a negative relationship between rank and capability in the officer corps of some units. The adverse effects are reinforced by the tendency to concentrate almost all effective decision-making authority at the senior grades.

Responsibility in the military establishments of many developing countries tends to be treated as a shared social phenomenon rather than as something pertaining strictly to the individual. Concepts of right and wrong may depend less on individual determination and

131

more on what is deemed right or wrong by the world surrounding the individual. Having to answer to society for all deeds generates an overriding concern for honor and creates pressures for officers and men to appear above reproach by keeping and saving "face." This collective approach to responsibility tends to produce people who are sensitive and subject to public recrimination but feel a lesser sense of personal culpability. The cumulative effect of concern for "face" and shared rather than individual responsibility vastly complicates the development of rationalized personnel systems. The concern for face has a pronounced effect on the predisposition to both offer and accept criticism. One result is that the ability to put on a good show may appear more important as a measure of success than a high operational readiness rating.[4] Other examples may include the failure to demote or discharge the inept and an unwillingness to report factually on politically threatening or career-threatening readiness and force improvement deficiencies. Although efforts to overcome such problems have been evident in the Gulf states for some time, actual progress has been exceedingly slow in most cases.

The most successful training programs appear to be those in which the trainee is removed from the inhibitions of his accustomed social milieu. Such values as acceptance of individual responsibility and criticism, innovative behavior, respect for manual endeavors, and willingness to work long hours may be more easily inculcated in settings where these traits are approved and rewarded. Previous studies have observed that Middle Eastern students often return from training stints in the United States fired with new attitudes and work styles. The use of bicultural liaison officers who are assigned responsibility for discipline and behavior and accompany their training contingents became an effective device for reinforcing the positive effects in the Iranian armed forces prior to the revolution in 1979. Saudi Arabia has recently installed similar procedures. This may explain why former U.S advisors rate the performance of the younger Saudi officers who trained in the United States and abroad as good and why they report that the Saudi soldiers have acquired technical skills more rapidly than many Third World forces with a far better educational base.[5]

---

[4] *Ibid.*, pp. 42-43.
[5] Abdul Kasim Mansur (pseud.), "The Military Balance in the Persian Gulf: Who Will Guard the Gulf States from their Guardians?" *Armed Forces Journal International*, November 1980, p. 72.

Military Problems

The most serious gaps and shortfalls that directly impact on the combat effectiveness of GCC forces are (1) the absence of an integrative strategy that can adapt indigenous social values and institutions to imported military technologies and its attendant strategic thought in order to effectively use the equipment; (2) the rapidity and apparent carelessness with which most of the smaller GCC states acquired new and sophisticated weapons, without giving adequate attention to combat support and combat service support; (3) the decentralized organizational structures and responsibilities that impede cooperation and coordination of military units even within the same military; and (4) the attendant dependence on foreign officers, advisors, and technicians whose value in wartime is open to question. East of these shortfalls is discussed in its perceived order of importance.

Lack of an Integrative Strategy

The foregoing discussion of social problems attending military modernization calls attention to an often unspoken assumption underlying the evaluation of the capabilities of any Third World military establishment—that successful absorption of modern weapons requires successful mastery of the doctrinal precepts of the country that originally designed and manufactured them, that the recipient country's forces must prepare to wage the type of war for which their imported weapons were originally designed. Otherwise, it is argued, the recipient will have no usable capabilities against the type of external threats it is likely to face. This assumption would be invalid for the GCC states even if their most probable adversary were a foreign army that enjoyed clear-cut technological superiority in the mastery of modern weapons. It is even less valid when the most likely adversaries are Iran or Iraq.

The assumption is a fallacy (as is clearly evident by Egyptian performance in the 1973 October War), because it confuses military modernization with military Westernization. The surprisingly successful performance of Egyptian troops in the first week of the October War involved, at the tactical level, the employment of a manpower/weapons mix that favored the Arabs' numerical advantage and enabled them to counter Israel's technological superiority. In so doing, the Egyptians limited Israeli tactical options, and forced the Israeli Defense Force to fight on Arab terms for the first part

133

of the war. They were successful in this strategy because Egyptian planners were able to draw on existing Arab/Islamic social values to motivate their troops. They were able to incorporate existing authoritarian social patterns and practices into training techniques; and they were able to structure existing elitist attitudes in the officer corps to achieve improvement in leadership.[6] They did not wait for modernization of their societies to reach a point where their troops could absorb Western weapons systems and employ them in the same manner that they were intended to be employed by Western armies (fighting other Western armies in Europe).

Essentially, this task involved the adaptation of non-Western strategies to Western weapons, converting the strengths of traditional social orders into weapons to be used against a superior enemy. The elements emphasized by non-Western strategists—mobility, time and space, kinship linkages, or honor—vary, but they all have the same purpose: the combination of a minimal technological infrastructure utilizing Western weapons with non-Western culture and behavior in a manner that produces acceptable battlefield performance.

In this context, Egypt's strategy for war with Israel was an attempt to both selectively assimilate Western military technology in certain critical areas and combine this with a strategy of large numbers. The consequence was a complex behavioral process by which the Arab recipient of Western arms learned to adapt both the imported technology *and* his own social institutions in order to effectively use the equipment.

Admittedly, the impediments to successfully achieving such an adaptation are more formidable for the GCC than they were for Egypt, since the GCC must develop a strategy based on inferior numbers and the compensating use of air power and anti-aircraft missile defenses. The concentration on the development of these capabilities, in turn, requires a higher absorption of Western technological infrastructure.

---

[6] The obvious limitations of this approach were demonstrated during the second week of the war. On the one hand, the vast resources of Egyptian manpower were put to effective use. On the other hand, the uses had to be tightly structured to fit existing pre-planned contingencies. As long as Egyptian troops could operate in a structured and memorized operational environment, they performed effectively. When they were forced out of it by Israeli tactics, they became tremendously disorganized. See John W. Amos II, *Arab-Israeli Military Political Relations: Arab Perceptions and the Politics of Escalation* (New York: Pergamon Press, 1979), pp. 193-197.

Purchase of Equipment Unsuited to Indigenous Needs

The absence of any adaptive strategy is evident in the major imbalances in weapons inventories that prevent or limit effective inter-service or combined arms operations in the GCC states, especially the smaller countries. High performance combat aircraft have been purchased without high performance missiles and munitions. Tanks are purchased without suitable armored fighting vehicle/armored personnel carrier (AFV/APC) and artillery support or transporters. In most GCC states the conversion rates at which their armed forces are being restructured and modernized, rates of over 20 percent annually in some cases, have proven impractical even for sophisticated Western military forces with long experience in the use of modern weapons. Many Gulf nations, for example, are attempting to convert to new types of fighter aircraft over much shorter periods that would be attempted by the Royal Air Force, the Luftwaffe, or the French Air Force.

By way of comparison, even Western and Soviet-bloc forces cannot increase their total holdings of major weapons systems like aircraft and tanks by more than 10 to 15 percent per year without sharply degrading the quality of their manpower or shifting their manpower base to a wartime footing. These equipment and absorption problems increase in direct proportion to the weakness in the military infrastructures of Third World countries and their inability to obtain adequate training and support. Thus the GCC states appear to be copying military technologies which are changing in the interim. They may never reach Western norms of battlefield performance because they will always be slightly obsolescent in their newly acquired military techniques. In trying to overcome these lags, conversion rates on major equipment items keep unit structure in constant turmoil. Training is erratic with units evolving in very different directions even in the same country. No common standard of readiness exists, and countries tend to improvise to meet particular needs.

Too often military modernization efforts appear to have been tied to individual major equipment purchases. Many of these purchases appear to have been made with little effort to examine their cumulative impact or potential for integration into an effective training and support system. This practice, in turn, aggravates a problem that characterizes most Middle Eastern military establishments, which must cope with shortages of skilled indigenous manpower—the inclination to strip the best human resources from the general units in order to man the elite forces or the most recently acquired

135

"prestige" weapons systems.[7] This tendency usually degrades the quality and capabilities of indigenous personnel in general units. The cumulative effect of these practices is that even those units that can fight effectively in set-piece defensive actions may collapse without warning in the face of unfamiliar contingencies that are not pre-planned.

Most of these problems and gaps are more apparent in the smaller GCC states than in Saudi Arabia. Between 1971 and 1978, when Saudi defense expenditures as a percentage of central government expenditures were at their highest, about 50 percent was spent on construction, 30 percent on training, and only 20 percent on hardware. The objective has been to create the skill and infrastructure necessary to allow the Saudis to effectively use the weapons they do buy. In the Gulf only the Saudis, however, have adopted this approach.

Decentralized Military Organizations

Two problems common to all GCC countries are (1) the problem of overcoming the organizational momentum in the direction of diverse and decentralized militaries that often preclude units of the same military from dealing with one another; and (2) the fairly small indigenous combat services and support capability reinforced by large numbers of foreign advisors and technical experts. These are two of the most serious problem areas attending the effective modernization of the GCC's armed forces. They also provide the clearest illustrations of the "dynamic tension" between the imperatives of internal security and control over the military, on the one hand, and the perceived urgency in modernizing the armed forces for external defense, on the other.

There is no conclusive evidence that GCC governments still fear the development of large, centralized and otherwise efficient armed forces. Circumstantial evidence indicates such fears are gradually diminishing.[8] Whether Gulf leaders are more confident of their ability to manage modernization and social change or whether fear

---

[7] On this, see Pascal, Kennedy, and Rosen, *Men*, pp. 44-45. The authors note, however, that in some instances this practice may have offered some advantages with respect to enhancing combat effectiveness. For example, the Egyptian policy of manning surface-to-air missile (SAM) and anti-tank units with their best personnel in 1973 apparently conferred some advantages on the Arab forces vis-a-vis Israel.

[8] Most of the GCC governments, for example, have now introduced the technological and organizational means of communication between air and ground forces.

of external attack and externally-supported subversion has simply supplanted other concerns does not matter. The existence of decentralized military organizations which are further diversified by different sources of equipment, different foreign expertise, and different tactical training, and that may even draw on different elements of their societies for their manpower, seriously impairs working together. Communications nets are usually vertical between individual units and indigenous high commands. These conditions make it extremely difficult to mount any combined arms exercises, or even to effectively utilize the latest C^3 technologies. This sort of inflexibility degrades training exercises, reduces adaptability on the battlefield, and virtually precludes effective maneuver of different elements in the same service and different service branches within the same military in combined arms operations.

Even if GCC leaders had complete confidence in military loyalty, the organizational momentum based on past practices impedes efforts to establish greater coordination among components of the same military forces. Organizational momentum or inertia in the direction of continued functional cleavages and decentralized responsibilities is undoubtedly reinforced by its interaction with indigenous social norms discussed earlier. These include rigid centralization of command and prescribed responsibilities which translate into a penchant for staying in conventional channels in military operations. An excessive compartmentalization of skills and duties to the point of near isolation results. The reluctance to share resources, the concern to protect oneself and one's unit from responsibility for failure, the lack of faith by superiors in the competence of subordinates, and the reluctance of subordinates to take any decision-making responsibility are further symptoms. Thus, the inefficiencies and bottlenecks that characterize GCC forces cannot be expected to disappear quickly.

The Reliability of Foreign Officers, Advisors, and Technicians

The presence of expatriate officers in senior command positions and foreign technicians in support and logistics operations as a device for diversifying government control over the military, as well as for transferring military technologies and skills, has already been discussed. These same expatriate contingents are a mixed blessing when it comes to developing the GCC forces' defense capabilities. Without the presence of effective foreign support, the GCC countries would not be able to field modern military forces for some time to come. However, the speed and haphazardness with which the smaller GCC states are modernizing diminish the usefulness of their indigenous skilled personnel, the best of whom are often switched to newer weapons entering inventory without their having absorbed previous systems. This situation places native pilots and technical personnel in a constant state of turmoil and increases host country dependence on foreigners.

The role of expatriate personnel may be indispensable to the modernization of the GCC's military forces, but it carries with it some very considerable dangers. First, there is no way to know whether expatriates will prove very capable in wartime. That they have superior training and more extensive combat experience than local personnel does not mean they will prove equal to the combat challenge, particularly when they are not fighting for a cause in which they believe or indeed even serving in the same conditions in which they originally entered the job. Second, apart from the question of capabilities, the question of dependability also arises. Will their countries "request" their departure? In the event of a conflict in the Gulf, will the United States government suggest that its nationals, including those in the defense sector, depart? Or will individuals in critical positions choose to do so as a matter of personal and family interests? These are questions of more than academic importance. Third, as long as training and tactical development are concentrated in the hands of foreigners, indigenous military forces will have little opportunity to work out a synthesizing strategy to adapt both their imported military technologies and their indigenous social institutions to the effective utilization of their equipment in combat.

These obstacles constitute an unavoidable list of the more important negative by-products that inevitably accompany rapid modernization of Third World military forces. Most of these hurdles can be overcome with enough time. The first step toward meeting this challenge is to recognize their implications for the development of an effective Gulf-wide defense effort. Such an assessment must be based on an evaluation of separate services.

GCC Air Forces

In the 1973 war, Arab forces performed best under conditions where the role of Western technology was minimal. Generally Arab forces were able to match the Israelis, reasonably well on the ground, less well in air defense, hardly at all in air-to-air combat, and not at all in naval engagement. The Egyptians, in particular, and the Syrians to a lesser extent, employed a strategy to exploit Arab numbers and minimize the effects of Israeli technological superiority. The GCC countries, however, do not have an adequate population base upon which to build large land forces. In fact, in any large-scale military confrontation the forces of the external threat countries will probably far outnumber the forces the GCC can muster in its own defense. However, the geography of the Gulf minimizes the need to maintain large ground forces in a defensive mode, and confers a special strategic importance on air power and air and sea mobility. Thus, it is not surprising that the Gulf states have given priority to the modernization of their air forces and air defense capabilities.

The difficulty of expanding and modernizing air forces can be appreciated by the fact that it takes up to three years for even a highly trained squadron to convert to a more advanced type of fighter. The success and speed of such conversions is highly dependent on related major improvements in C^3I capabilities, as well as on appropriate changes in training methods and facilities.

The proliferation of fighter aircraft types can be seen in Tables 5.1 A and B. Each additional system further strains the logistical and support capabilities of the recipient state. The number of different systems under consideration or on order as of July 1985 indicates that GCC progress toward purchase of common aircraft types is still limited.

A front line squadron in NATO usually consists of some 15 aircraft. Using the totals in Tables 5.1 A and B, that would give the GCC countries—*on paper*—about 9 fighter squadrons (there are 14 in NATO), one interceptor squadron (Saudi Arabia's Lightnings), and 14 FGA squadrons.

The actual air strength of the GCC is nowhere near that suggested by the totals in Tables 5.1. The modernization carried out by Saudi Arabia has been well planned and so has avoided many of the problems discussed above. As a result, Saudi Arabia has just enough pilots to fly the combat inventory of F-5s and F-15s.[9] The air power of Kuwait and the UAE, however, appears to be more for show than readiness. Almost total reliance on foreign support has done little to make these squadrons effective. Oman's air force is effective because of heavy reliance on foreign pilots and technicians. The small quantities of aircraft for some of the smaller GCC states

---

[9] Thomas L. McNaugher, *Arms and Oil: U.S. Military Security Policy Toward the Persian Gulf* (Washington, D.C.: Brookings, 1985), pp. 212-213.

TABLE 5.1A

INVENTORIES OF COMBAT AIRCRAFT IN GCC INVENTORIES OR ON ORDER, CIRCA 1985

			COUNTRIES			
SYSTEM INTERCEPTOR/ AIR SUPERIORITY	BAHRAIN	KUWAIT	OMAN	QATAR	SAUDI ARABIA	UAE
Mirage F-1C/D		29		14		
Mirage 5A/D						30
Mirage 2000					?#	36*
F-4E	12*					
F-15C					45	
TF-15D					15	
Tornado ADV			8		?#	
Lightning F-53		12+			15x	
COUNTRY TOTALS:	0	12	0	14	72	61
TOTAL INTERCEPTOR/ AIR SUPERIORITY AIRCRAFT:				159		

TABLE 5.1B

INVENTORIES OF COMBAT AIRCRAFT IN GCC INVENTORIES OR ON ORDER, CIRCA 1985

			COUNTRIES			
SYSTEM FIGHTER/ GROUND ATTACK AIRCRAFT	BAHRAIN	KUWAIT	OMAN	QATAR	SAUDI ARABIA	UAE
A-4KU		30				
F-5E/F	12				85	
Jaguar S Mk1			20			
Alpha Jet				8		6
Hunter FGA Mk6			12	2		
BAC 167			12		46	
MB-326KD/LD						10
Hawk		?*				
COUNTRY TOTALS:	6	30	44	10	111	14
TOTAL FIGHTER/ GROUND ATTACK AIRCRAFT				215		

*On order.
x An additional 17 Lightning F-53s are in reserve.
+ In storage or used as reserve.
# Under negotiation as of July 1985.
Sources: *The Military Balance* (London: IISS, 1984–85); and *SIPRI Yearbook*, 1985; recent press reports.

suggest a grossly inefficient use of technical personnel, if indeed any serious effort is being made to support these systems.

Given the diversity and number of fighter aircraft already in GCC inventories or on order, the purchase of a common GCC fighter is not going to add appreciably to these states' capabilities until the beginning of the 1990s at the earliest, and joint logistical arrangements would have to be worked out in advance and a uniform structure of support across the GCC created. Since the GCC can be expected to continue to field a diverse array of aircraft, a practical near-term alternative is the integration of these aircraft and surface-to-air missile systems into a common network, linked to one another by compatible communications and as well to the Saudi AWACS. Unfortunately, this is much easier said than done. C^3 is the weakest link in the GCC's defense chain. Apart from the very technical complexity this approach involves, there remains the political fear in GCC capitals of the type of unified command structure needed to make an integrated C^3I system effective.

Despite the drawbacks, pursuit of these options remains attractive. These are among the few options that may enable the GCC states to begin a synthesis of their imported military technologies with existing social values and with the attitudes of their indigenous manpower. That is, a truly integrated C^3 takes advantage of the indigenous preferences for centralized command structures and vertical LOCs at the expense of horizontal ones.

Leaving aside the fictions portrayed by the AOB of the totals in Tables 5.1, a major deficiency of the GCC air forces is the absence of a real strike capability for deterrence purposes. The training and aircraft diversity of the smaller GCC states, given their shortages of skilled manpower; the size and operational readiness of their individual forces; and the lack of any assets for air battle management—all these factors virtually negate the value in the short or intermediate term of these air forces. By contrast, the RSAF has adequate size, pilot training, coherence, and air battle management support in the Gulf theater (the last currently dependent on U.S. assistance) to play the key role in GCC defense. Little wonder, then, that the RSAF is, in fact, the key to that defense.

Yet the goal of the RSAF should be to deter battles rather than merely win them, and if deterrence fails to win behind the front (where the oil fields are), not over or at it. The American and Saudi planners have creditably developed a solid air arm for the kingdom over the past decade, but have left it short of strike capabilities that will deter attacks or defeat them on the other side of the Gulf. The Saudis are upgrading the strike capabilities of their aircraft deployed in the Gulf and southern Red Sea theaters, and wisely so,

141

but how much these efforts will yield is questionable unless the RSAF seeks and obtains more advanced radar for strike missions.[10]

Until the GCC is able to plan a more coherent and coordinated air defense, the burden of air defense in the Gulf will fall on Saudi Arabia. The considerable problems and hurdles confronting improvements in the GCC's air forces apply much less to Saudi Arabia than to any or all the other GCC countries. Recent Saudi acquisitions have been planned to balance between deterrence and defense capabilities, and have been accompanied by meticulously drafted training and support plans that have been followed reasonably well. Supplier reticence has been a much greater factor in RSAF diversification than Saudi intent.

The Gulf-wide role of the RSAF was revealed during the so-called tanker crisis, when Saudi Arabia enjoyed GCC consensus in defending the skies over the Gulf against Iranian aircraft attacks on petroleum tankers. While the GCC is making some slow progress on coordination, the short term will undoubtedly continue to equate GCC air defense responsibility with Saudi air defense responsibility. The bottom line is that the Saudi air force will remain the GCC's best hope to protect the freedom of the Gulf over, as well as the sovereignty of, the Gulf lands.

GCC Land Forces

Modernization of the GCC's ground forces has proceeded more slowly and less completely than that of air forces if for no other reason than that ground forces are more intimately connected with the responsibilities of internal security. Moreover, air forces are "capital-intensive," which at least reduces the problems of chronic manpower shortages. By contrast, ground forces are necessarily "labor-intensive," which plays to one of the GCC's most serious weaknesses—the manpower shortage.

Not surprisingly, the most serious problems in the GCC's ground forces concern problems of manpower recruitment and retention in one form or another.

Saudi Arabia, Oman, and the UAE are better able than the other Gulf states to offer opportunities in the military that are at least competitive with opportunities in the civilian sector. It is easier and more reliable to make inferences about qualitative shortfalls in the ground forces based on equipment acquisitions than it is to infer very much from sociological generalizations about manpower qual-

---

[10] See also equipment recommendations in Chapter VI.

ities. Many key assignments in most of the GCC countries are still filled by officers who lack the proper training or by expatriates. Manpower retention problems are compounded by political factors, "influence peddling," and nepotism, all of which can lead to the promotion of the incompetent and the alienation or resignation of the competent. These problems are exacerbated by the tendency to divert officers and NCOs with specialist training into general positions because they have superior ability and education.[11]

The rate of modernization of the ground forces is further constrained because the army has traditionally been a career path of those with little family influence or connections. Leadership problems flow from this legacy, since such personnel have the weakest ties to the regime. The Gulf states still must weigh the appointment to key positions of officers from such backgrounds against the imperatives of internal security. This trade-off frequently results in retaining expatriates (especially in Oman and the UAE) or political loyalists in key positions regardless of their competence.

The acquisition pattern of major weapons systems in the ground forces (i.e., tanks and other AFVs) suggests shortcomings similar to those noted in the air forces. Figures on key equipment changes and rates of equipment transfer, when contrasted with Western and Soviet-bloc data, provide an indication of the extent to which some GCC countries may be buying more equipment than they can absorb.[12] As noted above, no army can increase its holdings of key weaponry like tanks and aircraft by more than 10 to 15 percent per year without adversely affecting manpower quality and combat readiness or putting forces on a wartime footing. Since the Gulf nations lack the military infrastructure that exists in Western or Soviet-bloc forces, their effective absorption rates must be much lower.

The number of medium tanks in the active force structures of the Gulf states is a useful indicator of equipment trends and modernization rates because Israel's successful use of armor in 1956 and 1967 made the tank the dominant weapon system for ground forces in the Middle East. As a rule of thumb, a modern division in an industrialized state has between 300 and 350 tanks. There are about 6,000 to 7,000 medium tanks in all the NATO forces in the Central Region.

The total number of medium tanks suggests the GCC has at least three modern NATO divisions' worth of military equipment, or

---

[11] Cordesman, *The Gulf*, p. 521.
[12] This section draws heavily on discussions and data presented in Ibid., pp. 528-537.

TABLE 5.2

NUMBERS AND TYPES OF MEDIUM TANKS IN ACTIVE FORCES CIRCA 1984–1985

SYSTEMS	COUNTRIES					
	BAHRAIN	KUWAIT	OMAN	QATAR	SAUDI ARABIA	UAE
M-60A1			6		150	
M-60A3					100@	
Centurion		50+				
Vickers Mk 1		70				
Chieftain Mk 7		160	27			
AMX-30				24	300	100
OF-40 MK2						36
Scorpion		160*	?			20
COUNTRY TOTALS	0	200	33	24	550	156
TOTAL MEDIUM TANKS:			910			

@ In addition to 150 M-60A3 conversion kits for 150 M-60A1s already in inventory.
* On order.
+ Some in storage, or used as reserve.
Source: *The Military Balance* (London: IISS, 1984–85.)

about 15 percent of all the tanks in the NATO Central Region. As in aircraft inventories, the actual capabilities of the GCC are nowhere near the firepower suggested by the totals in Table 5.2. The lightly armored forces of Qatar and Bahrain serve to guard the countries' leaders and are unlikely to be deployed beyond token strength to confront external threats. Omani forces are battle-tested in counter-insurgency operations, but lack the armor for any useful deployment against potential threats from Iran or Iraq. Kuwait's 10,000-man army looks impressive on paper, deploying two armored brigades and three infantry battalions. However, given the Kuwaiti penchant for recruiting mainly relatively unskilled Bedouins, there is no reason to assume that they can effectively deploy their Chieftain and Vickers tanks against a determined external threat. That leaves Saudi Arabia with about two armored brigades and two mechanized infantry brigades, plus other infantry formations deployed at various points around the kingdom. Annual rates of expansion far greater than even the NATO and Warsaw pact can absorb, such as characterize some of the GCC states (e.g., Kuwait and the UAE), stand in contrast to the reasonably methodical military buildup by Saudi Arabia and Oman.

GCC Naval Forces

The development of modern naval capabilities is a very recent endeavor. Like the ground forces, it marks the conversion of GCC naval services from shore patrol and coast guard activities, which are essentially internal security responsibilities, to the acquisition of an effective sea denial capability.

Since navies are more technology-intensive than air or land forces, the attempt to develop any modern naval capabilities might seem to be adding just another line of logistic, service and combat support requirements that will further aggravate shortages of indigenous skilled manpower. That is misleading for at least four reasons.

● First, the state of development of most threat (Ethiopian, Iranian, Iraqi) navies means that the requirements to construct either a defensive naval force or a deterrent naval strike capability are quite limited. Tremendous turnover in the Iranian navy has gutted what was once the only real navy in the Gulf. Today, small investments in naval power can have out-sized impact.

● Second, because of the limited defensive capabilities of threat navies, individual platforms may have relatively high firepower, meaning the manpower requirements to support that firepower may be limited.

● Third, the development of precision-guided anti-shipping missiles increases the lethality of missile-firing fast attack craft without requiring a commensurate amount of operator skill. In most cases, the missile's guidance systems relieve the operators of all but initial lock-on responsibilities. Thus, it may be easier to absorb new weaponry in naval warfare than in other sectors of the GCC's military modernization effort.

● Finally, as the Falklands and the Gulf wars have demonstrated, sea denial missions do not have to be performed by ships alone. Aircraft, properly armed, can effectively perform anti-shipping missions. The Saudi navy reflects this fact with 24 Dauphine 2 helicopters on order equipped to carry Otomat anti-shipping missiles. Although the Kuwaiti navy still concentrates on coast guard activities, it has on order six Super Puma helicopters equipped with Exocet anti-shipping missiles.

Since Gulf naval modernization is so recent, and most GCC naval equipment inventories remain "on order," very few strong inferences concerning their capabilities can be made. Nevertheless, one problem can already be seen on the horizon—the splitting of the sea denial mission between the GCC navies and their air forces. With the exception of Saudi Arabia, rotary-wing aircraft equipped with anti-shipping capabilities are on order by the GCC states' air forces, not their navies. This is a prescription for the development in inter-service rivalries (not entirely unheard of in the United States) and an impediment to developing an effective C^3 between sea and air platforms in any combined arms sea denial operations.

Economic Problems

Economic problems in the quality or pace of military modernization are related to the decline in the price of oil. The most serious economic difficulty involves not the GCC's ability to afford its military modernization, but additional barriers to intra-GCC coordination and integration of their respective modernization enterprises as they find themselves competing for a share of the declining world oil market. This competition has tended to pit the smaller GCC states against Saudi Arabia. The smaller sheikhdoms argue that their markets can be sustained only if Saudi Arabia agrees to absorb most of the cuts in production necessary to equalize supply and demand conditions in the worldwide market. Saudi Arabia's oil revenues have dropped more than 75 percent since 1981. This cleavage is reinforced by Iranian pressure on the smaller Gulf states to support Iranian oil policy (i.e., higher prices and continued production), just as it exerted pressure on them to refrain from increased cooperation with and support for Iraq in the Gulf war.[13]

Until recently, Saudi Arabia was absorbing a disproportionate share of the worldwide decline in production. In the fall of 1978, it was producing 10.4 MBD. The average daily production for 1985 was 2.5 million barrels per day (BPD), well below the OPEC quota for the kingdom of 4.353 million BPD. Saudi Arabia has been alone among its OPEC partners in continuing to charge the cartel's official price while other members have offered deep discounts in an effort to increase demand and production. From an economic standpoint, Saudi Arabia can easily win a price war since it has the lowest production costs in the industry, but at the cost of intensifying

---

[13] Iranian proximity to Kuwait is sufficient to give it some clout in influencing Kuwait's oil policy. In the case of the UAE, the sheikhdom of Sharjah receives an annual payment from Iran as part of a settlement reached when the shah was still in power, allowing Iran to occupy the island of Abu Musa.

political tensions between Riyadh and the smaller Gulf states as well as Iraq and Iran.

Saudi Arabia and Kuwait had been marketing some oil (about 300,000 BPD from the Neutral Zone) for Iraq. An equivalent amount of Iraqi oil is now shipped through the Saudi Red Sea port of Yanbu via the Saudi pipeline, which Iraq expects to boost to 500,000 BPD in the near future (in exchange, Saudi Arabia and Kuwait are no longer marketing oil for Iraq from the Neutral Zone). Iraq had been producing some 1.2 MBD prior to the opening of the pipeline. Iraq's stepped-up production was preceded in mid-August 1985 by what Baghdad claimed was its biggest air strike against Iran's vital oil export outlet of Kharg Island since the war with Iran began in 1980.

If the Iraqi raid proves to be the beginning of sustained attacks to put Kharg Island out of business, it will both make more room for Iraq's increased oil exports and tie Saudi Arabia much closer to the Iraq war effort.[14] This in turn will introduce more cleavages in Saudi Arabia's relations with the smaller GCC states. Iran may well mount retaliatory attacks, since its relative economic advantage over Iraq depends entirely on its ability to ship its oil through the Strait of Hormuz. Unlike Iraq, Iran has no overland route to the outside, except through the Soviet Union. So far the Soviets have shown little interest other than in the Igat 1 gas pipeline. Thus, if Iraq were to embark on a campaign to cut off Iran's oil exports while increasing its own, Iran could try to retaliate through harassing attacks on any of the Arab Gulf states that support Iraq and carrying out its intermittent threat to close the entire Gulf to all oil shipments.

A less dramatic but no less serious problem stemming from the decline in oil revenues is the prospect of cuts in defense expenditures. In that event, it is likely that initial cuts may be made in the costs of foreign support activities rather than in the cancellation of weapons purchases previously ordered. Such a trend would only reduce the ability of the GCC states to effectively absorb their new equipment and so prolong their military weakness in the face of regional threats.

Conclusion

The principal problems confronting the evolution of a viable collective defense regime in the Gulf are (1) developmental, (2) geo-

---

[14] It is not known whether Saudi Arabia agreed to accept the extra Iraqi production for transit in its pipeline to Yanbu.

graphical, and (3) structural. This chapter has discussed political, social, military, and economic hurdles that impede rapid movement toward such a regime.

The developmental problems derive from the Third World nature of the Gulf environment. They reflect the disjunction between social patterns that have evolved over centuries and conflict with the requisites of modernization, on the one hand, and the elements of contemporary military development, which is equally dependent upon those requisites, on the other. Developmental hurdles also arise in opportunity-cost dilemmas—comparative estimates of cost and benefit as between weapons systems, as between weapons and men, and among different economic sectors. The political and strategic choices that confront Gulf leaders must often come back to difficult economic choices just as they often shape economic choices. Some of these trade-offs are central to any defense planning, anywhere.

Geographical problems arise from the multiplicity of threats facing the Gulf states, and particularly Saudi Arabia, which must pay attention to the Red Sea and Indian Ocean threats as well as to the Gulf. Indeed, this is one of the primary strategic problems of the GCC. While the most valuable and vulnerable GCC targets are clustered in the Gulf, the only member of the alliance with any substantial protective military power cannot concentrate its forces there, because that power, Saudi Arabia, must maintain readiness against an increasingly hostile group of countries over 1,000 miles from the Gulf itself. The GCC oil facilities remain attractive targets for capture, as well as for blackmail. Lying literally on the international frontiers, none of the GCC states has space to trade for time.

Finally, we have considered the structural problems of the GCC at some length. Saudi Arabia dominates the GCC, and it may certainly be said that without Saudi Arabia—without Saudi political leadership, economic strength, and military resources—there could be no GCC. The kingdom is the core of the GCC, and its military assets, limited as they are, undeniably constitute the security backbone of the organization. Yet, even as American domination of NATO provoked some jealousies and concerns in Europe, Saudi domination of the GCC, which is relatively far more one-sided, also raises concerns in the Gulf.

The GCC is a new institution. As such, its members have only begun to alter their defense decision-making patterns in order to reflect the commonality of concerns that the GCC symbolizes and the need for coordination that it lacks. Procurement patterns within the GCC vary markedly among its members: Saudi Arabia and

148

Oman, in particular, have begun to develop careful methods for systems evaluation that take into account national strategy, manpower constraints, training requirements, and the like; while some other GCC countries continue to acquire systems for "passive deterrence" (show) rather than "active deterrence" (performance). Integration of the wide diversity of weapons systems in the GCC into something like a coherent unified force structure is, at best, a long way off. Meanwhile, the key to GCC capabilities and deterrent credibility remains its dominant member Saudi Arabia: if Saudi plans and military development continue to move forward creditably, the GCC will have to be taken seriously, at least by potential threat nations in the Gulf. If Saudi military development loses momentum, direction, or coherence, the impact will necessarily be felt heavily within the GCC.

VI

THREAT AND RESPONSE: PROTECTING U.S. INTERESTS IN THE GULF

The GCC will be no more effective than Saudi Arabia is, for given the asymmetry of power in the organization it can never escape its dependence on the largest member. The United States should continue to support increased GCC coordination, should provide the kinds of support that might facilitate reinforcement from outside the Gulf, and should encourage further efforts at joint exercising and cooperative procurement. Saudi Arabia should seek improved C^3I for coordination and radar and other aircraft enhancements to provide the GCC limited strike capabilities as a deterrent, and should procure advanced technologies with limited operator skills and maintenance requirements.

Introduction

Important U.S. and Western interests are at stake in the Gulf, a region subject to increasing pressure hostile to those interests and where the recourse to violence has grown dramatically. The first line of defense of Western interests remains the countries in which those interests are located. As we have seen, the GCC has some

151

potential for achieving capabilities adequate at least to protect the most important U.S. interests in this regard. Realization of this potential will require time and some outside support and encouragement.

What is manifestly absent at this time is deterrent capacity. Yet, there are few environments in the world more clearly suitable for deterrence than the Gulf, given the location of primary targets. The essential platforms, or key weapons systems, already exist in Gulf inventories. However, these systems are not at this time equipped for or oriented toward the creation of a deterrence system.

A policy of enhancing the GCC's ability to deter regional threats is clearly beneficial to U.S. interests in the region. If, however, such a policy is to be effective, it must be designed and implemented in a way that does not inadvertently undermine the Gulf countries' political system in general and their internal security in particular. Thus, the protection of American interests in the Gulf must be considered in the context of some important "parameters" alluded to in earlier chapters, but which now must be made more explicit:

• A highly visible U.S. role in these states could more easily lead to a weakening of their internal security and their political cohesion by undermining the political legitimacy of the GCC governments.[1] Thus, the American role cannot rest exclusively on formal commitments which are often politically unacceptable to the U.S. Congress and to the Gulf leaderships alike.

• The GCC as a defensive alliance created with the purpose of bringing the organization's collective resources to bear on the security problems of any one of its member countries is a positive development from an American policy perspective; but it is not the GCC that adds to the member countries' defensive capabilities, it is Saudi Arabia and the Saudi armed forces. Saudi Arabia will survive without the GCC, but the GCC cannot exist without Saudi Arabia. Therefore, by concentrating on strengthening certain of Saudi Arabia's military capabilities, the United States can in effect strengthen the viability and effectiveness of Gulf defense as a whole.

• A practical point of departure for enhancing the deterrent and defensive capabilities of the GCC is to concentrate on the development of air power. This approach favors the resources of the low-

---

[1] Except, of course, in the most extreme crises that might confront the Gulf. In these cases, however, cooperation with and support from the United States would be readily sought by the Gulf leaders themselves.

population states, and facilitates the protection of the Arabian Peninsula as a whole, which is much easier militarily than defending individual states on it.

• Further steps toward coordination and integration of the conservative Gulf states' military forces must assume the continued diversity of equipment types across air, land, and naval systems for the near term and even longer, and accommodate themselves accordingly to that reality. The pace of further integration will be conditioned by the structural inertia imposed by time-honored practices of decentralized military establishments for a variety of reasons already addressed.

Every additional step the conservative Gulf states take toward further military cooperation will have two important effects on U.S. interests. First, it will reduce the need for American or any other Western intervention in the area. Second, it can make such intervention easier and more effective in "worst-case" situations where it becomes necessary. GCC cooperation in C^{3}I, in planning, in cross-basing, in creating a joint command, in development of an effective air defense system, and joint efforts in training and support will inevitably increase the risk to any adversary that an attack on the southern Gulf states will draw U.S. forces into the region. These same steps will increase the ease with which the United States can support a friendly Gulf state against a major military coup, terrorist campaign, or insurgency, and will allow the United States to increasingly substitute technical aid, technical support, or equipment transfers for the deployment of forces. Optimization of Gulf security resources by striving for a division of labor between the GCC states and the United States appears the most appropriate and feasible means to defend U.S. interests in the Gulf.

Optimizing Security Resources

The United States, in cooperation with other Western countries, can protect Western interests in the Gulf by focusing its security assistance policy on four interrelated objectives.

• First, it can encourage a division of labor among the GCC members, centered on Saudi Arabia, that provides at least the common air battle management and joint training necessary to allow Gulf forces to fight as a common unit and so to enhance their credibility

153

as a deterrent to regional adversaries. This aim focuses on the effective integration and coordinated use of existing assets.

• Second, in the event that deterrence fails, the division of labor should enable the Gulf states to buy time for outside reinforcement to occur. This objective focuses on the problems of waging an effective defense, especially an effective air and coastal defense. Such a capability is more than a matter of effective coordination of existing forces for a common defense. Other issues include the kind of equipment to be acquired that would enable the Gulf states to buy as much time as they can and to make outside reinforcement as timely and as effective as possible.

• Third, the United States can assist the GCC states in developing a portion of their ground forces to the point where they are capable of providing more effective protection of key oil installations and handling peninsular threats from the Yemens.

• Fourth, American assistance must make provision for the need to facilitate outside help to defend against large-scale overland attacks (e.g., an invasion by allied Iraqi and Iranian forces) or concentrated air attacks. The principal role of external reinforcement is to prevent outside intervention in peninsular conflicts.

The Development of Effective Air Power

The strategic advantages that geography confers upon airpower as an "equalizer" for low-population countries in the Gulf were noted in an earlier chapter. An effective, coordinated air defense is the sector in which surprise attack is the most likely and where the political damage to regime security from such harassing attacks can be far more extensive than whatever physical damage they may cause. Furthermore, the air forces are not seen as posing the type of internal threat associated with ground forces. Thus, it is not surprising that the GCC governments have already placed top priority on this defense sector. Service in the air force is sufficiently prestigious that recruiting and retention problems are relatively minor.

Gulf cooperation in the development of compatible C^3I links with appropriate IFF systems and Saudi AWACS-type sensors netting aircraft, land-based air defenses, and land-based command centers could evolve into a persuasive collective deterrent against local threats without sacrificing the member countries' sovereignty. It would increase the credibility of over-the-horizon reinforcement from the United States without making any formal arrangements or agreements with Washington.

Joint training for the GCC's air forces can be accomplished far more quickly than for land and naval forces. The development of C³I links between Saudi Arabia's AWACS and GCC air forces and land-based air defenses does not require the introduction of a common fighter aircraft as long as different aircraft have compatible communications equipment. Joint exercises to develop teamwork among pilots flying different aircraft are more important. Without such exercises, coordination even among pilots flying the same aircraft would be largely ineffective. Although the GCC states have diverse aircraft on order for the mid- to late 1980s, most of them will have the capacity to be equipped with compatible avionics, onboard computers and software, IFF and early warning (EW) systems, air armament, and refueling and outboard tank capabilities to support operation as a unified air screen. GCC joint air exercises have reflected rapidly developing capabilities in this regard. They can be fitted with sufficiently advanced avionics and munitions-carrying capabilities to enable them to operate effectively with the RSAF and AWACS. The negative effects of using diverse platforms can also be reduced if the GCC can cooperate on the standardizing of munitions they acquire with their aircraft.

While the individual air forces cannot cross-service each other, they can already cross-disperse, arm, and fuel one another's aircraft. It is possible that some cooperative maintenance organization could be developed, for aircraft procured by more than one state, with each state responsible for a set of key components. Even if this sort of cooperative effort could be implemented between only two states, the effect would be to make more efficient use of scarce manpower resources.

A similar sort of integration and coordination can be achieved with land-based air defenses, particularly around the Improved HAWK (I-HAWK) surface-to-air missile system. These are being procured by Saudi Arabia, Kuwait, Bahrain, Qatar, and the UAE. Kuwait and the UAE have expressed an interest in linking their I-HAWKS with Saudi Arabia's AWACS. A link-up with AWACS would improve the effectiveness of the I-HAWK and all other GCC ground-based radars. Area coverage can be expanded further if the UAE goes ahead with a decision to purchase the Grumman E-2C HAWKEYE, since parts of the UAE are sufficiently far from the Saudi AWACS umbrella to warrant an independent (but integrated) AEW capability. A rough sort of standardization can also be devised for shorter-range air defense missile systems such as the Crotale

155

(Qatar, UAE), Improved Crotale or Shahine (Saudi Arabia, Kuwait, Qatar), Rapier (Oman, UAE), or the RBS-70 Rayrider (UAE) SAMS. The GCC states could buy Improved Hawks and compatible C³I links for their anti-aircraft guns and missiles, standardized on the Shahine. Such a concentration would make the US (Raytheon) and France (Matra/Thomson-CSF) the "standard" suppliers for ground-based air defense. This sort of standardization would enable the GCC to use available data links and IFF systems to develop a credible collective deterrent against local threats without sacrificing their sovereignty. Even if some of the Improved HAWK batteries are undermanned or in storage for lack of qualified crews to operate them, it may still be useful for the GCC governments to procure more of them, on the assumption that, in times of crisis, these units could be manned by experts from various reinforcing nations, including the United States. French advisors are reportedly manning Kuwait's Shahine missile batteries deployed on Bubiyan Island, which is adjacent to Iraq.[2] These SAM batteries can increase the credibility of over-the-horizon reinforcement from the United States and France[3] without concluding any formal security arrangements with the United States.

Buying Time for Reinforcement to Occur

The GCC must be concerned with not only building local capabilities, but also facilitating the delivery of help against a major regional threat, including contingencies such as a land attack by Iranian or Iraqi forces driving south through Kuwait. The upgrading of local capabilities to meet such a threat and the advance planning necessary to permit timely external reinforcement are not mutually exclusive enterprises. The GCC forces must be able to delay, and deny any decisive victory to, the attacker before help can arrive. Presumably, the attacking force in such a scenario will be much larger than the forces the GCC can deploy for its defense. Low-cost powered munitions dispensers e.g., Messerschmitt-Bolko-Blom's MW-1, or Brunswick's Low Altitude Defense System (LADS), which could be adapted to current aircraft such as the F-5E (Saudi Arabia, Bahrain), the A-4KU (Kuwait), the Mirage F-1 (Kuwait, Qatar), or the Alpha Jet (UAE, Qatar),[4] can carry anti-armor and anti-per-

---

[2] Michael Collins Dunn, "Can the Gulf Secure Itself?" *Defense & Foreign Affairs*, June 1985, p. 9.

[3] The subject of over-the-horizon reinforcement is discussed later.

[4] The MW-1, however, is over 18 feet long and weighs 11,200 pounds when loaded with 8,800 pounds of submunitions, and therefore is too heavy for most aircraft

sonnel munitions. Others, such as MBB's Verbal/Syndrom,[5] combine sensors and low-cost anti-tank missiles or rockets in one pod.[6] The effect of these munitions dispensers is a "force multiplier" analogous to a flying shotgun. They would enable defending GCC forces to lace potential enemy routes of advance or choke points with sensor-activated anti-tank mines in advance of invading forces. They can also be used to take out enemy missile batteries. Self-powered munitions dispensers are area weapons and so require lower levels of pilot skill than point target munitions such as Maverick. The addition of weapons dispensers and the appropriate stocks of anti-armor submunitions to aircraft inventories should not impose additional manpower demands nor should their utilization require extensive training.

The use of smart area denial munitions can be applied to the GCC ground forces as well. Anti-armor munitions such as SKEET can be packaged in 155 millimeter (mm) artillery shells or used in LADS airborne munitions dispensers. The SADARM (Search and Destroy Armor) is a roughly similar eight-inch howitzer submunition. These and similar area denial submunitions can be adapted to artillery tubes already in the inventories of the Saudi and Kuwaiti armies. Therefore their introduction does not require converting to an entirely new system. Tactically, it could give Saudi and Kuwaiti ground forces charged with blocking an invasion from Iran and Iraq a significant boost in firepower. These munitions can be used to disrupt an enemy advance in enemy-controlled territory. They offer the potential of enabling GCC forces to "hold" enemy territory with firepower even though their prime targets—vehicles and armored forces—are movable. There is a sufficient array of airborne sensors that can accurately locate targets on the move—*and relay the location in real time*—so that they can be stopped by static defending forces when appropriately netted to an effective AEW&C system. Apart from the question of adequate C³I links, the incorporation of area denial submunitions offers tremendous enhancements in fire-

---

except the Tornado IDS and the F-15. Two LADS dispensers weighing 2,000 to 3,000 pounds each can be carried aboard an F-16 or an F-20, and the F-15 can carry four. Northrop has designed a dispenser, the ND-7, that is compatible with the F-5 family of fighters. Presumably, the LADS or the ND-7 could be compatible with the Mirage F-1 and the Alpha Jet. See Benjamin F. Schemmer, "NATO's New Strategy: Strike Deep," *Armed Forces Journal International*, November 1982, pp. 50-59.

[5] Verbal is a contraction of "Verbal Balistics," and Syndrom describes the synergistic effect of sensors and aircraft dynamics in aiming the munitions tubes. See *Armed Forces Journal International*, January 1984, p. 19.

[6] The possible political problems involved in the attempt by the GCC states to buy such equipment from West Germany are discussed below.

power while not requiring a commensurate upgrade in operator skills.

The adaptation of powered munitions dispensers to GCC strike aircraft and the licensed production of the submunitions they carry could provide a useful springboard for the further development of a GCC domestic armaments industry.

Development of Ground Forces for Peninsular Security

The conservative Gulf states' ground forces vary considerably in size and structure. For reasons discussed above, the pace of modernization will be slow. Therefore, it is not surprising that the missions of most of the GCC's land forces and the decentralized nature of their organizational structures are still tied rather closely to maintaining internal security.

The ground forces of Bahrain and Qatar are very small, and are unlikely to be deployed beyond token strength against external threats to the GCC. Similarly, for all practical purposes, the orientation of the federal forces of the UAE is almost exclusively toward internal security.[7] The structure of the Sultan of Oman's Land Forces evolved out of the Dhofar rebellion. They remain primarily light infantry forces geared for counter-insurgency warfare. They would be of little help to Saudi Arabia and Kuwait in facing threats from Iran and Iraq. SANG also remains essentially a tribally based internal security force. Its primary mission is to ensure the loyalty of Saudi Arabia's tribes. It has only gradually recruited new and educated personnel whose loyalties are to the service and not to a given tribal leader.[8]

The configuration of these forces to deal primarily with peninsular threats, as distinct from country-specific threats, does not appear to offer much pay-off for the foreseeable future. A concerted push by the United States to expand and accelerate the modernization of these forces for the purpose of meeting external threats could easily create internal political problems by highlighting closer ties between host governments and Washington. It could also exacerbate any social problems associated with recruitment and retention difficulties these forces already may be experiencing.

What remains to deal with external threats are the two armored

---

[7] See, for example, John Keegan, *World Armies* (2nd ed., pp. 603-604). The principal "regional commands" barely disguise the fact that the constituent forces remain almost semi-private forces of the sheikhdoms they represent.

[8] Cordesman, *The Gulf*, p. 365.

and one mechanized brigades of the Kuwait infantry and the RSA. Saudi Arabia cannot afford the political and military consequences of leaving a major base or front undefended. Therefore, the army is dispersed to cover (unreinforced) threats from the Yemens[9] (about two mechanized brigades at Khamis Mushayt and a smaller outpost at Sharar); to protect Tabuk in the northwest corner of the kingdom (most of its armored, paratroop, and commando units); and to block any invasion through Kuwait (at King Khalid Military City at Wadi al-Batin, with a capacity for three brigades). Other infantry units are dispersed about the kingdom, including outposts near the Iraqi border.

Many RSA units are under-strength. The most serious problem, however, is their lack of mobility. The Saudi army is so widely dispersed throughout the kingdom that it takes a week to ten days to concentrate significant forces on a given front. For example, during an outbreak of fighting between North and South Yemen in 1979, US Air Force C-5As had to be called in to airlift tanks from Tabuk for redeployment in the south.

U.S. assistance in developing air-mobile units provides a potential solution to this problem. This approach could be confined exclusively to Saudi Arabia (to which most of the assistance would be directed, in any case). It could build also on the limited progress the GCC has made in developing its own rapid deployment force and on the experience these units have gained in the two GCC-wide maneuvers, Peninsula Shield 1983 and 1984. Kuwaiti A-4s and Saudi F-5Es have demonstrated reasonably good coordination in joint air maneuvers. While coordination among the ground forces has not been as effective as the air exercises, there is no reason not to expect steady improvement with additional experience. Joint maneuvers of the ground forces are conducted at the battalion level, which does not require the degree of coordination of maneuvers at, say, the brigade level (a level which, for all practical purposes, is irrelevant to the GCC anyway).

This option involves a phased and integrated provision of attack and troop helicopters to equip air-mobile units and so provide for

---

[9] The quantity of aircraft and armored fighting vehicles that is being transferred to the PDRY is far in excess of what the South Yemeni forces can possibly absorb in the foreseeable future—e.g., the tank inventory equals or exceeds Saudi Arabia's— or needs to face any conceivable threat on the peninsula. And South Yemen, unlike some other Soviet clients, does not maintain an active re-transfer program of major end-items. Thus, it is difficult to escape the conclusion that the tank and aircraft inventories constitute a form of pre-positioning for external reinforcement from Cuba, Ethiopia, Libya, Syria, or even from the Soviet Union.

159

rapid concentration of force and compensate for the GCC's lack of experience in large-scale maneuver. The vast expanse of Saudi territory, the political and military imperatives requiring more than token coverage on a number of fronts, plus the capability to rapidly deploy in answer to crises in the smaller GCC states makes the idea of air-mobile forces appealing. Such a force, however, will require considerable unity of command over the air-ground battle and rapid and secure voice links with the Saudi C³I center in Riyadh to coordinate with air and coastal defenses.

One advantage of organizing air-mobile units on a GCC-wide grid is that such an organization will give the smaller states a stake in closer coordination of their defense efforts with Saudi Arabia while still preserving their sovereignty. In particular, this approach to structuring the ground forces should contribute organizational momentum toward an integrated and unified command structure to take advantage of the C³I infrastructure already in place in Saudi Arabia.

Facilitating External Reinforcement

The fundamentals facilitating external reinforcement from the GCC states' major power suppliers can be summarized in two words: overbuild and overbuy.

Reinforcement is facilitated by the availability of spare parts, support facilities, petroleum, oil and lubricants (POL) stocks, and munitions in the GCC countries in quantities that are far larger than those required for local forces alone. Bases need to be able to accommodate the logistics requirements of the supplier as well as the host forces. Runways at key airfields, for example, should accommodate oversized transport aircraft like the C-5A/B, not just C-130s. The need for a logistical base to support incoming forces makes it advisable to transfer or pre-position some major equipment critical to the reinforcing powers' forces. Some of the more prominent items might include tanks, surface-to-air missiles, communications equipment, and sensors. In this regard, the purchase of M-60A3 main battle tanks may prove to be a prudent investment, followed by the purchase of the M-1 (equipped with a 120MM gun) rather than the Leopard II. As a rule of thumb it makes sense, where possible, to transfer major equipment items that will be found in the projection forces of the external power. Whether by coincidence or design, the GCC states' equipment inventories are domi-

160

nated by weapons from the United States and France—the two countries most able to provide reinforcement in times of crisis.[10]

A policy of overbuy, overbuild, and pre-position is likely to increase the required number of skilled personnel needed for maintenance and support operations. The logical source of such manpower is from the external supplier—for two reasons. First, and most obviously, it is in the supplier country where the skilled people familiar with the weapons transferred are most plentiful. Second, the presence of expatriate personnel from the supplying power not only minimizes further strain on indigenous human resources, but puts in place a "skeleton crew" from the supplying power to interface local facilities with equipment and materials sent by the reinforcing power if necessary. The presence of such personnel is also visible evidence of the supplier country's commitment to supporting the security of the host government. That in itself can provide some deterrence against potential threats.

Undoubtedly, the most important area of development is an integrated C^3I apparatus compatible with U.S. Air Force (USAF) and U.S. Navy (USN) ability to operate with Saudi and American AWACS in providing over-the-horizon reinforcement in situations of high-density air threats. This approach presumes equipping the Saudi AWACS and an integrated Saudi C^3I network with frequency-agile, secure voice links (the Have Quick and Seek Talk frequency-agile voice links) and some kind of jam-resistant joint battlefield information system similar to but perhaps less advanced than the Joint Tactical Information Distribution System (JTIDS), necessary to manage high density air battles of the kind that could develop in the Gulf in the late 1980s. The absence of such equipment means reliance on slow communications without automated support and reduces an integrated AWACS-centered C^3I system's ability to handle high-density attacks. Given the location of so many key targets in the oil fields so close to the Gulf coast, secure and rapid communications between the ground and air are essential. Without adequate links between aircraft and radars, elements of the same system (especially if that system is suddenly reinforced by external elements) can threaten one another more than they threaten the common enemy.

Since it is air power that will bear the earliest and heaviest brunt of any sustained external attack, the reinforcement of GCC air

---

[10] For a description of French reinforcement capabilities, see Giovanni de Briganti, "Forces d'Action Rapide: France's Rapid Deployment Force," *Armed Forces Journal International*, October 1984, pp. 122-123.

assets can be expected to be one of the earliest demands for over-the-horizon reinforcement. The GCC countries would prefer to avoid direct intervention of foreign combat units on the ground unless such intervention is absolutely necessary to avert defeat and the collapse of one or more of the GCC governments. The United States would also prefer to avoid such direct involvement if possible. If an extreme situation materialized, the GCC would undoubtedly prefer the intervention of Egyptian and Jordanian ground forces (supported by American or French sea and airlift operations) to the intervention of American or French troops. Therefore, effective over-the-horizon reinforcement of GCC air capabilities will be crucial. Technical barriers to the rapid linking of USAF and USN assets to Saudi/GCC integrated C^3I could decisively degrade any over-the-horizon reinforcement that proves necessary.

Filling the Gaps, Meeting the Shortfalls: Options

Filling gaps and meeting shortfalls in the short term means building on what is in place in order to make it work more effectively for the common defense. A primary direction should consist of actions that encourage the GCC states to cooperate in developing—at the very least—the common air battle management capability and the joint training necessary to allow the air forces of the conservative Gulf states to fight in a coordinated manner. The smaller Gulf air forces are even more dependent on AWACS-type sensor and C^3I links than is the RSAF. The problems of air defense are almost insurmountable when a country has only one real air base, exceedingly small numbers of modern air defense fighters, if any, and no effective independent radar coverage of the critical targets it must defend. All the GCC countries will require an AWACS capability to provide C^3I links to their fighters, land-based command centers and air defenses and links to their neighbors to make up for their limited numbers of fighters. Without such links, Iran, Soviet long-range aviation, or even the Yemeni and Iraqi forces of the late 1980s may be able to attack the smaller conservative states at will. However, many of the weaknesses in the smaller GCC states will become significant only to the extent these states' armed forces are decoupled from their neighbors and from the possibility of U.S. reinforcement.

Development of an effective, modern military posture in the conservative Gulf countries is not possible in isolation of collateral measures to strengthen the GCC or some of its constituent members politically. The organization's most obviously indispensable political asset is Saudi leadership. The initial momentum achieved toward additional cooperation and coordination of efforts in defense matters between 1981 and 1983 did not take the form of a multilateral treaty signed by all member states. Instead, a series of bilateral treaties—signed by Saudi Arabia and four of the five other future members—led to the GCC.[11] Patient Saudi diplomacy played a decisive role in bringing together the GCC states to reach an agreement on the creation of a Gulf rapid deployment force and the announcement of plans to create a joint command. Recognition of this unique and core role of Saudi Arabia is central to strengthening the GCC politically and militarily.

Building on Saudi Arabia's Infrastructure

Effective development of a Gulf defense structure must be built on the Saudi armed forces. Saudi Arabia has made the most progress in absorbing Western military technology. Only Saudi Arabia has the military infrastructure on which to build an effective, integrated Gulf-wide defense force. Unlike Iran under the shah, Saudi Arabia has managed a reasonably smooth transition to modern armed forces. The Saudis have not tried to push the pace of their defense modernization so excessively as to disrupt their training system or hopelessly dilute their pool of qualified technical personnel. Consequently, the Saudi command structure has steadily improved since the early 1960s without disruptions in its continuity. The combination of an increasingly professional career structure, the increasing use of merit promotion (including promotion of people from non-traditional manpower sources, like the Nejd, without discrimination), good pay and privileges, and the avoidance of corrupt conscription and forced manpower retention measures, has eliminated much of the tension and moral difficulties within the armed forces that existed in the early 1970s.

---

[11] Kuwait remained "odd man out" of these arrangements partly out of fear of Oman's ties with the United States, partly in deference to the threat of increased radical or Iranian- or Soviet-backed activity if Kuwait supported too strong an effort toward collective defense. In addition, Kuwait appears to have objected most strenuously to the extradition clause of the proposed bilateral agreement with Saudi Arabia, on the grounds that it violates the Kuwaiti constitution. Kuwait also objects to a clause that would allow forces of one country to pursue suspects up to twenty kilometers inside the territory of another. See *Middle East Economic Digest*, XXVII, December 2, 1983, p. 6.

The result of this steady development has been the emergence of one of the most effective middle and senior grade officer corps in the region. Other Gulf and Arab military establishments have had greater experience with modern weapons and far more combat experience. However, constant political purges and rotations of all ranks have left most of them with a far weaker command structure than the extent of their experience with modern military technologies would suggest. The institutional coherence of the Saudi command structure is absolutely crucial to successful defense of the lower Gulf.

During the 1970s, about 90 percent of the military agreements Saudi Arabia signed with the United States were for the purchase of construction services, infrastructure, training, and other elements necessary to prepare the Saudi armed forces to operate large quantities of military equipment. Saudi Arabia as a result is now reaching the point where it can operate modern armed forces in a manner and on a scale that permit planning of effective and successful defense against most potential threats on its borders. During the 1970s, the RSAF successfully transitioned to modern fighters like the F-5E. In the 1980s it has managed the successful transition to the F-15. The Saudi Army has similarly moved to tanks like the AMS-30 and the M-60A3.

Whatever form a collective GCC security posture may ultimately take, only Saudi Arabia's military stands a chance of deterring most forms of regional aggression without the other GCC states should the occasion require it; but there can be no GCC without Saudi Arabia, even if the smaller members had made more progress in effectively absorbing their modern equipment and had made purchases that conformed more closely with their strategic and tactical requirements than they often have.

Upgrading Saudi A WACS-Based C³I for Gulf Defense

A final stage in Saudi Arabia's investment in basic infrastructure is in an integrated C³I system, based on the elements of the Air Defense Enhancements package already in place, that does much more than provide the necessary infrastructure for combined arms operations for the Saudi military: such a system constitutes the only logical foundation for an efficient, integrated approach to linking the air forces, the ground-based air defense units, and the command centers of the other GCC states to a military posture that can deter most forms of aggression in the Gulf and establish a sound basis for collective security with the lower Gulf states.

Therefore, Saudi Arabia must develop integrated C³I that nets the forces of the other GCC states and meets the needs of Gulf-wide defense, but that also respects the sovereignty of each GCC member. This approach is not only politically advisable for the sake of promoting cooperation within the GCC and placating the political sensitivities of the smaller members; it is crucial to avoid the degradation of the C³I system should one of the smaller member states be overwhelmed, even temporarily, by enemy forces in times of crisis. It is on this premise that all other useful options for filling current gaps rest.

The Strengthening of Passive Air Defenses

Passive defenses take advantage of the fact that the most serious regional threats confronting the conservative Gulf states are somewhat diminished by their own incomplete absorption of modern military technologies. Their problems are compounded by weakened command structures resulting from political purges and other sources of rapid personnel turnover.

Passive air defenses include dispersing aircraft, hardening of key aircraft maintenance facilities, and storage depots. They involve building shelters or runway revetments which are effective measures against harassing air attacks that can occur with little warning. Ideally, hardened shelters should be standardized so they could accommodate almost any of the major types of fighters in the GCC states' inventories, including those on order or currently under consideration. Standardized hardened aircraft shelters and maintenance facilities not only offer immediate protection; they provide some initial infrastructure for cross-servicing and ultimately cross-basing.

Such measures compound the weaknesses in threat forces. Aircraft in hardened shelters can survive near misses. Their destruction will require aggressor air forces to use point target munitions like air-to-surface missiles instead of area denial munitions. The former require much more pilot skill (and courage) and increase attacking aircraft exposure to ground-based anti-aircraft defenses.

The attacker's problems can be further compounded by hardening of key oil, air terminal, and port facilities, and of other strategic targets where feasible. An important feature of hardening key facilities is that, once built, they have no personnel requirements and are politically inert. Therefore, they comport well with GCC resource and political constraints discussed in earlier chapters.

The Need for Air Defense Aircraft Capable of Strike Missions

An active air defense includes effective battlefield air interdiction (BAI) capabilities. BAI usually involves disabling threat air forces by destroying the runways (if not some aircraft on the ground), anti-aircraft gun and missile defenses, and other support infrastructure required for sustained use of airpower. The mission also includes disrupting the advance of attacking formations on the ground by striking routes of march, staging areas, or choke points.

The development of such mission capabilities among the GCC air forces does not necessarily require the purchase of still more diverse aircraft types. As we have noted, some of the aircraft currently in inventory or on order could be adapted to utilized weapons dispensers such as LADS. Another obvious measure is the conversion of the RSAF F-15s to fly strike missions. This would utilize the conformal fuel tanks (for extended range) already procured, but would also include multiple ejection racks (MER) to carry a wider variety of munitions and an additional hardpoint on the fuselage. The Saudi and other GCC air forces must be able to effectively perform ground attack missions for the purposes of BAI as well as for counter-insurgency operations. Absent the development of an effective ground attack capability, the GCC may not be able to delay a full-scale invasion from Iran or Iraq (or a full-scale invasion of Oman from South Yemen) long enough for external reinforcement to do very much good.

Strengthening Air Defense Strike Capabilities and Oil Field Security with ESM

Oil field security is a clear American interest, and a major factor linking Gulf security to Western security. Oil field security and protection against external infiltration, especially by Iranian-supported terrorists, is an area in which the United States can provide important technical assistance. Specifically, such assistance could involve the use of electronic warfare support measures (ESM).

ESM refers to the detection and analysis of communications (including radio and radar frequency transmissions) to separate them into friendly, neutral, and hostile transmissions. Specific examples include tank radios, commercial taxi-radios, manual walkie-talkies, ship-shore radios, aircraft radios, IFF, and navigational aids,[12] search radars, and tracking radars. Thus, ESM is applied in operations undertaken to search for, intercept, locate, and identify immediately radiated electro-magnetic energy for the purposes of immediate threat recognition. Threat recognition includes not only the detection and location of covert transmissions by terrorist or insurgent groups, but the detection and location of hostile radars (especially the search and acquisition radars used by adversary surface-to-air missile batteries and radar-guided anti-aircraft guns, such as the ZSU-23/4), as well as communications among attacking formations across one's own border. ESM is critical in establishing the aggressor's electronic OB for the purpose of guiding friendly aircraft around hostile air defenses or vectoring them toward key targets.

An airborne radar surveillance platform such as the E-3A Sentry or the E-2C Hawkeye cannot perform ESM missions. First, combining ESM equipment with radar surveillance and tracking equipment interferes with the latter mission. Second, the ESM receiving and analysis equipment required for instant threat recognition is very heavy and takes up a considerable amount of space. Even if the two missions did not interfere with each other, a platform the size of a C-5A Galaxy would be needed to carry it all.

These technicalities, however, are not as important as the fact that neither the multi-role F-15s nor the F-5Es and Kuwaiti A-4s will be able to perform very effectively in ground attack missions without the intelligence gathered by ESM operations. Therefore, even with AWACS and an extended range F-15 configured for strike as well as for air superiority missions, the Saudi and other GCC air forces will not have the mobility to interdict enemy ground forces with what they have in inventory or on order. Moreover, should American forces be called upon to intervene in an emergency situation, USAF and USN units operating in or near the Gulf will need the battlefield intelligence that only ESM can provide in order to target enemy formations and to evade or destroy enemy air defenses.

However, one of the principal objectives of American support for the Gulf states is to avoid the necessity of direct U.S. intervention if possible. If it is not possible, then American policy would prefer U.S. assistance be limited to the provision of equipment and technical support. Moreover, crises may occur so suddenly that no time is available for external intervention. Conceivably, U.S. interven-

---

[12] For example, the IFF equipment in Soviet-built aircraft give off distinctly different emissions from those of the IFF and navigational aids on Western aircraft.

tion might actually compromise the GCC governments with their neighbors or—worse yet—with their own populations. In such situations, the enhanced ability of Saudi and other GCC air and ground forces to deal with threats on the ground as well as airborne intrusions may be critical.

The type of ESM measured to support Gulf-wide external defense and promote oil field security requires both airborne and land platforms, but linked together and netted to the C^3I system already envisaged for Saudi Arabia in the mid-1980s. An airborne ESM system does not carry with it the political liabilities for either the United States or the Gulf states of another AWACS/F-15 sale. It uses strictly off-the-shelf components, so that what is transferred is less sensitive on security grounds. An ESM system can be carried in a C-130 Hercules, a military transport already in service in Saudi Arabia, Oman, and the UAE. Therefore, no additional training is required of indigenous flight and maintenance personnel while the addition of foreign personnel is minimized. Particularly important is that fact that such an ESM platform will have the earmarks of a strictly *indigenously controlled* system, which AWACS does not.

ESM and the Saudi National Guard

While the United States has a manifest stake in the internal security of the GCC states, there has been a mutual reluctance on the part of both the United States and the GCC governments for the former to involve itself directly in the internal security affairs of the latter. One reason is simply that American expertise is far weaker than that of other countries whose involvement is well established. Another is that an American role in internal security would inevitably involve the United States in domestic political issues which could in turn easily diminish the political legitimacy of the very regimes that involvement was intended to strengthen.

The one exception to this pattern has been American assistance to SANG. This effort aims at converting a small portion of the guard (eight out of a total of 16 regular battalions) to a conventional, light mechanized infantry force to defend the oil fields. The program, under the direction of a U.S. advisory team, trains the guardsmen in up-to-date infantry tactics and the use of anti-tank missiles and anti-aircraft guns. The conversion units are re-armed with NATO rifles and machine guns. The original objective was to create "a lightly armored reconnaissance screening force . . . ideally suited for the security of the cities . . . or the oil fields."[13] To date the program has met with limited success.

SANG's progress is hampered by some ambiguity over its role. In many respects, it remains a means to interact with and maintain the support of tribal and Bedouin leaders at least as much as a modern combat or internal security force. It has yet to evolve into a force that can handle oil field security problems, urban disorders, or problems of border penetration. Politically essential to the kingdom, the Guard has yet to find a clear military mission. The role the Guard played in retaking the Grand Mosque in 1979 and in restoring order following Shi'a demonstrations in 1979 and 1980 suggests that SANG retains an important responsibility for internal security. How this continuity will affect U.S. support remains to be seen.

If the conversion battalions can be suitably trained for oil field and border security missions, their effectiveness may be enhanced by integrating them with whatever airborne and land-based ESM capabilities are developed. If these battalions become "a lightly armored reconnaissance screening force" in substance as well as in structure, equipping them with an ESM capability (linked to the rest of the Saudi C³I system) to help detect and locate covert transmissions by terrorist and subversive groups would help to make elements of internal and external security mutually reinforcing.

A Political Strategy for the Defense of U.S. Interests

Any strategy for the defense and advancement of U.S. interests means preserving Western access to Gulf oil. Even if specific regimes undergo change, the countries in the region will need to sell their oil in order to continue to function. A viable political strategy for the defense of American interests in the Gulf can succeed only if it defines friendly Gulf countries' security requirements (those that are supportive of those interests) on their own merits and demonstrates a realistic but unambiguous commitment to meeting them. A detailed discussion of such a strategy lies beyond the scope this work. Given the conclusions of the foregoing chapter, however, the main outlines of such a strategy are not difficult to pull together.

---

[13] See U.S. Congress, *Proposed Arms Sales for Countries in the Middle East*, Hearing before the Subcommittee on Europe and the Middle East of the House Committee on Foreign Affairs, 96th Congress, 1st Session, (Washington, D.C.: U.S. Government Printing Office), p. 35.

First and foremost, U.S. assistance to the GCC states must be defined in terms of what these countries need to improve their ability to handle their own security as much as possible, thereby reducing the need for or likelihood of U.S. intervention, and to make such U.S. involvement more effective in the event, this approach notwithstanding, that intervention becomes necessary. American security assistance must be defined in terms of these requirements as the most important criteria.

The possibility of denial of future access to American security support prompts the GCC countries to purchase their major weapons systems from a variety of suppliers. This action, in turn, complicates and diminishes their absorption of the weapons and places additional strains on limited manpower resources as well as training, logistic, and support capabilities. The cumulative effect is to blunt these countries' ability to defend themselves.

The second element of a political strategy consists of avoiding the inadvertent erosion of GCC member political systems. Thus, the United States should consciously provide only such aid as may enhance the appearance (to local nationals) of the GCC governments' autonomy. It is not merely a matter of maintaining the low visibility of foreign experts and advisors accompanying the introduction of new weapons; in addition, the weapons and other equipment transferred must contribute to the recipients' ability to act independently of the supplier. A related consideration is that the quality of American advice must remain high and American support teams must be seen to be seriously concerned with helping Gulf personnel effectively absorb their equipment, and not solely with securing follow-on sales of more equipment and services.

American advisory teams are frequently excellent. However, they are not always staffed with personnel chosen for tactical innovation. Advisors should, in conjunction with their local counterparts, devote time to the modification and adaptation of the tactics associated with imported military technology and equipment to optimize their use in local conditions. Such an effort involves thinking about how local social institutions might be adapted to using modern military technologies as well. The objective is to produce a synthesis that enables the recipient forces to absorb their equipment more rapidly and more completely as well as to use it on the battlefield more effectively.

The words of a U.S. congressman also bear remembering in considering any security assistance package to the Gulf:

> Part of the problem is that there is an asymmetry in arms sales. A nation does not get

170

> much from selling arms, but it could get hurt
> a lot if it announces that is thinking about a
> sale and then denies the sale.[14]

This is precisely what happened to the United States when it was considering supplying Saudi Arabia with the M-1 main battle tank and the M-2 armored fighting vehicle. Consummation of the sale would have lowered the unit cost of the two systems to both the United States and the Saudis. It would have standardized on a mix of armor that would serve both Saudi (and possibly other GCC) forces and U.S. reinforcements in an emergency. The result would have been a large pool of armor in the Gulf that American forces could use without major problems inherent in trying to deploy any such equipment over the horizon.

Publicization of the plans produced the cumulative impression that the United States was committed to an initial sale of 1,200 M-1s instead of the actual initial buy of 200. The embarrassment was compounded by categorical Pentagon denials of any sale at all, only to be followed by more detailed reports that the sale was in the works or that it involved the pre-positioning of about 1,000 M-1s solely for the use of CENTCOM.[15] One effect was to make Saudi Arabia appear willing to facilitate an American invasion of the Gulf—an impression Soviet and regional propaganda machines did not fail to promote.

The mishandling of this episode came at a time (March-April 1983) when Washington was actively trying to persuade the Saudis to put pressure on Jordan to support President Reagan's peace initiative and on Syria and Lebanon to reach an agreement on Israeli withdrawal from Lebanon. The United States was also trying to persuade Saudi Arabia to support the other GCC states in standardizing on American air defense systems. Needless-to-say, the M-1 fiasco did nothing to improve the chances of success of either of these other initiatives.

This episode underscores a final element indispensable to defending American interests in the Gulf and that must be kept in mind when planning for unforeseen contingencies in the region. Although a U.S.-supported buildup of GCC military capabilities in no way threatens the security of Iran, other Arab countries, or Israel, one of the most effective ways of protecting U.S. interests

---

[14] "Arms Sales: A Useful Foreign Policy Tool?" *AEI Forum*, No. 56 (Washington, D.C.: American Enterprise Institute, 1982), p. 8.

[15] The details of the M-1 episode are described in Cordesman, *The Gulf*, pp. 358-360.

in the region lies in ensuring that there is enough movement toward a just and lasting peace between the Arab states and Israel. This will avert the possibility that years of effort in the Gulf might be destroyed by the political and military consequences of the Arab-Israeli conflict.

SELECTED BIBLIOGRAPHY
AND FURTHER READINGS

Abir, Mordechai. *Oil, Power and Politics: Conflicts in Arabia, the Red Sea and the Gulf.* London: Cass, 1974.

————. "Saudi Security and Military Endeavor." *The Jerusalem Quarterly,* 33 (Fall 1984), pp. 79-94.

Akins, James E., et al. *Oil and Security in the Arabian Gulf.* New York: St. Martin's, 1981.

Ali, Assad Mohamed Mohsen. "Saudi Arabia's National Security: A Prospective Derived from Political, Economic, and Defense Policies." Unpublished Ph.D. dissertation, Claremont Graduate School, 1981.

Aliboni, Roberto. *The Red Sea Region.* Syracuse: Syracuse University Press, 1985.

Allen, Robert C. "Regional Security in the Persian Gulf." *Military Review,* LXIII, 12 (December 1983), pp. 17-29.

Amirsadeghi, Hossein, ed. *The Security of the Persian Gulf.* New York: St. Martin's, 1981.

Anthony, John Duke. "The Gulf Cooperation Council." *Orbis,* XXVIII, 3 (Fall 1984), pp. 447-450.

Axelgard, Frederick W. "The Tanker War in the Gulf: Background and Repercussions." *Middle East Insight,* III, 6 (November-December 1984), pp. 26-33.

Batatu, Hanna. "Iraq's Underground Shi'a Movements: Characteristics, Causes and Prospects." *Middle East Journal,* XXXV, 4 (Autumn 1981), pp. 578-594.

Blake, Gerald. "The Red Sea and the Arabian Gulf: Strategic and Economic Links." In Abdel Majid Farid, ed., *The Red Sea: Prospects for Stability.* London: Croom Helm, 1984, pp. 84-94.

Bloomfield, Lincoln P., Jr. "Saudi Arabia Faces the 1980s: Saudi Security Problems and American Interests." *The Fletcher Forum,* V, 2 (Summer 1981), pp. 243-277.

Chubin, Shahram. *Security in the Persian Gulf: The Role of Outside Powers.* London: International Institute for Strategic Studies, 1982.

_____. "Soviet Policy Towards Iran and the Gulf." *Adelphi Papers,* 157. Entire issue.

_____. "The Soviet Union and Iran." *Foreign Affairs,* LXI, 3 (Spring 1983), pp. 921-949.

_____. "U.S. Security Interests in the Persian Gulf in the 1980s." *Daedalus,* CIX, 4 (1980), pp. 31-65.

Cordesman, Anthony H. "The Crisis in the Gulf: A Military Analysis." *American-Arab Affairs,* 9 (Summer 1984), pp. 8-15.

_____. "Gulf Cooperation Council: Security Problems and Prospects." In Shireen Hunter, ed., *Gulf Cooperation Council: Problems and Prospects.* CSIS Significant Issues Series, VI, 15 (1984), pp. 10-15.

_____. *The Gulf and the Search for Strategic Stability: Saudi Arabia, the Military Balance in the Gulf, and Trends in the Arab-Israeli Military Balance.* Boulder, Colo.: Westview Press, 1984.

_____. "The Iran-Iraq War in 1984: An Escalating Threat to the Gulf and the West." *Armed Forces Journal International,* CXX, 10 (May 1983), pp. 36ff.

_____. *Jordanian Arms and the Middle East Balance.* Washington, D.C.: Middle East Institute, 1983.

_____. "The Oil Glut and the Strategic Importance of the Gulf States." *Armed Forces Journal International,* CXXI, 3 (October 1983), pp. 30ff.

_____. *Saudi Arabia, AWACS, and America's Search for Strategic Stability in the Near East.* Washington, D.C.: The Wilson International Center for Scholars, 1981.

_____. "US Military Assistance to the Middle East: National Security or Election-Year Politics?" *Armed Forces Journal International,* CXXI, 6 (January 1984), pp. 26-33.

Cottrell, Alvin J. and Michael L. Moodie. *The United States and the Persian Gulf: Past Mistakes, Present Needs.* New York: National Strategy Information Center, 1984.

Darius, Robert G., John W. Amos II, and Ralph H. Magnus. *Gulf Security into the 1980s: Perceptual and Strategic Dimensions.* Stanford: Hoover Institution Press, 1984.

Dawisha, Adeed. "Saudi Arabia's Search for Security." *Adelphi Papers,* 158 (1979). Entire issue.

Dessouki, Ali E. Hilal. *The Iran-Iraq War: Issues of Conflict and Prospects for Settlement.* Princeton: Center for International Studies, 1981.

Digby, James. *The Emerging American Strategy: Application to Southwest Asia.* Santa Monica: Rand, 1981.

Dunn, Keith A. "Constraints on the USSR in Southwest Asia: A Military Analysis." *Orbis*, XXV, 3 (Fall 1981), pp. 607-629.

Dunn, Michael C. "Gulf Security: The States Look After Themselves." *Defense & Foreign Affairs*, June 1982.

Eilts, Hermann Fr. "Security Considerations in the Persian Gulf." *International Security*, V, 2 (Fall 1980), pp. 79-113.

Epstein, Joshua M. "Soviet Vulnerabilities in Iran and the RDF Deterrent." *International Security*, VI, 2 (Fall 1981), pp. 125-158.

Fabyanic, Thomas A. "Conceptual Planning the the Rapid Deployment Joint Task Force." *Armed Forces and Society*, VII, 3 (1981), pp. 343-365.

. *The Red Sea: Prospects for Stability.* London: Croom Helm, 1984.

Feer, Frederick S. "Problems of Oil Supply Disruptions in the Persian Gulf." In George Horwich and Edward Mitchell, eds., *Policies for Coping with Oil Supply Disruptions.* Washington, D.C.: American Enterprise Institute, 1982, pp. 11-30.

Grummon, Stephen R. *The Iraq-Iran War: Islam Embattled.* "The Washington Papers." 92. New York: Praeger with the Center for Strategic and International Studies, Georgetown University, 1982.

Halloran, Richard. "Poised for the Persian Gulf." *The New York Times Magazine*, April 1, 1984, pp. 38-40, 61.

Hameed, Mazher. *An American Imperative: The Defense of Saudi Arabia.* Washington, D.C.: Middle East Assessments Group, 1981.

. *The Middle East In Review: 1984-85.* Washington, D.C.: Middle East Assessments Group, 1986.

Hanks, Robert J. *The U.S. Military Presence in the Middle East: Problems and Prospects.* Cambridge, Mass.: Institute for Foreign Policy Analysis, 1982.

Heller, Mark. *The Iran-Iraq War: Implications for Third Parties.* Tel Aviv: Jaffee Center for Strategic Studies, Tel Aviv University, Paper 23, 1984.

Hickman, William F. *Ravaged and Reborn: The Iranian Army, 1982.* Washington, D.C.: Brookings, 1982.

Hunter, Shireen T. "Arab-Iranian Relations and Stability in the Persian Gulf." *The Washington Quarterly*, VII, 3 (Summer 1984), pp. 67-76.

., ed. *Gulf Cooperation Council: Problems and Prospects.* CSIS Significant Issues Series, VI, 15 (1984).

175

Ispahana, Mahnaz Zehra. "Alone Together: Regional Security Arrangements in Sourthern Africa and the Arabian Gulf." *International Security*, VIII, 4 (Spring 1984), pp. 152-175.

Iungerich, Ralph. "US Rapid Deployment Forces—USCENTCOM—What Is It? Can It Do the Job?" *Armed Forces Journal International*, CXXII, 3 (October 1984).

Jabber, Paul. "US Interests and Regional Security in the Middle East." *Daedalus*, CIX, 4 (Fall 1980), pp. 67-80.

Johnson, Maxwell Orme. *The Military as an Instrument of U.S. Policy in Southwest Asia: The Rapid Deployment Joint Task Force, 1979-1982*. Boulder: Westview, 1983.

Kodmans, Bassma, ed. *Quelle securite pour le Golfe?* Paris: Institut française des relations internationelles, 1984.

Lenczowski, George. "The Soviet Union and the Persian Gulf: An Encircling Strategy." *International Journal*, XXXVII, 2 (1982), pp. 307-327.

Litwak, Robert. *Security in the Persian Gulf: Sources of Inter-State Conflict*. London: International Institute of Strategic Studies, 1981.

Long, David E. *The United States and Saudi Arabia: Ambivalent Allies*. Boulder: Westview, 1985.

_____. "U.S.-Saudi Relations: A Foundation of Mutual Needs." *American-Arab Affairs*, 4 (Spring 1983), pp. 12-22.

McLaurin, R.D. "U.S. Strategy in the Middle East and the Arab Reaction." *Journal of East and West Studies*, XI, 2 (Fall-Winter 1982), pp. 59-84.

_____, and Lewis W. Snider. *Saudi Arabia's Air Defense Requirements in the 1980s: A Threat Analysis*. Alexandria, Va.: Abbott Associates, 1979.

McNaugher, Thomas L. "Arms and Allies on the Arabian Peninsula." *Orbis*, XXVIII, 3 (Fall 1983), pp. 489-526.

_____. *Arms and Oil: U.S. Military Security Policy Toward the Persian Gulf*. Washington, D.C.: Brookings, 1985.

_____. "Principal Components of the Gulf Cooperation Council Security Strategy." In Shireen Hunter, ed., *Gulf Cooperation Council: Problems and Prospects*, CSIS Significant Issues Series, VI, 15 (1984), pp. 6-9.

Mansur, Abdul Kasim (pseud.). "The Military Balance in the Persian Gulf: Who will Guard the Gulf States from their Guardians?" *Armed Forces Journal International*, November 1980.

Martin, Lenore G. *The Unstable Gulf: Threats from Within*. Lexington, Mass.: D.C. Heath, 1984.

Nakhleh, Emile A. "The Gulf Cooperation Council: Political Challenges and Responses." In Shireen Hunter, ed., *Gulf Cooperation Council: Problems and Prospects*, CSIS Significant Issues Series, VI, 15 (1984), pp. 3-5.

———. *The Persian Gulf and American Policy*. New York: Praeger, 1982.

Neumann, Robert G. and Shireen T. Hunter. "The Crisis in the Gulf: Reasons for Concern but not Panic." *American-Arab Affairs*, 9 (Summer 1984), pp. 16-21.

Novik, Nimrod. *On the Shores of Bab al-Mandab*. Philadelphia: Foreign Policy Research Institute, 1979.

Noyes, James J. *The Clouded Lens: Persian Gulf Security and U.S. Policy*. Second Edition, Hoover Institution, 1982.

Olson, William J. "The Iran-Iraq War and the Future of the Persian Gulf." *Military Review*, LXIV, 2 (March 1984), pp. 17-29.

Peterson, J.E. "Defending Arabia: Evolution of Responsibility." *Orbis*, XXVIII, 2 (Fall 1984), pp. 465-488.

Plascov, Avi. *Security in the Persian Gulf: Modernization, Political Development, and Stability*. London: International Institute for Strategic Studies, 1982.

Quandt, William B. "The Crisis in the Gulf: Policy Options and Regional Implications." *American-Arab Affairs*, 9 (Summer 1984), pp. 1-7.

———. *Saudi Arabia in the 1980s: Foreign Policy, Security and Oil*. Washingotn, D.C.: Brookings, 1981.

Record, Jeffrey. *The Rapid Deployment Force and U.S. Military Intervention in the Persian Gulf*. Cambridge, Mass: Institute for Foreign Policy Analysis, 1981.

Ross, Dennis. *Considering Threats to the Persian Gulf*. Washington, D.C.: Wilson Center for International Scholars, 1981.

———. "Considering Soviet Threats to the Persian Gulf." *International Security*, VI, 2 (Fall 1981), pp. 159-180.

———. "Soviet Views Toward the Gulf War." *Orbis*, XVIII, 3 (Fall 1984), pp. 437-446.

Rubinstein, Alvin Z., ed. *The Great Game: Rivalry in the Persian Gulf and South Asia*. New York: Praeger, 1983.

Safran, Nadav. *Saudi Arabia: The Ceaseless Quest for Security*. Cambridge, Mass. and London: The Belknap Press of Harvard University Press, 1985.

Salameh, Ghassane. "Checkmate in the Gulf War." *MERIP Reports*, XIV, 6/7 (July-September 1984), pp. 15-21.

Shaw, John A. and Long, David E. *Saudi Arabian Modernization: The Impact of Change on Stability.* "The Washington Papers" 89. New York: Praeger with the Center for Strategic and International Studies, Georgetown University, 1982.

Sick, Gary G. *All Fall Down: America's Tragic Encounter with Iran.* New York: Random House, 1985.

_____. "The Evolution of U.S. Strategy Toward the Indian Ocean and Persian Gulf Regions." In Alvin A. Rubinstein, ed., *The Great Game: Rivalry in the Persian Gulf and South Asia.* New York: Praeger, 1983.

Stookey, Robert. *The Arabian Peninsula: Zone of Ferment.* Stanford: Hoover Institution, 1984.

Szaz, Z. Michael, ed. *The Impact of the Iranian Events Upon Persian Gulf and United States Security.* Washington, D.C.: American Foreign Policy Institute, 1979.

Tahir-Kheli, Shirin and Ayubi, Shaheen, eds. *The Iran-Iraq War: Oil Weapons, New Conflicts.* New York: Praeger, 1983.

Tahtinen, Dale R. *National Security Challenges to Saudi Arabia.* Washington, D.C.: American Enterprise for Public Policy Research, 1978.

Terrell, W. Andrew, Jr. "Jordan and the Defense of the Gulf." *Middle East Insight,* IV, 2 (March-April 1985), pp. 34-41.

Thompson, W. Scott. "The Persian Gulf and the Correlation of Forces." *International Security,* VII, 1 (Summer 1982), pp. 157-180.

United States Congress, 94th Congress, 1st Session. Senate, Committee on Foreign Relations. *Saudi Arabia.* A Report by Senator Mike Mansfield, October 1975.

United States Congress, 96th Congress, 1st Session. House of Representatives, Committee on Foreign Affairs. *Activities of the United States Army Corps of Engineers in Saudi Arabia.* Hearing, June 25, 1979.

United States Congress, 96th Congress, 1st Session. Senate, Committee on Foreign Relations. *The Future of Saudi Arabian Oil Production.* Staff Report, April 1979.

United States Congress, 97th Congress, 1st Session. House of Representatives, Committee on Appropriations. *Foreign Assistance and Related Programs Appropriations for 1982. Part 7: Proposed Airborne Warning and Control Systems (AWACS), F-15 Enhancement Equipment, and Sidewinder AIM 9L Missile Sales to Saudi Arabia.* Hearings.

United States Congress, 97th Congress, 1st Session. Senate, Committee on Armed Services. *Military and Technical Implications of the Proposed Sale of Air Defense Enhancements to Saudi Arabia.* Report of the Hearings on the Military and Technical Implications of the Proposed Sale of Air Defense Enhancements to Saudi Arabia, based upon hearings held before the Committee in accordance with its responsibilities under Rule XXV (C) of the Standing Rules of the Senate.

United States Congress, 97th Congress, 1st Session. Senate, Committee on Foreign Relations. *The Proposed AWACS/F-15 Enhancement Sale to Saudi Arabia.* Staff Report, 1981.

United States Congress, 98th Congress, 2nd Session. Senate, Committee on Foreign Relations. *War in the Gulf.* Staff Report, 1984.

United States Library of Congress, Congressional Research Service. Foreign Affairs and National Defense Division. *Saudi Arabia and the United States: The New Context in an Evolving "Special Relationship".* Report prepared for the Subcommittee on Europe and the Middle East, Committee on Foreign Affairs, U.S. House of Representatives, 1981.

United States Library of Congress, Congressional Research Service. *Western Vulnerability to a Disruption of Persian Gulf Oil Supplies: U.S. Interests and Options.* 1983.

Volman, Daniel. "Commanding the Center." *MERIP Reports*, XIV, 6/7 (July-September 1984), pp. 49-50.

Wenger, Martha. "The Central Command: Getting to the War on Time." *MERIP Reports*, XIV, 9 (Fall 1984), pp. 456-464.

Wiley, Marshall W. "American Security Concerns in the Gulf." *Orbis*, XXVIII, 3 (Fall 1984), pp. 456-464.

Wohlstetter, Albert. "Meeting the Threat in the Persian Gulf." *Survey*, XXV, 2 (Spring 1980), pp. 128-188.

Wolfe, Ronald G., ed. *The United States, Arabia, and the Gulf.* Washington, D.C.: Georgetown University Center for Contemporary Arab Studies, 1980.

Yodfat, Aryeh Y. *The Soviet Union and the Arabian Peninsula: Soviet Policy towards the Persian Gulf and Arabia.* New York: St. Martin's, 1983.

LIST OF ACRONYMS

AEW&C	airborne early warning and control
AFV	armored fighting vehicle
AMIO	Arab Military Industries Organization
AOB	air order of battle
APC	armored personnel carrier
AWACS	Airborne Warning and Control System
BAI	battlefield air interdiction
BPD	barrels per day
C^3	command, control, and communications
C^3I	command, control, communication, and intelligence
CENTCOM	U.S. Central Command
CENTO	Central Treaty Organization
ESM	electronic warfare support measures
FGA	fighter/ground attack
GCC	Gulf Cooperation Council
IAF	Israel Air Force
IFF	identification friend or foe
JTIDS	Joint Tactical Information Distribution System
KM	kilometers
LOC	line of communications
MBD	millions of barrels per day
MER	multiple ejection racks
MIDEASTFOR	U.S. Middle East Force
NATO	North Atlantic Treaty Organization
NCO	non-commissioned officer
NM	nautical miles
OAPEC	Organization of Arab Petroleum Exporting Countries
OB	order of battle
OPEC	Organization of Petroleum Exporting Countries
PDRY	People's Democratic Republic of Yemen (South Yemen)
PLO	Palestine Liberation Organization
POL	petroleum, oil, and lubricants
RSA	Royal Saudi Army
RSAF	Royal Saudi Air Force
SAM	surface-to-air missile
SANG	Saudi Arabian National Guard
SAS	Special Air Services (UK)
SEATO	Southeast Asian Treaty Organization
SLOC	sea lane of communications
SSM	surface-to-surface missile
UAE	United Arab Emirates
UDF	Union Defense Force (UAE)
USAF	U.S. Air Force
USN	U.S. Navy
YAR	Yemen Arab Republic (North Yemen)

INDEX

Abu Dhabi, 12, 84
Abu Musa, 5
  Iranian occupation of, 5pAnti-tank
    missiles, 118
Anti-Western politics, 27-28
  and religious belief, 45
Arab expatriates, 48-50, 120
Arab Military Industries Organization
  (AMIO), 115-116
Arab nationalism, 108
  oil wealth and, 110-111
Arab nationalist movement, 108n
Arab Revolutionary Brigades, 100
Arab-Israeli conflict. *See also* Palestin-
    ians
  airspace violations and, 66, 69, 88-89
  U.S. position in Gulf and, 28, 46
  Gulf security issues and, 77, 87-90,
    93
  Palestinian issue and, 45-46, 93
Arafat, Yasser, 93
Area (size) of individual Gulf states, 2
Armed forces, size of, in individual
    Gulf states, 2
Arms acquisition. *See also* Military
    modernization and Weapons pur-
    chases
  Iran-Iraq war and, 34
  by GCC states, 138-160
  by Saudi Arabia, 19, 72-73, 88, 127
AWACS. *See* Airborne Warning and
    Control Systems
Bab el Mandeb, 65
Baghdad Pact, 95
Bahrain
  coup attempt in 1981, 128-129
  general information on, 10-11
  Iran's claim on, 52
  military cooperation with Saudi Ara-
    bia by, 122-123
  military resources of, 140, 158
  tank inventory of, 144
  vital statistics of, 2
Baluchi people, 15
Barre, Siad, 115
Bedouin tribesmen, 80, 129
Border hostilities, 52, 53. *See also*
    Boundary disputes
Boundary disputes, 14

between Iraq and Kuwait, 35
  border hostility arising from, 52
Bradsher, Henry, 88n
Bubiyan Island, 101
Buraimi Oasis affair, 104
Camp David agreements, 90, 91, 116
Carter Doctrine, 30
CENTCOM. *See* United States Central
    Command
Central Treaty Organization (CENTO),
    29
Cold War, 3
Command, Control, Communications
    and Intelligence (C^3I), 161, 162,
    164-165
Cordesman, Anthony H., 25n, 68n, 72n,
    106n, 112n, 143n, 158n, 171n
Crotale, 155-156
Dahlak Island, 65
de Briganti, Giovanni, 161n
Dessouki, Ali Hillal, 111n
Dhofar rebellion, 158
Diego Garcia, 16, 61
Djibouti, 17n, 65
Dubai, 12, 84
Dunn, Michael Collins, 156n
Economic development
  modernization efforts of Gulf coun-
    tries, 42-43
  oil prices and, 44, 146-147
Education
  impact of social predispositions on,
    129-130, 132
  secular, 42, 129-130
Egypt
  effect of oil wealth on, 100
  as naval power in Red Sea, 17, 65
  1973 October war and, 133-134
  relationship with Jordan, 15
  relationship with Iraq, 15
Eilat, 65
Electronic warfare support measures
    (ESM), 166-168
  and Saudi Arabian National Guard,
    168-169
Eritrean Liberation Front, 66
Ethiopia, 17
  anti-Western posture of, 27-28
  possible targets of, 67

181

Social order in Gulf countries, 106-109
Socotra, 61
Soviet naval base on, 61
Socio-economic change. *See also* modernization
and capacity to mobilize for military purposes, 79-80
oil wealth and, 96
Somalia, 31
U.S. naval base on, 61
Southeast Asian Treaty Organization (SEATO), 29
Soviet Union
consolidation of control over Afghanistan, 94
interests in the Gulf of, 20-21, 30, 54-55
invasion of Afghanistan by, 15-16, 18, 30, 31
Iraqi arms provided by, 2-3, 5-6
presence in Indian Ocean of, 61, 63
relations with Iran, 2, 20
relations with Iraq, 8-9, 20
relations with Syria, 31, 92
rivalry with U.S. in Gulf, 29-31, 53
as threat to Gulf states, 19, 37-39, 53-55
as threat to Western interests in the Gulf, 37-39
Strait of Hormuz, 37, 147
Subversion, 47-48
and expatriate involvement in, 49
Sudan, 17, 65, 99
Sukkhio-24, 55, 63n
Sunni Muslims, 6
conflict with Shi'as, 35
in Iran, 7
Superpower balances, 94-95
Surface-to-surface missiles (SSMs), 34
Symbolic targets, 51
Syria
anti-Western posture of, 27-28
effect of oil wealth on, 100
re-emergence as power center, 91-93
relations with Iran, 14
relations with Iraq, 7, 71-72
relations with Jordan, 72
relations with Soviet Union, 31, 92
as threat to Gulf states, 71-72
"Tanker war," 19n-20n, 142
Tanks
number of, in individual Gulf states, 2, 144

types of, 143-144, 160
Terrell, W. Andrew, Jr., 72n
Terrorism
and interruption of oil flow, 37
Iran and, 28
religious extremism and, 40
as security threat to Gulf states, 50-51
targeted against Western citizens, 36, 51
Threat assessment, 54-55, 72-74
from Israel, 66, 69
from North, 54-55
from Red Sea, 63, 65-67
from South, 58, 61, 63
from Syria, 71-72
from Gulf, 55, 57-58
Tinnin, David B., 38n
Tornado Air Defense Variant (ADV), 127, 128
Tudeh party (Iran), 30
Tu-22 bombers, 55
Tu-26 Backfire bombers, 55
Tumb Islands, 5, 52
Turkey, 3
Turki, Prince (Saudi Arabia), 38
"Twin-Pillar" policy, 3-6
Umm al-Maradem, 83
United Arab Emirates (UAE)
air strength of, 139-140
expatriate workers in, 48
general information on, 11, 12
land force strength, 142, 144
military authority in, 129
military forces and internal competition in, 123
military resources of, 117, 139-140
oil revenues of, 97, 98
relations with Soviet Union, 21, 30
rivalries within, 83-84
United States
and GCC members, 94-95
interests in the Gulf, 17-19. *See also* U.S. interests, protection
involvement in Gulf security, 26
issues undermining position of, 28
oil dependence of, 96
presence in Indian Ocean of, 61, 63
protection of citizens of, 36
relations with Iraq, 8-9
relations with Jordan, 92-93
relations with Oman, 12
relations with Saudi Arabia, 9, 19, 95

ABOUT THE AUTHOR

Mazher A. Hameed, a specialist in international security affairs, has been Executive Director of the Middle East Assessments Group (MEAG) since 1982. Based in Washington, D.C., he also serves as a consultant to a number of public and private sector organizations. From 1980 to 1982, Mr. Hameed was Director of the Oil Field Security Studies Program at the Center for Strategic and International Studies (CSIS) of Georgetown University.

Mr. Hameed's writings on political and military developments in the Middle East appear regularly in the MEAG Bulletin and Perspective Series as well as in newspapers and periodicals. He is the author of *An American Imperative: The Defense of Saudi Arabia*, a study prepared at CSIS, and *The Middle East in Review: 1984-85*. At present Mr. Hameed is completing an in-depth survey of political conditions in the Middle East, to be published in late 1986, and a major report on Gulf security to be presented in May 1986 before the Middle East Studies Group of the Council on Foreign Relations.

Among the institutions where Mr. Hameed has lectured on regional security issues are the Middle East Institute, the National Defense University, the Foreign Service Institute, and American University.

Mr. Hameed was educated at the King George's Royal Military College, the Barking Regional College of Technology, Merritt College, the Fletcher School of Law and Diplomacy, and the University of California at Berkeley.